The

Long-Term Care Insurance Product

Policy Design,
Pricing, and
Regulation

The Health Insurance Association of America
Washington, DC 20004-1204

© 2002 by the Health Insurance Association of America
All rights reserved. Published 2002
Printed in the United States of America

ISBN 1-879143-65-8

≫ Contents

⟫ Figures and Tables

The Health Insurance Association of America (HIAA)

This book is published by the Insurance Education Program of the Health Insurance Association of America (HIAA) in conjunction with the American Association for Long-Term Care Insurance (AALTCI).

The Health Insurance Association of America is the nation's most prominent trade association representing the private health care system. Its more than 300 members provide health, long-term care, dental, disability, and supplemental coverage to more than 123 million Americans. It is the nation's premier provider of self-study courses on health insurance, managed care, and related topics.

The mission of HIAA's Insurance Education Program includes the following goals:

- to provide tools for insurance company personnel to use in enhancing the quality and efficiency of services to the public,
- to provide a career development vehicle for insurer employees and other health care industry professionals, and
- to promote general understanding of the role and contribution of the health insurance industry in the financing, administration, and delivery of health care services.

The Insurance Education Program provides the following services:

- a comprehensive course of study in the fundamentals of health insurance, medical expense insurance, supplemental health insurance, long-term care insurance, disability income insurance, managed care, health insurance fraud, HIPAA, and customer service in the health care environment;
- certification of educational achievement by proctored examination for all courses;

■ programs to recognize accomplishment in the industry and academic communities through course evaluation and certification, which enable participants to obtain academic or continuing education credits; and

■ development of educational, instructional, training, and informational materials related to the health insurance and health care industries.

The Health Insurance Association of America (HIAA)
Insurance Education Program
1201 F Street NW, Suite 500
Washington, DC 20004-1204
800-509-4422
Web: www.hiaa.org
E-mail: mgrant@hiaa.org

❯❯ The American Association for Long-Term Care Insurance (AALTCI)

The American Association for Long-Term Care Insurance (AALTCI) is proud to be working together with the Health Insurance Association of America on the development and promotion of the premier designation for the long-term care insurance professional.

AALTCI is a nonprofit professional organization with the singular focus of meeting the needs of long-term care insurance agents, brokers, and insurers.

We invite you to join with thousands of leading LTCI professionals who are members of the association.

For more information on member benefits, including our program of regional LTC symposiums, our magazine, *Long-Term Care Insurance Sales Strategies*, or other programs, visit our website at *www.aaltci.org*.

The American Association for Long-Term Care Insurance
National Headquarters
3835 East Thousand Oaks Boulevard, Suite 336
Westlake Village, California 91362
818-597-3205
Web: www.aaltci.org
E-mail: info@aaltci.org

>> Preface

Long-term care is a continuously changing field. New providers of care emerge, and the traditional providers develop new ways of meeting needs. Legislators and regulators step in to protect the interests of the public and to address specific problems. Consumers, concerned with rising costs, look for better ways to finance those costs.

In response, insurance companies continue to develop the long-term care insurance (LTCI) product. By adapting to changing conditions and devising new solutions, insurers strive to provide consumers with the best protection possible against the financial risk of long-term care costs.

This book, *The Long-Term Care Insurance Product*, looks at these changes and at long-term care policies as they exist today. It discusses the recent evolution of the product, including the impact of HIPAA, and it examines LTCI policy provisions, including benefit eligibility, benefit amounts, inflation protection, elimination periods, policy maximums, nonforfeiture, renewal, lapse, and others. It also provides an explanation of how the premium is calculated.

The Long-Term Care Insurance Product serves as the textbook for the third of HIAA's four self-study courses in long-term care. Those completing these courses earn the designation of Long-Term Care Professional (LTCP).

This book has been written and organized to make ideas and information easy to learn and to facilitate study and review. Focus questions and review questions draw attention to important points and engage the reader in active learning. Key terms appear in boldface and are marked in the margin with this symbol: ▣.

The Long-Term Care Insurance Insurance Product is intended for educational purposes. Its contents are not a statement of policy. The views expressed or suggested in this and all other HIAA textbooks are those of the contributing authors and are not necessarily the opinions of HIAA or of its member companies. In addition, this book is sold with the understanding that HIAA is not engaged in rendering legal, accounting, tax, or any other professional service. If legal advice or other expert assistance is required, the services of a professional should be sought.

Finally, it should be kept in mind that the insurance industry is continuously changing and the information in this or any book may be superseded by the latest trends and innovations. For information on current developments, the reader should visit HIAA's website at *www.hiaa.org* and the AALTCI website at *www.aaltci.org*.

Gregory F. Dean, JD, CLU, ChFC
Executive Director, Insurance Education Program
Health Insurance Association of America

» Acknowledgments

Author

Jason G. Goetze

Reviewers and Contributors

Margie Barrie
LTCI Consulting Group, Inc.

Judith Bass, MHP, FLMI, ACS, HIA, ALHC
State Farm Insurance

Sharil L. Baxter, MSM, CLTC, CSA, MHP, CTM
LTCI Partners, LLC

Mary Frances Bertucci, FLMI, ACS, AIRC, ALHC
Guaranty Income Life Insurance Company

David Brenerman
UnumProvident Corporation

Marie Bucci
John Hancock Life Insurance Company

Winthrop S. Cashdollar
Health Insurance Association of America

Timothy P. Cassidy
Long-Term Care Group, Inc.

Susan A. Coronel
Health Insurance Association of America

Steffani Crawley
AEGON Insurance Group

Harry Crosby
GE Capital Assurance

Gregory F. Dean, JD, CLU, ChFC
Health Insurance Association of America

Dave Donchey, CLU
Leisure Werden and Terry

Phyllis Felser
Felser Insurance Services, LLC

Barry J. Fisher
Barry J. Fisher Insurance Marketing

Kathy Gabor
Brokerage Services International, Inc. (BSI)

Carol Gardner
LifeStyle Insurance Services, Inc.

Jocelyn F. Gordon, Esq.
Life Plans, Inc.

David Gregg
Mutual of Omaha

Allen Hamm
Superior LTC Insurance Agency, Inc.

Andrew E. Hanson
Hanson Financial Services

Patrick E. Hoesing
Art Jetter and Company

Edward S. Hutman
BISYS Insurance Services

Arthur C. Jetter, Jr., CLU, CFP, RHU, FLMI, REBC
Art Jetter and Company

Roy W. Kern, LUTCF, CLTC, CSA, RFC
Roy W. Kern and Associates

Jim Knotts, FLMI, FLHC, HIA, ACS
State Farm Insurance

Diane Lavin
Metropolitan Life Insurance Company

Sally H. Leimbach, CLU, CEBS
LTC Insurance Specialists, LLC

Terry Lowe, HIA, CLU, ChFC, FMLI, FLHC, ACS
State Farm Insurance

Beth M. Ludden, FLMI
New York Life Insurance Company

Christine McCullugh
LTC Solutions, Inc.

Deirdre A. McKenna, JD
Health Insurance Association of America

Glenn Miller
Physicians' Mutual Insurance Company

Sam Morgante
GE Capital Assurance

Susan C. Morisato
Bankers Life and Casualty Company

Raymond Nelson, ASA, MAAA
Bankers Life and Casualty Company

Ann Gillespie Pietrick, JD
Conseco Services, LLC/Bankers Life and Casualty Company

Lee Sacks, CLTC, CSA
Daniel Charles, Inc.

Abe Scher, MSW, LCSW
Scher Long-Term Care Insurance Services, Inc.

Beth Singley
Assisted Living Federation of America (ALFA)

Jesse R. Slome, CLU, ChFC
American Association for Long-Term Care Insurance (AALTCI)

J. Eugene Tapper, MS, NHA
Glocal Insurance Marketing

Eileen J. Tell, MHP
Long-Term Care Group, Inc.

Michael Thresher
J. T. Ryan and Associates

General Reviewers

Terry Lowe, HIA, CLU, ChFC, FMLI, FLHC, ACS
State Farm Insurance

Raymond Nelson, ASA, MAAA
Bankers Life and Casualty Company

Eileen J. Tell, MHP
Long-Term Care Group, Inc.

Editors

Michael G. Bell

Aziz Gökdemir

» About the Author

Jason G. Goetze has worked exclusively in the long-term care insurance industry since 1989. In a variety of home office positions, he has been involved in long-term care insurance product development; successfully influenced changes in regulation and legislation; strategized and implemented an integrated marketing and training program that grew a seller of individual long-term care insurance into a leading seller with the highest per agent sales for a life insurance agent distribution system; conducted over 350 consumer seminars on behalf of agents; and provided competitive analysis of companies' products.

Mr. Goetze is recognized throughout the industry for expertise and leadership qualities. He has spoken at many industry conferences on training, marketing, market conduct, and Medicaid planning. He chaired LIMRA's Health Insurance Committee twice and their long-term care subcommittee for seven years, and he served on committees at the Health Insurance Association of America (HIAA), the American Council of Life Insurers (ACLI), and the Society of Actuaries (SOA). His articles have been published in trade journals, he has been quoted in national publications, and he has written other books on long-term care insurance.

1

The Evolution of The Long-Term Care Insurance Product

» Overview

Long-term care insurance (LTCI) is a relatively new insurance product. Since its beginnings as skilled nursing home coverage in 1965, long-term care insurance has broadened its scope and depth of coverage considerably while adding important consumer protections; it is thus approaching mainstream acceptance. It has not been easy for those involved with the product—insurers, regulators, and consumers. Although there is healthy tension among all three groups, they have worked together to make the product more reliable and meaningful over time.

More insurance companies are entering the LTCI business in one way or another each year. Consumers and consumer advocates are always searching for a properly priced policy that provides meaningful benefits for a broad range of services and providers. The regulators are constantly seeking ways to maintain the delicate balancing act between the needs of the consumers and insurers. While there is much common ground among these groups, they each have some different views of what long-term care insurance is or should be. Readers of this book may also have their own views. Therefore, it is important for this text to provide a common understanding and definition of long-term care insurance

» Defining Long-Term Care Insurance

Long-term care insurance means many things to many people. Some view it as reimbursement for receiving medical attention at home. Some expect it to pay for housekeeping, delivery or preparation of meals, or transportation services to get to and from the grocery store. Others see it as a way to pay for someone to go to the "old folks home to die."

Even within the insurance industry there are different opinions. Some think of it as a stand-alone, individually sold insurance product that is purchased at the kitchen table. Some want it available from their employer under a group offering with the decisions made by corporate benefits managers. Others like it combined with other products they're more comfortable with, such as life insurance or annuities.

The NAIC Definition

Because this text focuses on the long-term care insurance product, a common definition is needed. The National Association of Insurance Commissioners (NAIC) plays an important role in setting uniform standards for insurance products and promoting state adoption of those standards. The NAIC is perhaps the best place to look for a common definition, since establishing a common definition of "long-term care insurance" is part of the organization's ongoing work.

The Definition of Long-Term Care Insurance of the NAIC Model Act

Long-term care insurance means any insurance policy or rider that is advertised, marketed, offered, or designed to provide coverage for not less than twelve (12) consecutive months for each covered person on an expense incurred, indemnity, prepaid or other basis; for one or more necessary or medically necessary diagnostic, preventive, therapeutic, rehabilitative, maintenance or personal care services, provided in a setting other than an acute care unit of a hospital. Such term includes group and individual annuities and life insurance policies or riders which provide directly or which supplement long-term care insurance. Such term also includes a policy or rider which provides for payment of benefits based upon cognitive impairment or the loss of functional capacity. Long-term care insurance may be issued by insurers; fraternal benefit societies; nonprofit health, hospital, and medical service corporations;

prepaid health plans; health maintenance organizations or any similar organization to the extent they are otherwise authorized to issue life or health insurance. Long-term care insurance shall not include any insurance policy which is offered primarily to provide basic Medicare supplement coverage, basic hospital expense coverage, basic medical-surgical expense coverage, hospital confinement indemnity coverage, major expense coverage, disability income or related asset-protection coverage, accident only coverage, specified disease or specified accident coverage, or limited benefit health coverage. With regard to life insurance, this term does not include life insurance policies which accelerate the death benefit specifically for one or more of the qualifying events of terminal illness, medical conditions requiring extraordinary medical intervention, or permanent institutional confinement, and which provide the option of a lump-sum payment for those benefits and in which neither the benefits nor the eligibility for the benefits is conditioned upon the receipt of long-term care. Notwithstanding any other provision contained herein, any product advertised, marketed or offered as long-term care insurance shall be subject to the provisions of this Act.

FOCUS QUESTION 1

Name some entities that issue long-term care insurance.

_____

_____

_____

_____

_____

_____

_____

_____

Many insurers recognize the unprotected financial risk associated with needing long-term care. They have worked diligently over many years to develop the right insurance option to protect such needs of their customers. But insurers also face a risk in entering this market. That risk is the potential financial loss due to excessive claim payments from a product that is not properly designed, priced, underwritten, or administered. Some companies have entered the long-term care insurance market not adequately prepared for these challenges and have subsequently been forced to leave the market. The NAIC definition gives insurers the flexibility to find innovative approaches to solving the needs of the insurance-buying public. And insurers have looked at several alternatives for providing long-term care insurance.

The Components of the NAIC Definition

As the definition states, long-term care insurance is available as a **stand-alone product** or in combination with other insurance products. The advantage of a stand-alone policy is that insurers need only focus on establishing and refining the tools, contract language, and technology to support one type of risk. Other insurance-related factors do not cloud the long-term care need or analysis of the product's experience. Stand-alone products are also easier for both the distribution system and consumers to understand.

The stand-alone product is available as an individual or group insurance product. The **individual long-term care insurance product** is one that is typically sold by an agent to an individual or couple. The individual product currently makes up the lion's share of the market. Because the stand-alone product is the option that provides the clearest basis for understanding long-term care insurance, it receives the most attention in this text.

The **group long-term care insurance product** is gaining increasing acceptance with employers. Many of the nation's largest employers currently offer long-term care insurance in their employee benefit package, typically as an employee-pay-all, voluntary benefit. A growing number of smaller employers also currently offer or are considering it. More than eight million federal employees and annuitants, including the nation's military, will have a long-term care insurance program available in the fall of 2002. The number of employees electing to buy long-term care insurance through the workplace, however, remains small. One factor for the relatively low participation rates in this voluntary benefit is the challenge of making a younger, working-age population aware of the need for this type of insurance. Another factor is that employees must usually pay the entire premium. Furthermore, at the time of this writing, those consumers considering the purchase of long-term care insurance offered through their employer cannot use the same payment method for their long-term care insurance as they use for their medical insurance—either their cafeteria package or flexible spending arrangements. Chapters 13 and 14 of this book go into more detail on the group long-term care insurance product.

Because long-term care insurance is a relatively new insurance product, some insurers do not feel comfortable getting involved in this side of the insurance business at all, or may not be comfortable entering the market with a stand-alone product. Some insurers prefer to gain experience with the underwriting, administration, and claims process by integrating the long-term care risk with other insurance products with which they have more extensive experience. In this way, the potential financial loss is minimized while the insurer learns more about the long-term care component of the risk. Long-term care insurance is most often combined with life insurance, although other combination products link long-term care with disability insurance or annuities.

Long-term care insurance is integrated with life insurance, annuities, and even disability income policies. As the NAIC spells out in its definition, only certain riders to a life insurance policy meet the standards of long-term care insurance. Annuities are receiving more attention as a product that can be designed to also address long-term care needs. And insurers are coming up with innovative conversion privileges or dual benefit eligibility options on disability income policies to enable them to also cover long-term care. These and other combination product options are discussed in the last chapter.

FOCUS QUESTION 2

What other kinds of insurance do we often see packaged with long-term care insurance?

_____

_____

_____

_____

_____

_____

There is another type of coverage available that looks just like a long-term care insurance policy but makes benefits available for less than one year. **Short-term care insurance** is available to individuals who either cannot afford a long-term care policy or do not think they will ever need more than one year of benefits. They have limited availability—many states do not allow this coverage. Where they are available, they are usually regulated as limited benefit plans. Because this coverage does not fall under long-term care insurance, it is not addressed in this text.

The most common benefit arrangements available with a traditional long-term care insurance policy are expense-incurred or indemnity. The **expense-incurred design** reimburses for actual expenses for services received up to a fixed dollar amount per day, week, or month; this amount is selected by the insured at the time of purchase. The **indemnity** or **per diem design** pays a flat dollar amount regardless of the actual expenses. The indemnity design takes two forms in today's marketplace. The most common form pays a flat dollar amount, but only pays benefits when long-term care services are received by the claimant; the other type of indemnity policy pays benefits simply when someone is impaired, regardless of whether long-term care services were received (or of what type, if they were).

Long-term care services covered under these insurance policies are diversifying and evolving rapidly. Early policies focused largely on facility-based care, mostly care in a nursing home. There was little or no at-home care covered. Today, it is typical for an LTCI policy to pay for care in a nursing home or assisted living facility, at home, or in a variety of community-based settings such as adult day care. Benefits are no longer limited to just skilled care, as in the early policies. Personal care from both skilled and nonskilled providers is also covered, usually with no distinction made in terms of the amount of benefit payable.

To avoid stifling the product development opportunities inherent with a new product such as LTCI, the NAIC's definition describes the types of services considered within "long-term care" in general terms rather than identifying specific types or providers of services. The definition includes ". . . for one or more necessary or medically necessary diagnostic, preventive, therapeutic, rehabilitative, maintenance or personal care services. . ." These terms are frequently found in policies along with additional clarification on the actual types of services covered.

Basing benefit payments on a cognitive impairment or the loss of physical capacity is now the standard for long-term care insurance. It took years of research, most of which was conducted by the provider community and academia, before the insurance industry felt comfortable adopting these concepts as the criteria for determining eligibility for long-term care benefits. Cognitive impairment and functional loss (as measured by the inability to perform activities of daily living) are now established as the most valid, objective, and reliable measures of when someone needs long-term care. As such, they are now standard criteria for long-term care insurance, whether offered on a stand-alone basis or as part of a combined insurance product. Other types of insurance (for example, disability income insurance) are also exploring using these same concepts to help define the insured event.

A wide variety of organizations may offer long-term care insurance. Again, the NAIC wanted to allow for innovation by opening the field to virtually all those able to offer life or health insurance. This text uses the term **insurers** to summarize this collection of types of organizations, which might include insurance companies, HMOs, fraternal benefit societies, continuing care retirement communities, and others.

The NAIC definition goes on to ensure there is no confusion between what constitutes long-term care insurance and other forms of insurance. These other types of coverage have a specific risk they insure against. Given the general public's limited understanding of all insurance products, adding a layer of complexity by integrating these different products is simply inappropriate. This also clearly differentiates long-term care insurance from the type of rider options that have the potential to give consumers a false sense of security that their entire long-term care risk is addressed by a significantly limited policy or rider design.

The NAIC definition concludes with a catchall phrase to cover all the products that truly are designed for long-term care as opposed to those that cover a different risk. This is an essential component of the NAIC's work—to maintain the integrity of the long-term care insurance marketplace.

» The Evolution of Long-Term Care Before LTCI

People have always gone to some type of home when they were unable to care for themselves. In the "old days," they went to live with one of their children—that is, if they weren't already living together in a multigenerational household. Facilities designed to care for impaired people started to emerge as life expectancies increased and as the family structure began to change in various ways—children pursuing career interests away from their family farm or hometown, parents retiring to warmer climates, or marriages not lasting a lifetime. These facilities were called nursing homes.

Care in this type of facility was affordable for many. The facility did not typically provide much more care than a family member would be able to provide—assistance with getting dressed, personal hygiene, and moving about. The facility also provided a quality nutrition program combined with exercise or therapy opportunities to help maintain the resident's physical strength, and social activities enhanced the resident's emotional well-being. Medical treatment was left to hospitals to provide.

This began to change after World War II. The cost of hospitalization and nursing home care was increasing. This was especially burdensome for aging people, who needed more medical treatment and nursing services than younger people required. Medical insurance costs reflected this need for additional care with rates that were unaffordable for many in their retirement years. There were even cases of people spending their savings on copayments and deductibles plus treatments or medications that were not covered by the type of insurance that was available at the time.

» The Impact of Government Programs

These factors led to a sweeping change in the way health care providers were reimbursed for their services to the elderly. Medicare and Medicaid were signed into law in 1965.

Medicare

Medicare is Title XVIII of the Social Security Act. It is an entitlement program available to just about everyone over the age of 65. It is available to individuals and their spouses who have worked for at least 10 years at a Medicare-covered employer and are citizens or permanent residents of the United States. It is also available to self-employed persons who have paid into the Social Security system for a sufficient amount of time. In addition, many of those who do not meet these qualification criteria may purchase Medicare coverage. People under 65 can apply to Medicare for benefits if they have received disability benefits under Social Security for two years or have a chronic kidney disease in need of dialysis or kidney transplant.

FOCUS QUESTION 3

Who is entitled to Medicare?

People over the age of _____ .

People (and their spouses) who have worked for at least _____ years for an employer covered by Medicare. To qualify, these individuals have to be US citizens or _____ .

Name others you can think of:

_____

_____

_____

Medicare's two components are designed to pay for hospitalization, medical care, and physician services. Part A, paid for by the federal government, focuses on hospitalization including inpatient care, skilled nursing facilities, hospice care, and limited home health care. Part B is an optional program covering doctor services, outpatient hospitalization, medical-oriented therapies, and some additional home health care. The cost of Part B is heavily subsidized by the government, and consumers pay an additional monthly premium ($54 in 2002).

The services most pertinent to long-term care insurance are Medicare's skilled nursing home, home health care, and hospice benefits.

Medicare Nursing Home Benefits

Skilled nursing home services under Medicare are only available to those who:

- have had three days of hospitalization,
- enter a Medicare-certified skilled nursing facility within 30 days for the same diagnosis, and
- need skilled care.

The requirement that the patient needs skilled care means they need specialized treatments and therapies to help them recover from the condition causing the hospitalization.

Medicare pays for all covered services for the first 20 days of skilled nursing home treatment. From days 21 to 100, the patient must make a large daily copayment ($101.50 in 2002 and increasing annually with inflation), and Medicare pays the rest. After the 100th day, Medicare pays no benefits.

FIGURE 1.1

Timeline of Medicare Nursing Home Benefits

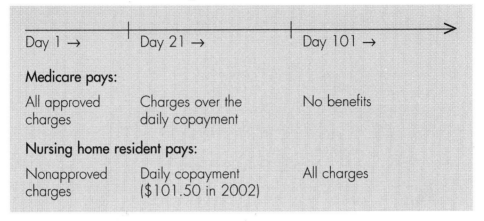

Day 1 →	Day 21 →	Day 101 →
Medicare pays:		
All approved charges	Charges over the daily copayment	No benefits
Nursing home resident pays:		
Nonapproved charges	Daily copayment ($101.50 in 2002)	All charges

Medicare Home Health Care Benefits

To qualify for home health care benefits under Medicare, four criteria are required:

■ There must be a physician's plan of care that includes the need for medical care at home.

■ Intermittent (not full-time) skilled nursing care, physical therapy, occupational therapy, or speech language pathology services must be needed.

■ The patient must be confined to their home except for short trips such as for medical treatment or religious services.

■ Care must be received from a Medicare-certified home care agency.

The services available under Medicare are skilled nursing services, physical therapy, occupational therapy, speech language pathology services, medical social services, specified medical supplies and medical equipment, and part-time home health aide services in conjunction with the skilled services. This does not include full-time care, prescription drugs, home-delivered meals, homemaker services, or stand-alone personal care.

What are some of the home health care benefits covered by Medicare?

_____

_____

_____

_____

_____

_____

_____

What are some others that are not covered?

_____

_____

_____

_____

_____

Home care is payable as long as a physician continues to include the services in the plan of care when care is needed for less than seven days a week or eight hours a day. The original intent of providing just 21 days of service was successfully challenged in the courts and now remains a guideline rather than a maximum.

Most people who need long-term care at home do not often satisfy these Medicare criteria, or if they do, they don't meet them for very long. Someone who suffers a cognitive impairment or condition such as Alzheimer's disease might need constant supervision and help with personal care, but would not be homebound or in need of medical care. Similarly, someone who needs help with bathing and dressing for a prolonged time because of physical loss from a stroke would not satisfy the requirement to be homebound.

Medicare Hospice Benefits

Medicare's hospice benefits are available to those who:

- have a life expectancy of six months or less,
- waive their rights to other Medicare-covered services,
- have hospice services included in a physician's plan of care, and
- receive care from a Medicare-certified hospice program.

The hospice services available include physician services, skilled nursing services, home health aide and homemaker services, physical therapy, occupational therapy, speech language pathology services, drugs for symptom control and pain relief, medical social services, specified medical supplies and medical equipment, dietary counseling, and grief counseling for family members. Medicare hospice benefits will not cover treatment to attempt to cure the terminal illness.

Medicaid

Medicaid is Title XIX of the Social Security Act. It is a joint federal and state means-tested program administered by state and county governments. To receive benefits, applicants must prove that they do not have the financial resources to pay for the necessary care. County governments assess applicants' assets and, in many states, income. If the applicant is married to someone living outside a hospital or nursing home, this husband or wife becomes part of the analysis as a "community spouse." If the individual or couple has more than the state-mandated allowable limits, the Medicaid applicant must reduce (or spend down) their assets and income to below those limits before Medicaid will provide benefits.

Medicaid is the primary payer for many nursing home residents. States have the option to apply for a Medicaid waiver to cover nontraditional Medicaid providers such as assisted living facilities and home health care. However, a lack of funding generally limits the availability of these benefits, and the vast majority of Medicaid long-term care expenditures nationally are for nursing home care.

Medicaid has had less of an impact on long-term care insurance than Medicare because it is means-tested. Medicaid-eligible individuals generally cannot afford to own a long-term care insurance policy. In fact, the NAIC Model Regulation requires insurers to include on their application a question regarding the applicant's status with regard to Medicaid. Insurance companies should not issue a policy to someone who is covered by Medicaid because the individual would not be able to pay the premium. It is not likely a suitable sale because the insurance policy duplicates some of the coverage available from Medicaid. However, it should be noted that some people who do have the means to purchase long-term care insurance instead decide to spend down to meet Medicaid requirements when the need for care arises. Because of this, Medicaid does have some impact on the LTCI field.

» The Initial Long-Term Care Insurance Products

When Medicare was introduced, there were many who thought that the role of private insurance companies in paying for seniors' health insurance was over. But Medicare was never intended to replace private insurance. In fact, Medicare created many opportunities for creating **wraparound products** (products that address the limitations of the program).

Medicare supplement insurance was the most common type of private insurance found to coordinate with and not duplicate Medicare. Even with the seemingly small copayments and deductibles Medicare initially had in place, many consumers preferred to have those paid by insurance. The thinking goes something like this: "I would rather pay what might be a little extra in insurance premiums each year and know for certain what my out-of-pocket costs will be, rather than have situations where my medical costs are high one year and low another." That was how their previous insurance program had worked—in essence, they were paying a little extra for peace of mind. Insurance companies recognized this desire of their consumers and developed Medicare supplement policies to cover those copayments and deductibles inherent in the Medicare program and other health-related items not covered by Medicare.

One innovative insurance company took a deeper look at the limitations of Medicare and developed an insurance product that covered the skilled nursing facility benefit copayment and then continued to pay benefits beyond what Medicare was paying. This policy was the beginning of what we know today as the long-term care insurance industry.

Benefit Eligibility

Early policies mirrored Medicare's benefit eligibility requirements. First, the insured needed at least three days of hospitalization. Back then, physicians could have their patients admitted to the hospital for just about any reason. For someone who needed nursing home care (and remember, facilities during this time provided mostly assistance with daily tasks and not the rehabilitative medical treatments we see today), physicians and hospitals could easily find a battery of tests or procedures to perform.

The next criterion for insurers' benefit eligibility was just as easy to satisfy — enter a Medicare-certified skilled nursing facility. Nursing homes were eager to gain such certification. They recognized that worrying about checks not clearing the bank or receiving payments late would be a thing of the past if the facility could get the government to pay for the residents' care. Having additional paperwork in the form of reporting requirements to Medicare and having a governmental watchdog ensuring quality care was a small price to pay in exchange for the peace of mind of knowing a stable payment source was in place. Most facilities back then were smaller than they are today and were operated by local owners who recognized a need in the community for a facility to care for older residents with pride and dignity. There were few corporate owners and fewer facilities that didn't want to meet Medicare's requirements to become certified. Someone who was going to enter a facility and get Medicare or these new policies to pay benefits could select just about any nursing home in their community.

The final criterion to qualify for benefits under this new form of insurance was to receive **skilled care** as defined by Medicare. Generally speaking, skilled care occurs when someone receives specialized treatments and therapies from a health care professional as they recover from an acute condition. The key is that people must always show signs of progress in their recovery efforts. Once their condition stabilizes, they no longer meet Medicare's definition of receiving skilled care, and thus they would not meet the insurance company's definition for benefit qualification.

List the benefit eligibility requirements of early long-term care policies.

_____

_____

_____

_____

_____

_____

_____

_____

A good illustration of how skilled care operates is when a broken hip is replaced. A person who is discharged from the hospital following hip replacement surgery almost always needs additional recovery and rehabilitation time before they can once again walk on their own. Entering a nursing home to receive rehabilitative care and physical therapy is significantly less expensive than staying in the hospital for the same services. The nursing home actually saves Medicare and private insurance in claim costs, and the patient is in a more desirable setting than a hospital and receiving the same type of treatment that was formerly available only in a hospital setting.

While this person is getting better, they are receiving skilled care—treatments and therapies designed to restore their physical condition to the point it was before the hip replacement surgery. This treatment has a sunset—it will eventually end.

Compare this situation to that of someone who needs assistance resulting from a chronic condition such as arthritis. It is not likely such a person will find restoration of their abilities as a result of any type of treatment or therapy. It is possible to take medications to lessen the pain and participate in therapy to assist in flexibility or mobility, but someone inflicted with arthritis will not regain the full function of the affected area.

This requirement for skilled care became especially problematic for individuals suffering from dementia, senility, or Alzheimer's disease. While progress has been made in slowing down the progression of such conditions, there is currently no therapy, treatment, or medication that will enable those suffering from them to fully regain their abilities. People expected their policy to pay benefits when they needed nursing home care for this type of cause. But in fact, coverage was denied based on the provisions and language of these initial policies.

Once someone did meet the long-term care insurer's benefit qualification criteria under these initial policies, benefits were available to the insured for at least six months but no longer than three years. The daily benefit maximum was extremely low when compared to today's standards, and inflation protection was not even considered an option. These early products were so risky for the insurance company that the policy was only conditionally renewable. By today's standards, these products are primitive and lack any real value, but back in 1965, a skilled nursing home insurance policy was innovative.

» Summary

Long-term care insurance has a short history, with its beginnings coinciding with the establishment of the federal Medicare and Medicaid programs in 1965. The early products were primitive by today's standards, but they represented a first step. The insurance industry followed the Medicare model in designing benefit qualification criteria by requiring a claimant to first be in a hospital before receiving care. This has changed over the years to provide consumers with easier access to more diverse services with payments for longer periods of time, and essentially to better fit with people's real long-term care needs, which include the need for care of a nonskilled and ongoing nature.

The next chapter looks more closely at some of the factors and entities that have influenced product design over the years.

Expense-incurred design	Medicare
Group long-term care insurance product	Medicare supplement insurance
Indemnity design	Per diem design
Individual long-term care insurance product	Short-term care insurance
Insurers	Skilled care
Long-term care insurance (LTCI)	Stand-alone product
Medicaid	Wraparound product

Key Terms

» Review Questions

1. What is the minimum length of coverage provided by long-term care insurance as defined by the NAIC?

2. What is the advantage (compared to combined products) of issuing a stand-alone long-term care insurance policy? Answer from the respective perspectives of insurers and consumers.

3. Characterize an individual who might find short-term care insurance useful.

4. Is short-term care insurance available across the United States?

5. Which two conditions are considered to be the most valid, objective, and reliable measures of when someone needs long-term care?

6. When were Medicare and Medicaid established?

7. What is the maximum length of nursing home care paid for by Medicare?

8. Do Medicare hospice benefits cover any treatment attempting to cure a terminal illness?

9. What is the desirable outcome of skilled care as defined by Medicare?

10. How many days does a patient need to have been hospitalized to qualify for Medicare nursing home benefits?

» Answers

1. Twelve consecutive months.

2. For insurers, the advantage is that they need only focus on establishing and refining their strategy to support one type of risk. For consumers, a stand-alone policy is easier to understand.

3. A person who cannot afford a long-term care policy may benefit from short-term care insurance. An individual who thinks they need coverage for a year at the most (perhaps while waiting for their job-related long-term care coverage to take effect) would also find short-term care insurance useful.

4. No, some states do not allow it.

5. The first criterion is cognitive impairment; the second is functional loss, measured by the inability to perform activities of daily living.

6. 1965.

7. One hundred days.

8. No.

9. According to Medicare's definition, skilled care is care that results in improvement during a patient's recovery effort.

10. Three days.

2

Factors in the Evolution of the LTCI Product

    Consumers
    Regulators
    Insurers
    Providers

» Overview

Today's LTCI products have evolved greatly from their beginnings. Quali-fication for benefits no longer resembles Medicare's requirements or the arbitrary and ill-defined medical necessity criteria of early policies. Prior hospitalization is specifically excluded from benefit triggers in the NAIC Models and state regulations. Today's policies no longer differentiate bene-fits by level of care, paying more for skilled care than nonskilled care, as early policies did. The types of covered facilities and providers continue to expand to keep pace with the rapid rate of change in the long-term care delivery system. And every policy is at least guaranteed renewable, with a few companies experimenting with noncancellable policies that guarantee the premium for the life of the contract.

How did long-term care insurance products get so much better? This resulted from the efforts of many people working together. Input came from:

- consumers,
- regulators,
- insurance companies, and
- those who provide care for the impaired.

» Consumers

Consumers have had a marked impact on the LTCI field. It is not adequate to consider consumers simply as those who purchase a policy. Consumers encompass everyone who is involved in the purchase of long-term care insurance, including:

- those who purchase,
- those who consider purchasing,
- those who regularly spend time with consumers and sell the product,
- those who provide advice to potential buyers of the product, and
- most important, those who own a policy and then go into claim status.

Consumers in Claim Status

LTCI claimants find out how their policy actually operates. Actually, seldom are those who purchase a policy the ones who file the claim. It is most often the spouse or children of the insured who initiate and manage the insurance claim process. When in claim status, insured individuals' primary concerns are more with their condition and the care they're receiving than with how the provider of that care is reimbursed.

Who is most likely to find out if there is a clause in a policy designed to keep someone off claim? Not those who read the fine print of their policy—which rarely occurs. It is those who work through the system to see how the policy performs at the time of claiming benefits. Once that language is found and a claim denied, word spreads quickly about that company, the type of insurance they offer, and how it treats claimants. A reputation is created.

At the same time, as claims are delivered, insurers find out whether the original intent behind the policy design is adequately supported by the contract language, whether the policy language has kept pace with changing delivery options, and whether provisions are indeed working as intended and meeting the needs of both the insurer and the consumer.

The agent who sold the policy should assist their client in facilitating timely claim payment to the degree the insured seeks assistance from the agent. This value-added service is especially helpful during the time of crisis leading up to the filing of a claim. Agents know others in the business, and word of this will spread rapidly through the tightly knit agent community. Whether the end result is positive or not, the agent's experience, communicated to those responsible for product development, will influence future policy design and changes in the claim process.

The claimant and the claimant's family are also the ones to preach about the value of owning such insurance. If the experience of dealing with the insurance company and its agent at claim time is a positive one, this too is known among those who know the claimant. Because LTCI is a relatively new insurance product, there are relatively few people who know someone receiving benefits. This causes a great amount of curiosity about the product. A positive experience with the workings of a policy is the best way to satisfy that curiosity.

Policyholders Who Never Make Claims

Those who purchase a policy but never receive benefits from it also contribute to product enhancements. These are people who believed in the idea of taking responsibility for payment of their long-term care needs by shifting the risk to an insurance company. Although they received no benefit payments in exchange for their premiums, they did gain peace of mind from the arrangement. Agents and insurers recognize these situations as contributing to the success of the product line—if everyone filed a claim, we would see a significant increase in premiums. For people in this situation, there are now several options for receiving some monetary reward for their loyalty over the years, as outlined below.

Nonforfeiture benefits arose out of the concern that someone might hold a policy for years, never receive benefits, but then be unable to maintain their coverage and be forced to lapse. Also, some consumers expressed concern that although they paid premiums for many years, they got back nothing tangible from the insurance company, having not needed long-term care by the time of lapse or death. (It is hard for the consumer to recognize the value of peace of mind inherent in owning all forms of insurance.) They expressed their concerns in the appropriate circles and got the NAIC to carefully evaluate nonforfeiture options. Now a specified nonforfeiture benefit option is part of the NAIC Model and many states' insurance regulations. All federally tax-qualified policies must offer a nonforfeiture option.

A fairly recent offshoot of this negotiation was the recognition that there is the potential of significant premium increases in the future. For those affected by such increases, the NAIC developed the **contingent nonforfeiture benefit**, and many states have adopted this language as part of their regulations. This benefit may be included in the insurance contract, but this is not common today. Instead, the benefit is part of the insurance company's administrative function and is a requirement of the state for an insurer to be allowed to offer the product in the state.

The contingent nonforfeiture benefit becomes effective only after a premium increase has been submitted that exceeds the limits spelled out in the regulation. The benefit works just like the other NAIC-mandated nonforfeiture option in that it provides a shortened benefit maximum based on both the daily benefit and the amount of premiums paid. However, it is different in that it is only effective if the insured's policy lapses after a substantial premium increase. Typically, a contingent nonforfeiture benefit is automatically included in a policy when the insured has declined the standard nonforfeiture benefit. Unlike the standard nonforfeiture benefit, which has a significant premium cost, the contingent nonforfeiture benefit is included without an additional premium cost, making it an attractive approach.

FOCUS QUESTION 1

Describe how the contingent nonforfeiture benefit works.

TABLE 2.1

Contingent Nonforfeiture Premium Increase Guidelines from the NAIC Model Regulation

Issue age	Percent increase over initial premium*	Issue age	Percent increase over initial premium
29 and under	200%	72	36%
30-34	190%	73	34%
35-39	170%	74	32%
40-44	150%	75	30%
45-49	130%	76	28%
50-54	110%	77	26%
55-59	90%	78	24%
60	70%	79	22%
61	66%	80	20%
62	62%	81	19%
63	58%	82	18%
64	54%	83	17%
65	50%	84	16%
66	48%	85	15%
67	46%	86	14%
68	44%	87	13%
69	42%	88	12%
70	40%	89	11%
71	38%	90 and over	10%

* The percentage is cumulative—that is, it applies to the combined amount of any rate increase and any previous rate increases.

Insureds Who File Complaints

There are also some consumers who express their dissatisfaction with the LTCI policy they purchased by submitting a formal complaint about the policy or its operation. Complaints are received at state insurance departments, agent offices, and insurance company home offices. They come in either written or oral form. These complaints state how the insureds felt they were injured as a result of owning or considering the purchase of these policies. Companies now record their complaints related to all product lines and report them to the many states that require complaint reports. Some states then make the complaint information available to consumers in a qualified report listing insurers. Complaints can serve as a learning tool for insurance companies interested in improving the way they do business.

The primary cause of complaints to insurance departments is premium increases. Long-term care insurance has always been sold with the intent of having the premiums remain the same throughout the life of the contract. But, in a guaranteed renewable contract, insurers have a limited right to adjust premiums as experience warrants. When rates increase, some insureds understand, others are disgruntled, and still others are irate.

In the event of a premium increase, the insured can choose to pay the higher premium or not. If they choose not to, they might be given the option of reducing their benefits until the premium is about the same as their original premium or simply lapse their policy. Furthermore, they can always complain about the increase to their state insurance department. And they do complain. These complaints have led to significant changes to the NAIC Model Regulation and the way insurance companies design and price their products.

Consumer Purchasing Decisions

The ultimate consumer input is how the consumer's money is spent. A company can develop what seems to be the perfect policy based on consumer research and never sell a single one. When a company develops an innovative policy feature that consumers find worthy of spending their money on, the company finds success. Normally, other companies will recognize this consumer desire and integrate these features into their next product. Such was the case when coverage was expanded to include assisted living facilities. A true competitive edge does not last long in the long-term care insurance industry.

Agents

Agents working in the LTCI field also serve as a conduit for consumer input. These people meet with individuals and business owners in offering long-term care insurance and serve as intermediaries between insurers and consumers. As the eyes and ears for insurers, they have the opportunity to understand the buying public's concerns and objections. Many companies conduct agent "input councils" to obtain feedback on consumer needs and product design.

Independent agents have the option of not selling a company's product if the product does not in their view meet the needs of their clients. Sales results have a direct impact on product development. As an example, agents will offer a client the company's product with the best nonforfeiture options if the client feels that this is the most important aspect of the policy. Companies offering products that an agent does not find value in offering will not see the sales results they might have expected. Offering the product to meet the needs of the producers and consumers is paramount to an insurer's success.

FOCUS QUESTION 2

In what ways do independent insurance agents have an impact on an insurance company's long-term care insurance products and sales?

» Regulators

Regulators have the enforcement mechanism to ensure that quality LTCI products are offered. State regulators working through the state insurance department are able to approve and disapprove products submitted for sale in their state. For this text, the term "regulator" goes beyond the people reviewing the filings at the state insurance departments. It also includes the National Association of Insurance Commissioners (NAIC) and the federal government.

State Insurance Department

State insurance departments are the principal watchdogs of the insurance industry. They control insurer activities through the following means:

- licensing,
- review and approval of product filings,
- review and approval of rates,
- guaranty associations, and
- ongoing reports.

Licensing. An insurance company applying for a license must provide the insurance department with proof that it has the financial resources to insure the risks under consideration. The department might even review the experience of the principal officers or the board of directors, including performing criminal background investigations. This scrutiny is relatively easy for an established, ongoing enterprise. For new companies, it might prove difficult.

A company selling long-term care insurance normally has a life and health insurance license, although there are some using a property and casualty license. Each state has requirements of the insurer before a license is granted.

Product Filings. The next way the insurance departments help to maintain consumer confidence is to review and approve product filings. Long-term care insurance falls under most states' accident and sickness regulations.

Every state and the District of Columbia have LTCI regulations. All have adopted at least a portion of the NAIC's Model Act and Model Regulation. Generally speaking, if an insurer meets the NAIC's requirements, the product approval process is less difficult. But few states accept a company's initial filing without some modifications.

▣ The **policy form filing** is where states spend most of their time reviewing. There are many aspects to the product for which states have established minimum standards that insurers must meet before having their product approved. Even within individual states, these standards can vary depending on who performs the review.

▣ A **disclosure form** is documentation from the insurer given to the purchaser or prospective purchaser of long-term care insurance. The state reviews and approves these forms. The forms have become mostly standardized across the industry, but certain states want to see specific language or a variance if it is significant. These disclosures include the following:

■ an outline of coverage — a description of the policy's principal benefits and exclusions;

■ a 20-year graphical demonstration of the differences between having inflation protection and not having it (normally a part of the outline of coverage);

■ an application to obtain the individual's medical history;

■ a replacement form (including the name and address of the company whose policy is subject to replacement);

■ a personal worksheet (designed to assess the suitability of the sale);

■ "Things You Should Know Before You Buy Long-Term Care Insurance";

■ a form explaining the risk of rate increases; and

■ a shopper's guide. (The NAIC has developed one to meet its standards; some states allow companies to use their own.)

Some states approve advertising materials; some simply require the insurer to submit them, while others do not require filing them. Advertising materials include anything that is intended for use with a consumer. This includes the product brochure, prospecting letters, consumers' seminar materials, small brochures, and even sales scripts from training materials. Some states require the advertising to be submitted with the product filing, while other states won't review the advertising until after the product has been approved. This review of advertising materials has been known to lead to a regulator's desire to review the product filing again.

FOCUS QUESTION 3

From the perspective of a state regulatory agency, what are some of the things that can be construed as insurance "advertisement"?

_____

_____

_____

_____

_____

_____

_____

_____

Review and Approval of Rates. States require submission of premium rates. Some states approve the rates, while others simply review them. This is true both of initial rate filings and filings for adjustments to premiums.

Companies formerly had to represent that they would pay out at least a specific minimum portion of the premiums collected for claims. Normally this claim payment to premiums ratio, or **loss ratio**, was 60 percent. The NAIC adopted new requirements for rate submissions as part of Section 10 of the Model Regulation that eliminated the loss ratio standard in new rate filings. Now an actuary is required to certify "that the initial premium rate schedule is sufficient to cover anticipated costs under moderately adverse experience and that the premium rate schedule is reasonably expected to be sustainable over the life of the form with no future premium increases anticipated. . ." Under the current Model Regulation, loss ratios only come into play if a rate increase is filed.

Guaranty Associations. For companies that become insolvent, the insurance department operates a type of safety net called a **guaranty association**. The guaranty association board is normally made up of officers from insurance companies, and their duty is to ensure that policyholders of the failed insurer are not adversely affected. Another company normally takes over the operation of the failed insurer and receives a financial subsidy from the guaranty association to administer its business.

Reports. State insurance departments also require ongoing reporting that includes both financial results and product experience. Companies file what is commonly referred to as a "Blue Book" showing annual financial results. This is a detailed analysis of the company's income statement and balance sheet. Many areas of the common accounting reports show the specific reserves held for product lines and the incomes of the key officers of the organization.

LTCI insurers are required by state insurance departments to file a number of annual reports. The NAIC Model Regulation suggests a number of reports that states should review. A rescission report is required to ensure that companies are performing their underwriting tasks when a policy is issued rather than waiting until claim time and then canceling the policy. A few rescissions each year are understandable, but an excessive number on a regular basis is likely to be an indication that the company's operation is in need of review.

Lapses and replacements are a potential problem area. If companies or agents have an excessive number of either, churning business to gain first-year premiums is suspected. The NAIC Model Regulation spells out the reports used to monitor this activity. These include the following:

- a list of the agents with the greatest percentage of lapses and replacement activity,

- the number of lapsed policies as a percentage of total sales,

- the number of lapsed policies as a percentage of the total in force as of the end of the preceding calendar year,

- the number of replacement policies as a percentage of total sales, and

■ the number of replacement policies as a percentage of the total in force as of the end of the preceding calendar year.

Consumers are also concerned about having claims evaluated fairly. No company wants to deny a valid claim or pay for an inappropriate claim. To ensure that companies are treating their insureds fairly, the NAIC Model Regulation has a form for companies to submit to insurance departments showing their experience with denying claims. (Denials resulting from not satisfying the elimination period or because of a preexisting condition are shown in this report, but they are excluded from the final denial ratios.)

Suitability reporting is also part of the Model Regulation, to help ensure that long-term care insurance is being sold appropriately to those who can financially benefit from what it has to offer. In the states that have adopted this part of the Model, insurers are required to submit:

■ the total number of applications received from residents of the state,

■ the number of those who declined to provide the information requested on the personal worksheet,

■ the number of applicants who did not meet the suitability standards, and

■ the number of those who chose to confirm that they felt the policy was suitable for them after receiving a suitability letter.

All these reports have an indirect influence on product development. If a company's in-force business is being replaced regularly, it should introduce a new product or modify its existing policies. If many policies are lapsing, this is likely an indication that there is either something wrong with the product or the way it is sold (although it may be due to a rate increase). If too many claims are denied, there is probably a problem with the way the qualification for benefits language is written or administered. If the financials show an unprofitable product line, the product could be in need of repricing (or this could result from poor underwriting or claim-paying practices).

Insurance fraud has become a major concern of regulators. Some states now want to know what companies are doing to curb the frequency of fraud and require an organized plan. They ask companies to report the frequency of claims investigated for potential fraud and the results of the investigation. They may assist in prosecuting fraudulent activity through the judicial system. These experiences and reports can influence the type of policy language they feel companies need to include to minimize the potential for fraudulent activity.

Summary of State Regulation. All states have long-term care insurance regulations. It wasn't always this way, which made it difficult for insurers to know what standards their product needed to meet to gain state approval. Also, consumers did not receive the protection they deserved from the regulators in their state. States recognized the need for such regulations as more companies submitted filings, and states desired a more consistent and fair review process. Developing the appropriate guidelines was facilitated as the NAIC Models improved. Most states have adopted the Model Act and Model Regulation in whole or in part.

State insurance departments are in a difficult situation. They represent the citizens of their state, so they would like to see the products provide as many benefits as possible. On the other hand, they want the insurance companies to maintain their financial stability, ensure a competitive marketplace, and continue to offer affordable insurance coverage to state residents. This balancing act is difficult and at times puts the department in a situation that requires expertise and the judicious exercise of power.

The National Association of Insurance Commissioners (NAIC)

The **National Association of Insurance Commissioners (NAIC)**, mentioned above, is an organization made up of the insurance regulators from all 50 states, the District of Columbia, and four US territories. The NAIC provides a venue for debate, negotiation, and consensus building on issues in need of uniform policy. At quarterly and interim meetings, the NAIC receives input from regulators, insurance company representatives, producers, and consumer representatives to develop the types of legislation and regulations state insurance departments can use as a model in their respective states. Regulators look to the NAIC for assistance on issues as broad as life insurance illustrations, fraud investigations, workers compensation, insurance company accounting, and long-term care insurance. (See www.naic.org.)

The NAIC recognized the need for such assistance for long-term care insurance in the mid-1980s and developed their first **Long-Term Care Insurance Model Act** and **Long-Term Care Insurance Model Regulation** in 1986. This was the result of input from consumers, organizations representing consumers (such as the American Association of Retired Persons — AARP), insurers, and state insurance department representatives. These same parties continue to provide input to the NAIC as it develops its LTCI models.

FOCUS QUESTION 4

Name stakeholders providing input to the NAIC.

_____

_____

_____

_____

_____

_____

_____

The NAIC Model Act is designed for use as legislation — language written and passed by a state legislature and then signed by the governor to become law. The Model Regulation is for use by the insurance department in regulating long-term care insurance (although in some cases provisions of it are enacted into law). Because it is regulatory in nature, the Model Regulation is more detailed and undergoes more changes than the Model Act.

Both Models are subject to regular scrutiny. Over the past years, there have been great debates on their content. The latest version of the Model Regulation is the result of a lengthy and sometimes controversial debate on how to best regulate for rate stability. The end result is based on a consensus that grew out of many discussions. The new model is in the process of adoption in many states.

Throughout this text, the NAIC's influence on the product evolution of specific features is noted. There are times the NAIC has led insurers into a specific policy direction. The two most significant regulator-initiated policy features are the 5 percent compounded inflation protection and nonforfeiture benefits that are required options.

The Health Insurance Portability and Accountability Act (HIPAA)

The **Health Insurance Portability and Accountability Act (HIPAA)** is an extensive piece of legislation passed by Congress and signed into law in August 1996. This federal law was a breakthrough for the LTCI industry. It established qualified long-term care insurance (thus redefining or codifying many commonly held practices) and clarified the tax treatment for long-term care insurance.

In order to manage the tax implications of tax-free benefits, the drafters of HIPAA wanted assurance that only those who actually need long-term care services, versus those who just want the services, would receive reimbursement for them. They require clear definitions on policies that expect to receive favorable tax treatment. Both the physical and cognitive benefit qualification criteria are spelled out in detail and most companies use the language from HIPAA verbatim. In large part, most major insurers were previously using most of the concepts and definitions embodied in HIPAA—the act simply codified the best and most appropriate current practice in the industry. HIPAA's impact on actual features and contract language is discussed in Chapter Four.

HIPAA made allowances for long-term care insurance policies that met state requirements issued before the January 1, 1997 effective date. Because qualified contracts were, for some carriers, such a departure from the way they previously wrote their policies, these older policies received the same favorable tax treatment as those designed with the new requirements. These policies are now considered **grandfathered policies**. However, they cannot be subject to material changes and still maintain their qualified status.

Some insurers, agents, and consumers feel the benefit qualification criteria required of a qualified plan are too stringent. They prefer the old way of doing business. There are nonqualified policies available that do not meet HIPAA's definition for long-term care insurance but do meet state insurance departments' requirements for approval. The tax treatment of these policies remains ambiguous.

Many were concerned that HIPAA would not sufficiently allow for creativity on the part of insurers. There was a sense that all products would be standardized, and innovation would become a thing of the past. However, since HIPAA's passage, there has been extensive movement toward offering new benefits while maintaining the core principles found in the legislation. What HIPAA has done is establish a base coverage with which companies, consumers, and regulators can work while the provider community changes and insurers gain more confidence with the long-term care risk.

» Insurers

Insurers too have influenced the evolution of the LTCI product. A wide variety of organizations are included in this text's definition of "insurers." The NAIC names some of the types in the Model Act: "Long-term care insurance may be issued by insurers; fraternal benefit societies; nonprofit health, hospital, and medical service corporations; prepaid health plans; health maintenance organizations; or any similar organization to the extent they are otherwise authorized to issue life or health insurance." There are even companies with property and casualty licenses offering long-term care insurance. Not all of these company types offer a policy, but the potential exists.

The product development process insurers go through is an interesting one. Some insurers want the most innovative products. Using manufacturing environment terminology, they have a large budget for research and development. They are in direct contact with the provider community, making visits to their facilities and meeting with them in their offices. They rely on provider trade journals to keep current on recent developments. Cutting-edge companies study the current long-term care and gerontology-oriented research. Most important, they listen to the needs and desires of their claimants. All this is done to ensure that the company's product design is current with the provider community and that the latest frequency of utilization data is considered in their pricing assumptions.

These companies have brought new ideas from the long-term care provider community to the insurance market through conducting research and evaluating claimant feedback. They are the companies that first eliminated the prior hospitalization requirement; included benefits for assisted living facilities and adult day centers; recognized the value of benefits for bed reservations, respite care, and caregiver training; and began using activities of daily living and cognitive loss as objective and reliable benefit triggers.

Innovation also comes from a deep understanding of the insurance product. Companies designed an inflation protection option that provided meaningful benefits for those who file a claim long after they purchase a policy. They included a feature to help ensure that a claimant's policy would remain in force during a period of long-term care—the waiver of premium. They tinkered with the administration of the elimination period to better meet insureds' expectations at claim time. They put two lives on a single policy to make better use of the scarce financial resources of many applicants.

FOCUS QUESTION 5

Name some innovations introduced by insurance companies to improve their LTCI products.

_____

_____

_____

_____

_____

_____

The innovative companies frequently find it difficult to gain state insurance department approval of their creative product features. They must educate the person reviewing the filing as to how it will work and why it is a benefit to the consumer. There is no regulation or sample language when it comes to a first-time offering. Gaining approval is a challenge.

Many insurers receive feedback from producers marketing their product. They might have a formal committee made up of their top producers who come to the home office a couple of times a year to discuss product issues. Home office employees might spend time in the field with agents to better understand the buying public. No matter who visits whom, there is an open, ongoing dialog among those looking to enhance their product offerings and provide a better product to consumers.

Insurers must "listen to themselves" in the product development process. The innovative companies have their product development people in close contact with both the underwriting and claims functions. These are the people who see the practical application of the theoretical product development designs. They also see people in difficult situations finding creative solutions to their problems. The claims and underwriting areas at innovative companies pay attention to provider trade journals and gerontology-oriented research. This is another way they find out about cutting-edge assessment techniques, providers, treatments, and medications used with chronically ill individuals.

When product development takes on a broader meaning than just what the policy says, the claims and underwriting people are in constant communication. A better understanding of how a claimant gets to the point of needing services is essential for both functions. Companies have different philosophies on this. One company might find cause for concern with issuing a policy to a diabetic using a certain level of insulin, while another company is confident in accepting the same applicant. The same is true for cancer survivors, those with a recent heart attack or stroke, overweight and underweight people, and other common ailments and conditions. The key ingredient is research and communication to improve the process.

Finally, companies need good financial results from their product offerings. Long-term care insurance is a very expensive product for insurers, requiring a large capital investment in the early years. The product development costs are extensive. Included in the cost are expenses for the people and computer systems to design, gain approval, market, underwrite, issue, administer, and pay claims. There is a large financial commitment by the insurance company before a policy is issued and later in administering the ones that are issued. These expenses go far beyond just paying claims.

Consider all the expenses when a policy is issued—the underwriter's time, obtaining the medical records and assessments, the issuing and distribution of the policy, the agent's and field manager's compensation, the billing and collection systems setup, the funds required for reserves for future claims. Remember that many of these costs are fixed costs that are incurred even when the policy is not issued and that no premiums are received to offset those costs. It takes many years for a company to recover its initial expenses with long-term care insurance.

If a company loses money with each policy it issues, it cannot make up losses with volume. Companies look more toward persistency combined with volume and investment results to maintain a financial model that will keep them profitable. This is the reason producers receive compensation when a policy remains in force—a renewal commission. This is why underwriting is essential to the success of the line—without it, people could delay the purchase until they are ready to file a claim, and the company would not collect adequate premiums to pay the claim. Even the various premium payment modes contribute to the persistency by allowing insureds to make smaller incremental payments more frequently to better fit their budget.

» Providers

The last, and arguably the most important component in the evolution of the LTCI product is the provider community. The provider community is defined as the people and enterprises that care for chronically ill individuals. This includes entities covered by current insurance options and those who might be covered in the future. The entities are the traditional providers, such as nursing homes, and the unconventional providers that have appeared on the scene in the past decade, such as assisted living communities, adult foster care homes, independent in-home care providers, and the like.

Providers receive some of the best new ideas from researchers looking at best practices in providing care throughout the world. Adult day services arose from Dr. Lionel Cosin's geriatric day hospital programs in England during the 1950s.[1] Providers get ideas from researchers seeking practical application to theoretical models. This is where the popular and successful Program of All-inclusive Care for the Elderly (PACE) originated.[2] How these changes have affected the long-term care insurance industry is discussed in subsequent chapters.

Nursing Homes

The **nursing home** industry has seen dramatic changes in the last two decades. In the past, nursing homes were the place people went for limited care when they lost their ability to remain independent in the community. Today they provide much of the rehabilitation and recovery services that formerly took place in hospitals. As the cost of hospitalization continues to increase, the payers of services (be they the Medicare program, insurers, or patients) are always in search of less expensive alternatives that do not jeopardize the quality of care received.

It is proven that nursing homes are able to provide many of the therapies that lead to recovery from acute conditions that were once performed only in hospitals. The equipment designed for therapy and for monitoring the progress of the patient is smaller, while nurses and therapists are better trained to use the equipment. A hospital setting is no longer always needed. Nursing homes frequently have a pharmacy on site and staff with the ability to administer medications. This has allowed physicians to discharge their patients from the hospital before recovery is complete—sometimes referred to as "quicker and sicker" discharges—and this has led nursing homes to become a "post-acute" class of provider.

Nursing homes used to classify the care they provided as skilled, intermediate, or custodial care. They have moved away from these confining definitions to recognition of the therapies and other services received by the residents. What was formerly known as skilled care now consists of such things as physical therapy, speech therapy, intravenous feeding or hydration, and changes of bandages and dressings.

FOCUS QUESTION 6

Describe the functional changes nursing homes have gone through in the last two decades.

_____

_____

_____

_____

_____

_____

_____

_____

Assisted Living Communities

Some of the services traditionally provided by nursing homes are now available in **assisted living communities**. These include providing a personal space (either a private or semi-private room), three meals a day, housekeeping and laundry services, assistance with bathing and dressing (some provide assistance with more activities), access to medical services and medication management, wellness programs, and planned outside activities. Assisted living communities do not have the equipment to provide rehabilitative services or to provide medical care for residents who need ventilators or catheters or help with continence problems. When a resident's impairment progresses beyond the capabilities of the assisted living community, she must receive such services in a hospital or nursing home.

There are people who remain functionally independent, yet nonetheless find assisted living communities a desirable alternative to living on their own. Lives are simplified by having someone else responsible for the grocery shopping, cooking, and cleaning. They are able to come and go as they please and have many friends in the community for personal interaction. The planned activities offer opportunities that simply aren't available living alone at home. (Such people are a challenge for long-term care insurers. Some are able to perform many tasks, but they aren't willing to do them. Others don't understand they need to exhibit a level of impairment, not just the receipt of services, before qualifying for most LTCI benefits.)

States have various regulations for assisted living communities. States regulate such things as the minimum number of beds in a facility, the types of services allowed, and the staffing requirements. Some states have different names for such facilities, and some have encouraged alternatives to assisted living. For example, California calls such facilities "residential care facilities for the elderly," while Oregon has smaller facilities providing the same limited services available under the name of "adult foster care." Minnesota even has different levels of assisted living facilities identified by a letter depending on the level of services the community provides.

LTCI policies began to recognize the need to expand their covered providers in the early 1990s. Claims on nursing home policies were scrutinized because claimants found assisted living communities more desirable than nursing homes — initially because they were less expensive. Companies recognized that these communities provided appropriate care services. The cost was significantly less, ranging from about half to three-quarters of comparable nursing homes in the area. The cost savings helped claimants with a "pool of money" benefit maximum better utilize their limited benefits. This evolution of care providers was a significant change for insurers and opened their eyes to the need to continually stay current with the provider community and to build flexibility into the policies they issue.

The long-term care provider landscape is changing. Hospitals, which traditionally have provided more care than nursing homes, are shifting care to nursing homes. At the same time, people who used to need nursing homes are shifting to assisted living facilities. Another component of this move to and from nursing home care is congregate living with very limited care. This is frequently referred to as "board and care homes."

Board and Care Homes

Board and care homes are facilities that provide less care than assisted living communities. People working in these places can provide limited ·assistance or supervision. Medical personnel are normally not on staff. Administering medications is not usually available. Limited personal care services are provided.

Although assistance in board and care homes is available around the clock, help is typically provided on a schedule. In other words, a resident can receive assistance with a shower and getting dressed in the morning and then with changing into sleepwear in the evening. These services are scheduled each day. Once someone needs assistance or supervision on a full-time or "on demand" basis, as with using the toilet or moving about, they need to move to a facility providing a higher level of care.

Board and care homes are a true wild card for insurers. Some of these facilities provide the types of services appropriate for an insurable event, while others do not. State licensing is inconsistent. Even the names vary. Unfortunately, this is where the most experimentation is occurring in the care provider community. Insurers cannot categorically deny or accept all claims in these facilities. There is much uncertainty surrounding board and care homes.

Alzheimer's Facilities

It seems contradictory, but those suffering from Alzheimer's disease and other forms of dementia have a wide variety of providers available but limited choices. The care these people receive is primarily from social workers, aides, or others who are not medically trained, so there is a wide variety of licensing options for the providers. But these individuals need full-time assistance similar to that provided by a nursing home. There are few choices because those licensed for lower levels of care seldom are staffed with the number of workers necessary to properly care for someone with Alzheimer's disease. These people are in a service gap, and as a result some specialty facilities are popping up under different licensing arrangements.

These **Alzheimer's facilities** (for lack of a better term) are different from nursing homes and assisted living facilities. The staff to resident ratio is high (about one to four), and there are purposeful, rewarding interactions throughout the day. The design offers smaller spaces for multiple, ongoing activities. The doors are normally locked from the inside to minimize the frequency of residents wandering away and to lessen the need for restraints. The hallways are designed in a loop rather than dead ends to provide wanderers an area free of frustration. If a facility cares for those with physical and cognitive impairments, there is a separate area or wing to care for individuals with Alzheimer's because their needs are vastly different from other chronically ill people. When these types of facilities are licensed as an assisted living community or nursing home, insurers are able to provide benefits for the cognitively impaired residents. Insurers struggle with the decision whether to pay benefits when these facilities are licensed in the board and care category. And when states have specific licenses for Alzheimer's facilities, insurers scrutinize the licensing requirements to ensure that their provider requirements are met.

FOCUS QUESTION 7

What are some special features that are found in Alzheimer's facilities?

_____

_____

_____

_____

_____

_____

_____

_____

Home Care Providers

With all the advances in the quality of care provided in facilities, most people still prefer remaining at home. Home care is not immune from the care provider evolution. Home care began providing nursing services ranging from prenatal care to nutritional counseling to treatment of infectious diseases such as typhoid, measles, and diphtheria. Nurses would travel from home to home providing counseling or checking vital signs and administering medications (including injections) to those in need. This changed dramatically with the rising cost of care in hospitals after World War II and the passage of Medicare in 1965.

Initially Medicare covered only nonprofit home care agencies and health departments. The services focused on discharge planning from hospitalization in order to maintain a continuity of care. Home care agencies expanded to include therapists, home health aides, homemakers, and nutritionists to meet the service needs of their patients. This was the beginning of the recognition that home care is a cost-effective alternative to institutionalization for health care.

Today, home care providers perform many services formerly available only in a hospital—from intravenous feeding or medication to taking X-rays. Therapists provide physical, speech, respiratory, and occupational services at home. Some specialty agencies will provide services unexpected in a home, including dental, optical, podiatric, and laboratory work. Although infectious diseases are rare these days, home care agencies have not forgotten their roots and still assist with nutritional counseling and administration of medications for people with a variety of diseases and ailments.

Homemaker services are also available from home care agencies. You can find on today's home care agencies' menu of choices items such as assistance with shopping, meal preparation, light housekeeping, medical supply or prescription delivery, and transportation to medical appointments or to run errands. Full-service **nutrition services** have expanded from simply advice on the right foods to eat to others, including menu planning, grocery shopping, and cooking. **Personal care services** are common. This is the assistance with such common tasks as taking a bath, getting dressed, or moving about the residence. Training for caregivers to help make their role more effective and efficient is also available.

Insurers cut their teeth on home care during the 1980s. The original coverage encompassed a post-confinement benefit available only after a nursing home stay. The number of home care benefit days was often equal to the number of days the nursing home portion of the policy paid in benefits. This has all changed with today's modern policies. Insurers no longer require prior institutionalization (treatment in a hospital or nursing home) to qualify for benefits. They have expanded the types of services they cover as home care agencies made more services available. The LTCI industry has embraced the home care industry, and insureds are grateful.

Adult Day Centers

Adult day centers are a new type of provider that has developed out of the need for primary informal caregivers to have a break during the day. These centers started out being called "adult day care," but it was found that the phrase "day care" had a negative connotation to potential consumers. Their trade organization now refers to adult day centers and adult day services. Although they do provide care, that part of their name is beginning to be a thing of the past.

In researching who was providing care to chronically ill individuals, there was recognition that many times a working adult child provided the care. This person often had to quit their job or take a part-time position to accommodate caregiving responsibilities. When a spouse was the primary caregiver, there was a high level of stress in taking on this new role. These individuals had little opportunity for a break from their new duties to address their other responsibilities. Adult day centers provide just the type of relief both the caregiver and care recipient needed from one another.

Adult day services include both personal care and medical attention. The personal care ranges from assistance with personal hygiene, to help with eating and walking, to nutritious meals and snacks designed specifically for the guest. There are therapeutic activities provided, including recreational exercise programs and social interaction with other guests. Many facilities offer educational opportunities—some invite business leaders or members of the local academic community to speak. They might offer transportation services for doctor appointments as well as for getting to and from the center and home.

The medical attention focuses on nursing care such as administering medications, monitoring blood pressure, food and liquid intake, plus physical, speech, and occupational therapy. The medically trained staff assist with a plan of treatment and monitor the guest's status and progress. Part of the reason for these regular assessments is to ensure that the guest's needs are not beyond the center's available services. Care management assistance, including referrals to various providers, is often available. The larger centers might offer counseling services for the guest, family members, and caregivers.

FOCUS QUESTION 8

Outline personal care and medical services provided by adult day centers.

_____

_____

_____

_____

_____

_____

_____

_____

_____

_____

_____

Adult day centers are normally open from the early morning to late afternoon or early evening Monday through Friday. The design is to have someone in need of care brought to the center in the morning, allowing the primary caregiver an opportunity to mind their other responsibilities or personal needs—such as grocery shopping, housekeeping, exercising, or visiting friends. If the primary caregiver is still working, they can leave the person under care at the center and go to work knowing that the care is provided in a safe and secure environment by well-trained people in a cost-effective manner.

Although the majority of guests have physical impairments, the programs have been found worthwhile for some people who are still independent and searching for increased social activities. There are adult day centers that specialize in the needs of individuals with dementia and their caregivers. Some centers recognize the challenges of the sandwich generation (those caring for parents and children) and provide childcare nearby with joint programs for the young and old alike.

Some centers are freestanding, but most are affiliated with nursing homes, assisted living facilities, or medical centers and hospitals. County- or community-based senior centers might have an adult day center affiliated with them that is partially funded by tax receipts. Registered nurses, nurse practitioners, social workers, counselors, program coordinators and assistants, administrators, directors, and volunteers staff these centers.

» Summary

Long-term care insurance has seen many changes in its relatively short history. The joint work of consumer representatives, regulators, providers, and insurers has resulted in a continuously improving long-term care product. These same four groups are likely to continue to seek modifications and enhancements to the types of policies offered in the future. This is only natural for a business in a growth cycle, as is long-term care and long-term care insurance.

What will long-term care insurance policies cover in the future? What new providers will evolve? No one is certain. But research continues, and insurers are remaining flexible in their product design. Most policies include a provision that allows for benefit payments not specifically listed in the policy. As long as the insured, the insured's physician, and the insurer all agree that the care is appropriate given the circumstances, benefits are payable. This allows the insured and insurer to maintain a meaningful relationship in this rapidly evolving field.

Adult day centers	Long-Term Care Insurance Model Act
Alzheimer's facilities	
Assisted living communities	Long-Term Care Insurance Model Regulation
Board and care homes	
Contingent nonforfeiture benefit	Loss ratio
	National Association of Insurance Commissioners (NAIC)
Key Terms Disclosure form	
Grandfathered policies	Nonforfeiture benefits
Guaranty association	Nursing home
Health Insurance Portability and Accountability Act (HIPAA)	Nutrition services
	Personal care services
Homemaker services	Policy form filing

» Review Questions

1. Who usually handles the insurance claim process on behalf of an individual who purchases long-term care insurance?

2. What is the most common consumer complaint about long-term care policies received by insurance departments?

3. What are the tools available to state insurance departments to regulate the insurance industry?

4. Do all states approve insurance premiums?

5. When did the NAIC develop its first Long-Term Care Insurance Model Act and Model Regulation?

6. When did Congress pass the Health Insurance Portability and Accountability Act (HIPAA)?

7. Is it more difficult for insurance companies to obtain state insurance department approval for product features that do not have a precedent?

8. What type of facility is available to the individual who does not need the level of care provided by nursing homes or assisted living communities, but requires some kind of assistance?

9. Would an Alzheimer's patient be well served by a traditional long-term care facility?

10. What role do adult day centers play in the long-term care equation?

» Answers

1. The insured's spouse or children, in most cases.

2. Premium increases.

3. Licensing, review and approval of product filings, review and approval of rates, guaranty associations, and reports.

4. No, some states only review these rates.

5. In 1986.

6. In 1996.

7. Yes, it is often a challenge to gain state approval for a first-time offering without an established precedent.

8. Board and care homes.

9. No. Owing to needs that differ substantially from those of other long-term care patients, Alzheimer's patients are better served in specialized centers or wings of traditional facilities.

10. These centers were developed to address the need for primary informal caregivers (such as adult sons or daughters caring for ailing parents) to have a break during the day. In fact, the center and the informal caregiver work in "shifts."

NOTES

1 http://www.ncoa.org/nadsa/ADSchron.htm.

2 For additional information, see http://www.hcfa.gov/medicaid/pace/pacegen.htm.

Benefit Qualification Criteria

» Overview

All insurance products have **benefit qualification criteria**. Some people refer to these as **benefit triggers**. There are three basic components of an insurance policy's benefit qualification criteria:

- an **unexpected loss** covered by the policy (also known as the **insured event**),
- repair of the loss, and
- a financial contribution by the insured for the loss.

Long-term care insurance uses this same concept when determining whether benefits are payable. The unexpected loss or insured event is the inability to independently function physically or cognitively. The repair of the loss is the receipt of services necessary to assist with the physical or mental functioning tasks that the individual is unable to do on their own. Finally, there is a financial contribution or payment for such services. This chapter considers how an insurance company determines whether the unexpected loss or insured event has taken place. Subsequent chapters discuss the repair of the loss and the financial contributions required when services are received from a covered provider.

» Determining an Insured Event

There are many people who know they have a problem maintaining their independence. These people might find doing routine tasks around their home more difficult than before. Difficulties with simple tasks such as housekeeping, laundry, and preparing meals are early signs of someone losing their ability to care for themselves. This can progress to an inability to safely complete the more advanced activities healthy people take for granted. Upon investigation of the cost for services to provide the necessary assistance, panic sets in. There is a realization that the expense for these services is high and can deplete a person's assets quickly. These people may look for a funding source such as an insurance company to pay for these expenses.

Clearly there is a loss in this situation. But it is not an unexpected loss if the individual waits until after impairment sets in before seeking insurance coverage. One principle of insurance is that it is protection that must be obtained *before* the unexpected loss or insured event takes place. Once the event takes place, it is no longer an unexpected loss and, therefore, it is not insurable. If this were not the case, no one would consider the purchase of insurance until they needed the benefits. Insurers would not have the opportunity to collect enough money to pay out benefits. For this reason, long-term care insurance companies conduct an analysis of an applicant's current health and ability to function before issuing an insurance policy. They want to be sure that there is not an existing loss, but rather that the person who is currently healthy and independent might someday have an unexpected loss.

This analysis is called **underwriting**. The basis of underwriting is pooling like risks. There are companies that specialize in automobile insurance for 16-year-olds—they pool those risks together. There are companies that like to provide life insurance to people whom other companies will not want, such as those who recently underwent treatment for cancer. Long-term care insurers pool people with similar levels of independence. This is identified through an analysis of the information provided on the application and in the applicant's medical records, a phone call to the applicant, and/or a nurse asking questions about and observing the applicant's independence during a face-to-face meeting.

FOCUS QUESTION 1

Outline the analyses that may be part of the underwriting process.

_____

_____

_____

_____

_____

_____

_____

_____

_____

Insurers are not the only ones who underwrite. Underwriting also occurs when someone applies for a mortgage or other credit. The lending institution must make sure that the borrower can afford the debt payments and has a consistent repayment history. Rather than an investigation of one's medical history or driving record, banks perform financial underwriting. If they are unsure of the applicant's ability to manage a debt, they may require the applicant to obtain mortgage insurance or charge them a higher rate of interest. Many nursing homes perform a type of financial underwriting in asking questions about the potential residents' ability to use private funds rather than government funds to pay for their care.

In pooling like risks, insurers are able to offer insurance coverage at the lowest rate possible for those participating in the risk pool. For example, people who have a good driving record and own a sedan will seek an insurer that provides good rates for them—they want to find an insurer with a risk pool designed for them. If they purchased their coverage from a company specializing in 16-year-olds who drive sports cars, they would pay too much for their auto insurance. Someone who has not had a life-threatening illness is not likely to buy life insurance from a company specializing in substandard risks.

The same holds true for long-term care insurance. Healthy people want to purchase their insurance from companies that offer discounts for preferred risks. Some companies are willing to accept certain marginal risks—such as the applicant being an insulin-dependent diabetic—while other insurers will not. A company that is willing to issue a policy to someone with one type of medical condition may not find another condition acceptable, while another company might issue a policy to someone with that condition. As an example, there are LTCI companies that accept applicants taking medication to control a mild heart condition while others do not.

Most long-term care insurance companies publish underwriting guidelines for use by agents. These are not as extensive as an underwriting manual but rather offer a general outline of the types of risks the company is willing to accept. Producers who have experience in the LTCI business and who sell the products of more than one insurer know the risk tolerance companies are willing to accept and will place their clients with the appropriate company. Talking with a company's underwriters or an experienced managing general agent about borderline cases will help the newer agent gain that experience.

The key to the underwriting process is to pool like risks and charge rates appropriate for those risks. This ensures that claim payments are made only to those with an unexpected—rather than imminent—loss. When an insurer is able to achieve the goal of consistent underwriting, the insurance premium is more likely to remain constant, while allowing the insurance company to make a profit.

The early pioneers in LTCI did not have any experience in assessing the needs of individuals to determine whether care was needed. They had experience with medical insurance where the doctor determines which tests and treatments are needed. They had experience with disability insurance, which relies on an assessment of a medical condition and loss of income. They also had extensive experience with life insurance—death is the easiest assessment of any type of insurance.

» The Evolution of Medical Necessity

Rather than experimenting with an unknown that could lead to unintended results with their long-term care insurance, the companies that went into this business in the early years decided to follow Medicare's requirements. The insured needed at least three days in the hospital before entering a Medicare-certified skilled nursing facility to receive skilled care. Although some of these policies remain in force, none are being sold today.

As the policies moved away from Medicare's requirement, the traditional medical assessment was retained. The term **medical necessity** was combined with prior hospitalization for someone to qualify for benefits. Although few companies attempted to define "medically necessary" in their policies, this became the standard benefit trigger during the 1970s and 1980s.

For some companies, medical necessity merely meant that the insured's physician had to certify that the individual needed long-term care. Other companies attempted to determine according to their own standards when long-term care was medically needed. The difficulty, of course, arises from the fact that long-term care needs have little if anything to do with medical need; they have to do with the ability to carry out everyday activities like bathing and dressing, or with being cognitively intact. Some companies began with loose definitions of medical necessity, but then tightened the interpretation as claims arose. This arbitrary definition of the insured event was bad for both the insured and the insurer, and gave regulators some concern with early policies that made what seemed like (and often were) inconsistent and arbitrary benefit determinations.

In the search for a policy that was friendlier to consumers, companies liberalized the prior hospitalization requirements. Originally, an insured had to enter a facility immediately after leaving the hospital. Qualifying for benefits was easier when companies allowed the insured to attempt their recovery at home for 14 or 30 days before entering a facility. Some companies tinkered with the number of days of prior hospitalization to find a competitive advantage.

Levels of Care

Companies also liberalized the types of care required to receive benefits. The initial requirements mirrored Medicare's requirement of skilled care. As discussed in the previous chapter, **skilled care** can be defined as daily care prescribed by a physician and delivered by skilled personnel designed to assist with the recovery process. An example is when someone who has had a hip replacement needs wound treatment from a nurse twice a day and services from a physical therapist. **Intermediate care** is when a person needs care less frequently than five days a week (Medicare's definition of "daily") but still received the same treatments.

When someone does not need medical attention or therapy required in skilled and intermediate care, they receive **custodial care**. This is more or less assistance care—assistance with common activities healthy people take for granted. Those receiving custodial care have help getting dressed in the morning and undressed in the evening; someone helps them take a shower or bath; they might need a little boost in getting out of a chair; or they may find having someone prepare a meal in bite-sized pieces necessary.

The evolution of the levels of care started with benefits for intermediate and custodial care in addition to the traditional skilled care Medicare required. The design was such that someone would need skilled care and three days of prior hospitalization before benefits for intermediate or custodial care were payable. The cutting-edge policies of this bygone time paid benefits for all three levels of care without prior hospitalization, as long as the care was medically necessary.

FOCUS QUESTION 2

Describe the three traditional levels of care, pointing out the differences setting them apart from one another.

_____

_____

_____

_____

Hospitalization

About this time, the federal government was considering dropping the prior hospitalization requirement from Medicare's requirements. In 1988, Congress passed and the president signed the Medicare Catastrophic Health Care Act. This act extended Medicare's payments for skilled nursing home benefits from a maximum of 100 days to 150 days and eliminated the need to enter a hospital first. (There were many additional benefits included in the act besides the long-term care benefits.) The act was repealed in 1989, once it was understood that the beneficiaries were to pay for a portion of the additional charge for this expansion. This repeal was the end of any discussion of a federal program to cover seniors' long-term care needs.

Although the prior hospitalization requirement was reinstated in Medicare's requirements, the majority of LTCI companies stopped putting this requirement in any new policies. By this time, the public and insurers better understood that many people need long-term care services without entering a hospital first. Hospital stays were beginning to shorten. The fact that someone had been in a hospital or even the length of their stay seldom gave a clear indication of a need for long-term care services. Consumers and some state regulators wanted the prior hospitalization removed from the insurance policy. Companies simply required that the care be medically necessary without the prior hospitalization requirement.

The medically necessary benefit trigger is mostly obsolete, although it is still included in some non-tax-qualified long-term care policies today. (It is not allowed in qualified policies.) Agents are reluctant to give up this type of benefit criterion, as it is more easily understood by consumers — their physician simply has to say that they need care. While there certainly are medical conditions that lead to a need for long-term care services, in the vast majority of those cases, those individuals also have the functional loss or cognitive loss that would qualify them for benefits under today's predominant benefit trigger. While some advocates of medical necessity as a benefit trigger suggest that physicians are the most appropriate assessors because of their relationship with the insured over many years, it is actually not typical for a physician to be trained to recognize the functional limitations that can cause a need for long-term care.

This traditional approach of relying on physicians for determining when benefits are payable served the LTCI industry for many years since no better criterion was available or known to insurers at the time.

» The Evolution of Benefit Qualifications

Many long-term care insurance companies began to recognize that relying on a term such as "medical necessity" was inappropriate to the concept of long-term care and inadequate for the future success of their product line. Requiring three days of hospitalization combined with the medical necessity trigger provided a certain comfort level because many claims would be eliminated because of the prior hospitalization requirement. Insurers were uncomfortable with medical necessity serving as a benefit trigger on its own, however, because it is too vague and hard to define. Defining it resulted in additional scrutiny from insurance departments that approve the products before they are made available for sale. The feeling was that physicians were not always impartial in the assessment of their patients. Questions arose regarding physicians' liability if they stated that long-term care services were not medically necessary for an individual.

The companies concerned with medical necessity felt that something more objective and more reliable would give them greater confidence in pricing and administering policies and would better serve the needs of consumers, ensuring that benefits are provided fairly. The insurers looking for an innovative solution insisted on the existence of a well-documented history of the new measures that provided adequate data for pricing assumptions. They did not want to experiment with an untested, newfangled concept. The most basic questions that needed an answer were:

- What are the most important factors to measure?
- Can these factors be measured objectively?
- What technology or tool is available to measure these factors?

Experienced companies reviewed their claim files for the answers. This raised the awareness that the task that lay ahead would not be easy. All the existing claims were evaluated as to whether the insured had been in a hospital before the nursing home and the level of care they needed in the facility. There may have been some claimants in facilities without the prior hospitalization, but the analysis of the appropriateness was still based on medical necessity. (Meaningful insurance coverage for home care was not yet available.) There were no consistent themes contained in the claim files.

The primary challenge in finding the answer to these basic questions was recognition that a multidimensional assessment was needed to isolate the traditional medical diagnosis for diseases and injuries from the new factors. People with a traditional diagnosis needed varying degrees of care depending on factors physicians seldom used in their practice. There was no single assessment to provide the objectivity and consistency necessary for insurers. The factors under review were too interrelated to provide the necessary accuracy with a single assessment. The cutting-edge insurers looked to geriatric research and the long-term care provider community for assistance with this measure and found that tools and technologies well suited for measuring long-term care need had existed for years.

Research had begun many years before long-term care insurance had been thought of. The research focused on measuring the needs of the elderly so they could receive better care as they aged. Long-term care providers used this research to develop new options for providing care in innovative settings that were appropriate for the individual. The providers were taking the theoretical models from the researchers and giving them the practical application insurers needed to validate the usefulness and effectiveness of such measures.

The conventional wisdom of the day held that the appropriate measure for someone's need for long-term care services was based on the relationship of three primary components: physical, mental, and social.[1]

Physical Measures

The physical measures considered a wide array of tasks people do on a daily basis. The list of items evaluated included moving out of a bed, taking a bath or shower, getting dressed, grooming, performing a range of motion, paying bills, washing clothes, reading books or magazines, writing, using a telephone, managing medications, cooking a meal and then eating the meal, driving a car or using public transportation, and shopping for groceries or clothing. A healthy person would have no difficulty in completing these tasks, while someone who needed long-term care services would need assistance.

Researchers lumped these common duties of life into two general categories: **instrumental activities of daily living (IADLs)** and **activities of daily living (ADLs)**. Research on physical limitations tended to focus on these terms, which varied slightly from study to study. They became recognized as easily learned and used measures that developed into a common language for generalists and geriatric specialists. Many medical schools and hospitals found that these assessments were an essential component in developing treatment plans for older patients.

Common Activities of Daily Living (ADLs)

- Bathing
- Dressing
- Toileting
- Transferring
- Continence
- Eating

Common Instrumental Activities of Daily Living (IADLs)

- Cooking
- Cleaning
- Using transportation
- Managing money
- Using a telephone
- Shopping
- Laundry
- Administering medications
- Walking outdoors

FOCUS QUESTION 3

Define ADLs and IADLs, explaining the difference and giving three examples of each. (You may wish to return to this question and review or elaborate on your explanation of the difference after reading the section titled "The Evolution of ADLs" below.)

_____

_____

_____

_____

_____

_____

_____

_____

_____

The mental measures looked at both intellectual ability (cognition) and depressive state (affective functioning). The terms "senility," "dementia," "senile dementia," or even "Alzheimer's disease" do not capture the full extent of the wide variety of performance abilities. But they do recognize when a chronic loss of mental capacity leading to a need for assistance exists. Frequently, acute medical conditions—such as visual or hearing impairments, heart conditions, brain tumors, or infections—affect an individual's mental health or effective functioning. Overmedication with prescription drugs can cause someone to display signs of disorders that are reversible when properly diagnosed and treated.

There is much overlap between a cognitive impairment and depression. One way to differentiate the two is recognizing improvements in mental functioning (rather than levels of impairments) indicative of a reversible impairment. Indications of improvement are a sign that the condition is treatable or even curable with medical treatment. The irreversible deterioration of cognitive abilities is found in individuals who have gradually lost their intellectual capability because of an undiagnosed organic defect within the body or the brain.

Social Measures

Social measures look at human relationships and activities surrounding an individual and their physical living environment. Today the vast majority of long-term care assistance is provided by informal caregivers such as family members and friends while the person still lives in a home or home-like setting. When professionals are asked to assist the informal caregivers with physical or cognitive problems, the formal caregivers strive to minimize the disruption of the positive social interaction inherent in the natural, family-oriented caregiving process.

Social analysis is a replacement for clinical hunches and subjective judgments. The assessment considers the appropriateness of a subject's living environment, the subject's ability to maintain the environment (including cleanliness and other IADL-oriented tasks), the structure and frequency of their contacts with others, and the activities they engage in during waking hours. The series of questions used to make these evaluations has varying levels or grades that measure an individual against a standard.

When someone has a strong level of independence as reflected in the social analysis, they are able to influence and adapt to the current living environment. When assistance is needed, the constraints of the living environment increase proportionally to the amount of care needed. This continuum progresses to the point of needing care in a facility that has few opportunities for creativity, including a loss of control over when and what to eat. This continuum varies considerably depending on many components of an individual's social measures.

FOCUS QUESTION 4

Outline assessments involved in conducting a social analysis.

_____

_____

_____

Interdependency

The physical, mental, and social measures operate independently for some; for others, there is interdependency among them. Someone who is physically challenged might find their mental and social well-being intact. The same holds true for someone with a mental or social challenge — the other two may be fine. Research shows that there are also varying levels of crossover of the factors with some people. Someone who has mental challenges might also experience physical challenges. Any combination of the three is possible.

The Evolution of ADLs

What did insurers find in this analysis of physical, mental, and social measures? What were the most important factors to consider at claim time?

Many long-term care insurance companies hired consultants to help them sift through all the assessment options available. They discovered that some assessment measures were useful in determining whether an insurable event triggering benefits had occurred, while other measures could contribute to the analysis of the appropriateness of the services claimants received. All these measures excluded the inconsistent medical diagnosis that was traditionally used with long-term care insurance. Because there was extensive research on most of these measures, adequate amounts of data on the general population (rather than an insured population) provided insights that were usable in making pricing assumptions. But there was no single method that provided all the information necessary to evaluate the appropriateness of a claim, so a multidimensional approach was needed.

The physical measures were relatively easy to determine. ADL measures were the standard used in most research and provider assessments. ADLs were well defined in research, almost to the point of using standardized terms. One challenge with assessing ADLs is that there are varying degrees of one's ability to complete a task. IADLs provided some insight as to the need for long-term care services but generally showed impairments before ADLs and also captured some needs that were not due to physical limitations, but more to social preference, learning, and social roles. For example, an elderly woman may have difficulty balancing her checkbook, not because of a disability, but because it isn't something she has ever had to do or wanted to do. Similarly, a man might be unable to cook or clean, but not because of the physical inability to do so. Because there are cultural and social influences that affect whether or not someone can perform an IADL, they are not considered reliable indicators of the need for long-term care. The care needed because of impairments with IADLs was normally available through a social network of friends and family members. Insuring against IADL losses was difficult both in terms of designs of meaningful benefit eligibility and providing accurate pricing data. Consistency and objectivity in an IADL claims assessment process was in scarce supply.

Breakpoints

Even the original research recognized that impairments with ADLs are not like a light switch—there is no clear-cut line defining whether the person is impaired or not. It is more like a light with a dimmer switch—some people need a little assistance, while others need a little more, and some cannot perform the task at all. There is a wide gray area between a pure impairment and pure independence. There is not only an impairment continuum of ADLs but also an impairment continuum within each ADL.

The ADL of dressing provides a good example of this. Independent people are able to get their clothes from a closet or dresser, put them on, and manage the fasteners (buttons, zippers, snaps, etc.). They do this without thinking about it. It is a very natural process. As people begin to become physically impaired, they may struggle with the fasteners, with getting an arm in their shirtsleeve or leg in their pants, or with pulling a shirt over their head. As the impairment progresses, additional parts of the task become difficult. They might adapt to this challenge by changing the types of clothes they wear—slip-on shoes instead of ones with laces to tie, velcro replacing buttons on shirts, or stretch pants rather than those with a zipper and snap.

The innovative insurers needed to establish **breakpoints** for each ADL indicating when they would consider a claimant impaired with that ADL. This was essential to maintaining consistency and objectivity in evaluating potential claims. One easily identifiable breakpoint that some policies acknowledged was whether individuals needed **hands-on assistance** from another person to perform the activity or if they could perform the activity with only some mechanical help like grab rails or ramps or velcro. Some people can perform an activity but are unstable at it and need **standby assistance** to keep them safe. That means someone is nearby to assist if needed, but that hands-on help is not always necessary.

These breakpoints were not always part of policy language but rather found in the insurer's claim manual. The manual described each ADL and the level at which the insurance company would consider an insured impaired with that activity. These detailed guidelines narrowed the gray area of the impairment continuum for a more reliable claims administration process and helped the actuaries with their pricing assumptions. For example, some carriers would consider an insured dependent in bathing if the insured could not perform any aspect of bathing, while another carrier might consider them dependent only if they could not perform the entire function on their own. And some chose a middle ground.

FOCUS QUESTION 5

Describe the two different kinds of ADL-related assistance.

_____

_____

_____

_____

_____

_____

Choosing ADLs

Insurers also had to establish which ADLs they were going to use and how many would constitute an impairment that would justify paying a claim. Research has shown that ADLs have a natural impairment continuum that occurs in about three-quarters of the people with a chronic condition. The first ADL that shows a level of impairment is bathing, followed by dressing. At this point, care is available on an intermittent basis. Assistance is needed in the morning as someone gets dressed for the day and in the evening to get into sleepwear. A shower or bath is normally provided during the dressing transition. (Such regularly occurring care is sometimes referred to a **scheduled care**.)

Moving down the impairment continuum, everything changes. The individual cannot schedule when they will need to use the toilet. They cannot sit in one place without transferring for too long without getting sore. Care must be met on demand during the normal course of a day.

With knowledge and assistance from their consultants, the pioneering insurance companies set out to determine the number of ADLs they would assess and the number of impaired ADLs that would trigger benefits. The opportunity to provide a unique product was found in the number of potential ADL combinations. Insurers found that having at least five ADLs was important to maintain objectivity and more than seven was unnecessary. (A few states required that seven be assessed.) Basing benefit qualification on just one ADL did not provide consistency, and four seemed excessive. Companies settled on the fact that either two or three ADL impairments were appropriate. A policy triggered benefits anywhere from impairment with two of five ADLs to three of seven. Because the numbers of ADLs did not tell the whole story, one was required to look at which ADLs were assessed. For example, qualifying benefits with a two-of-five-ADL design might pay benefits later in the impairment continuum than a two-of-six design if bathing or dressing is dropped from the list of ADLs assessed.

Ambulation is an important component of several of the ADLs, but it is not considered an ADL by research gerontologists working in long-term care. Insurers considered it and found that it had varying definitions depending on the researcher. Ambulation could be defined as walking indoors, walking outdoors, or negotiating stairs. Some research measured ambulating with and without assistance from a device such as a quad cane, walker, or wheelchair. Some people would have difficulty ambulating in the beginning of the impairment continuum, while others would need help later on. It did not meet the requirement of a consistent measure for most insurers.

Some insurers experimented with integrating IADLs with ADLs in their physical assessment. Utilizing an IADL trigger proved challenging for the company for a variety of reasons. Most notably, IADLs normally show signs of difficulty before ADLs, thus benefits were available sooner in the impairment continuum. This caused upward pricing pressure without a corresponding competitive advantage with consumers or agents. What is more important, as mentioned before, is that the inability to perform an IADL does not always correlate with a need for long-term care or a physical or mental loss; it might just reflect a learned pattern of social behavior.

Cognitive Impairment

Many people in need of long-term care show few signs of physical challenges. They need care because of problems with their mental or cognitive ability. In the old days, companies did not use a mental screen for claims assessment with the three-day prior hospitalization or medically necessary models. There was fear that people with senility or dementia would not qualify for benefits because they didn't need hospitalization or medical treatment before needing care. For this reason, regulators required companies to disclose in their policies that conditions such as Alzheimer's disease were covered.

In their search for better mental assessments, the innovative insurers, with help from their consultants, studied the research available. Given the insurer's desire to move away from the inconsistent medical model, it did not seem appropriate to consider an insured's level of depression or affective functioning. These people have an acute condition with medical treatments available for their condition. The potential for a cure is covered by their medical insurance or Medicare. For long-term care insurance to cover the same treatment would simply provide duplicative insurance benefits. For this reason, insurers' care assessments gravitated toward the deterioration of cognitive abilities not covered by other types of insurance. This is found with individuals who have a chronic condition causing a gradual loss of their intellectual capability. Although medical science is finding some treatments and prescription medications to slow the progress of cognitive impairments, there is currently no cure.

Individuals with senility, dementia, and Alzheimer's disease need assistance to ensure their safety and well-being. They might leave a burner on after cooking, which may cause a fire. They may forget to complete personal hygiene tasks. There are cases of people going into freezing temperatures without proper outer garments. These people are able to do many tasks but forget the importance of them. They simply need reminders when and/or how to do them. This is indicative of someone with a cognitive impairment.

FOCUS QUESTION 6

Describe ways in which people with cognitive impairment may endanger themselves.

_____

_____

_____

_____

_____

_____

_____

_____

Social Needs

Social measures were the most difficult challenge for insurers seeking consistent measures. Comparing an impaired person's socialization needs against an independent person does not necessarily reflect a need for long-term care services. The absence of frequent contact with family or friends is not an insurable event. However, this same absence when someone exhibits a physical or cognitive impairment does result in a need for additional services from long-term care providers.

Some insurers do make social assessments at the time of the claim. This gives an indication of the appropriateness of some of the services the insured is receiving. Increasing social activities or minimizing household maintenance activities can enhance an insured's well-being. When assistance from family and friends is inadequate, outside support is needed. Professionals and community-based volunteers are available. Senior centers have a variety of programs available, as do many churches and other religious congregations. Many people find moving from living alone to a group environment provides them with the level of social support they desire.

Unbeknownst to many LTCI applicants, a social assessment is part of many companies' underwriting process conducted when the applicants apply for coverage. The application might ask about activities or hobbies. The face-to-face assessments utilized by many insurers with certain applicants are designed to not only ask the applicant questions about their functional and cognitive abilities, but also to observe their current living environment. Casual conversation between the applicant and the assessor gives an indication of the applicant's activities and nearby social support opportunities. Many agents selling LTCI have found positive results when including a description of the applicant's socialization activities with an application.

Although the social analysis is not part of the policy language, long-term care insurers do find it an essential component in analyzing long-term care insurance risks and services received during a claim. In fact, most insurers reduce premiums when the insured is married—this is commonly called a spousal discount. That is a reflection of a level of positive social support available at home and the possibility of receiving fewer services.

» The Development of Functional Assessment

Pioneering insurers in search of a new benefit trigger now knew what to assess — activities of daily living and cognitive impairments. These measures moved away from the medical diagnosis that had presented problems for the insurers. This new tool is called a **functional assessment.** It looks at one's ability to remain independent (or function independently) in the community. This research dates back to the early 1960s, so it is well documented and provides meaningful pricing data.

How to assess physical and cognitive abilities was the next hurdle. Trying to determine the best method led to questions regarding which tool to use and who was best qualified to perform the assessment. Research provided a wide range of options but not a single perfect solution.

What Assessment Tool Should Be Used?

In working with consultants and network organizers, insurers developed tools to analyze physical and cognitive well-being. These were determined to provide the most pertinent and reliable measures for an LTCI claim. Social observations were a part of the tool used by home office claim administrators, although they were not part of the policy language. Social measures are difficult to quantify and can vary for healthy people. Making observations of social indicators helped the claims administrator at the insurer's home office to better understand the types of services that might be appropriate for the claimant or, in rare situations, helped make a definite benefit determination when the other indicators were inconclusive.

There were a great many assessment tools for both the physical and cognitive assessment. Careful consideration was given to both the user of the measure and the purpose of the measurement. The user groups included case managers, geriatric providers, nongeriatric care providers, and researchers. The purpose of the measurement included a description of the individual, screening for services, pure assessment, monitoring over time, or developing a prognosis. Because the potential tools were part of research long before insurers found a need for them, the researchers were not designing and testing tools specifically for insurance companies.

Researchers narrowed the choices and categorized the various tools by user and purpose. Then consultants helped the long-term care insurers with selecting the right measures and designing the appropriate measurement tools. The physical assessment tools used by companies leaned toward the original research on ADLs. This resulted in the provider perspective for the insurer and the most diversity for purpose. Insurers recognized that ADL loss offered two options for assessment: observation and self-assessment. Requiring an insured to demonstrate their inability to bathe or dress would clearly cross the line of good taste. Asking detailed questions of a claimant and the primary caregiver (either formal or informal) seemed adequate. With proper training and experience, an assessor would observe the indications of physical loss to provide insurers with the necessary objectivity and consistency.

The cognitive assessment was much more difficult to select and design. In the medical community, a definitive diagnosis of Alzheimer's disease is found only during an autopsy of the brain. Tools for mental health focused on how the person felt, while for cognition they focused on what they remembered. Testing memory is tricky when the person has a low intellectual capacity. The researchers worked diligently to identify effective tools that produced consistent results across social and economic boundaries long before an insurance application was considered.

The tests used in exploring cognitive abilities varied from as few as 10 questions to over 30. The goal was to get a read on the person's short- and long-term memory, as well as their ability to think, perceive, and reason. Another important check was their orientation as to time and to where and who they were. It is almost an insult to ask someone with normal abilities the questions that are used to determine impairment with any of these criteria. Yet someone with a cognitive impairment may find it hard to come up with the correct answer. Researchers found that an arithmetic test, counting forward or backward by sevens, gave an indication of cognitive abilities. Even today there is no single definitive tool to achieve the perfect result in assessing for a cognitive impairment, although most insurers use Delayed Word Recall (DWR), which has been developed and thoroughly tested to provide reliable and verifiable results. The scientific literature on the tool's accuracy and validity justifies its use in the major measuring tools for early cognitive loss.

Questions to Assess Cognitive Abilities

- What is the date today?
- What day of the week is it?
- What meal did you eat last?
- Is it now morning, afternoon, or evening?
- What is the name of this place?
- What is your room number?
- Where is the bathroom?
- What is your telephone number?
- What is your street address?
- How old are you?
- When were you born?
- Do you have children?
- If "yes," what are their names?
- Who is the current president of the United States?
- Who was the president just before him?
- What is your father's first name? Mother's first name?
- What was your mother's maiden name?

(These are typical questions to assess cognitive abilities from various tools used in research. Questions will vary depending on the person's living arrangements.)

Where Should the Assessment Be Done?

One important factor in performing these tests is where they are done. It is important that they are performed in familiar surroundings to minimize disorientation and anxiety. The best place is where the claimant resides and not in the assessor's office or clinic. When done in the claimant's own home, the person doing the assessment is given the opportunity to make noninvasive observations of the person's ability to maintain a healthy living environment. They view the claimant's functioning in their home and can identify the use of home-based medical equipment.

FOCUS QUESTION 7

Summarize the benefits of conducting an ADL assessment in the claimant's residence. Can you think of disadvantages associated with doing this in the assessor's workplace or a clinic or facility?

_____

_____

_____

_____

_____

_____

_____

Keep in mind that the assessment process is done by asking questions about the person's ability to maintain independence. The assessor is not there to act like a drill sergeant, forcing the claimant to demonstrate how they perform each ADL. This is simply inappropriate with many of the more personal ADLs. But casual observation will allow the assessor to have first-hand knowledge of the claimant's difficulty with walking, moving in and out of a chair, or cognitive functioning.

Having the primary, informal caregiver present during the assessment is usually a good idea. Older people possess much pride and dignity. When asked about their ability to complete a task that healthy people take for granted, they might answer how they'd like to do the ADL rather than how they actually do it. Someone with experience caring for the claimant can offer gentle reminders and give examples on how they help the claimant throughout the day.

Who Should Perform the Assessment?

For insurers, the next challenge was to identify who would perform the assessment. Although ADLs and IADLs were more readily accepted in medical colleges and hospitals, this language was not found in most claim or underwriting medical records received by the insurers. Insurers found that physicians were seldom trained with a structured functional assessment tool and less often integrated one into their daily practice. If a physical assessment was performed on a patient, it was normally a nurse who conducted the screening.

Insurers and their consultants agreed that the right person to perform the assessment must have:

- the proper motivation to maintain objectivity,
- the education or experience to perform the assessment, and
- an opportunity to observe the potentially impaired person.

Consultants and home care providers began to put together networks of assessors for insurers. They found that registered nurses, practical nurses, and Master's-trained social workers who specialized in geriatrics knew and understood the importance and various methods of identifying physical loss. There were people from coast to coast with the proper background and the willingness to contract into a network to perform this assessment service for insurers. The network organizers then trained their staff on the specific tools they used.

This network provided the information insurers needed. But did it provide the objectivity? To gain some assurances of objectivity and consistency, insurers and those developing the assessment networks for them determined that the best way to work with nurses or social workers in the claimant's community was to insulate them from the benefit determination process. They would collect the data regarding the claimant's physical and cognitive abilities and forward that information to the network provider. The network would in turn forward the assessment information to the insurer. The insurer would have the policy language at hand to determine whether benefits were payable. The individuals conducting the assessment did not need to know which company they were performing the assessment for or how the company determined benefit eligibility. They could simply do what they do best—assess people's abilities in an objective manner.

These networks brought consistency to the assessment process. Assessments can vary because not everyone asks identical questions in the same manner or they may accept varying answers as adequate. Having an effective tool minimizes the likelihood of error or deviation of results from assessor to assessor. A good assessment tool and proper training and testing in the use of the tool also allow less expensive personnel with fewer qualifications to conduct the assessment without jeopardizing the validity of the assessment. The individuals in this network worked with insurers in developing the tool. Then they provided extensive training to their assessors in the field on the use of the tool and observation techniques.

Insurers found this process of using an outside network invaluable. They did not have any of the hiring or training challenges common when expanding their employment base into areas beyond their expertise. Safeguards were in place for an unbiased analysis of an individual's physical and cognitive abilities. Competition followed insurers' acceptance to provide options in pricing and level of detail obtained from the assessor. Some companies have found this service useful to the underwriting process as well. This is especially true for older applicants who have not seen a physician recently or when the medical records are inconclusive regarding an individual's independence.

» Summary

Long-term care insurers have come a long way in developing their criteria for benefit qualification. Work done in conjunction with providers of care, researchers of impaired people, and consultants has resulted in a more objective and consistent method of accurately determining when someone needs care.

Key Terms 🔑

Activities of daily living (ADLs)	Insured event
Ambulation	Intermediate care
Benefit qualification criteria	Medical necessity
Benefit triggers	Scheduled care
Breakpoints	Skilled care
Custodial care	Standby assistance
Functional assessment	Underwriting
Hands-on assistance	Unexpected loss
Instrumental activities of daily living (IADLs)	

» Review Questions

1. Describe LTCI underwriting in terms of what it does.

2. Name institutions that conduct underwriting as part of their evaluation process.

3. Why did most LTCI companies stop requiring prior hospitalization as a benefit eligibility criterion?

4. What criterion helps us differentiate between a cognitive impairment and depression?

5. Who provides long-term care in most cases?

6. Can an ADL assessment come up with a clear-cut, either/or result?

7. What is the term for the criteria used by insurers to help deal with gray areas in determining whether an individual was impaired with an ADL?

8. What do we mean by a "functional assessment" conducted by an insurer? What does it measure or determine?

9. In measuring an individual's ADL loss, which option is preferable — an assessor's observation and/or the insured's self-assessment?

10. What is the benefit of having an informal caregiver (such as a member of the claimant's family) present during the ADL assessment?

» Answers

1. LTCI underwriting is the analysis of an applicant's current health and ability to function. An insurance company thus makes sure before issuing a policy that the individual is in good health and a loss would be unexpected.

2. Insurers, lenders, banks, and so on.

3. An understanding gradually emerged that many people need long-term care services without entering a hospital first.

4. Reversibility. When there are indications of improvement in mental functioning, that is a sign that we are dealing with depression—the condition is treatable or even curable with medical treatment. The irreversible deterioration of cognitive abilities, by contrast, is found with individuals who have gradually lost their intellectual capability because of an undiagnosed organic defect within the body or the brain.

5. Informal caregivers such as family members and friends.

6. A black-and-white determination is often impossible. There are several points of assessment—shades of gray—between a pure impairment and pure independence. There is not only an impairment continuum of ADLs but also an impairment continuum within each ADL.

7. Insurers use ADL-specific "breakpoints" to determine the point beyond which an individual is considered impaired with that ADL.

8. A functional assessment gauges an individual's ability to remain independent (or function independently) in the community.

9. The former is clearly preferable because asking an individual to prove their inability to bathe or dress would be inappropriate. A well-trained

assessor can glean the necessary information by asking detailed questions and observing the individual.

10. An older person, when asked about their ability to complete a simple task, might answer how they would like to do the ADL rather than how they actually do it—out of a natural urge to preserve their pride or dignity. Someone with experience caring for the claimant can offer gentle reminders and give examples on how they help the claimant throughout the day.

Note

1 Kane, Rosalie A., and Robert L. Kane. 1981. *Assessing the Elderly: A Practical Guide to Measurement*. Lexington Books.

The Health Insurance Portability and Accountability Act of 1996 (HIPAA)

» Overview

In the 104th Congress, Senators Nancy Kassebaum and Edward Kennedy sponsored a bill that had a far-reaching impact on the entire insurance industry. The **Health Insurance Portability and Accountability Act (HIPAA)** became law on August 21, 1996, with the long-term care portions of the bill effective on January 1, 1997. The primary focus of the bill was to ensure that people would have access to major medical insurance without proving evidence of insurability. But its reach goes far beyond medical insurance, with special importance for the long-term care insurance industry.

The discussion of HIPAA can go in many different directions. This landmark legislation went beyond the goal of having guaranteed medical insurance for certain people by integrating important provisions for:

- providing access to health insurance for small businesses,
- requiring insurers to renew coverage to groups and individuals,
- guaranteeing access to health insurance when someone's employment status changes,
- restricting the use of preexisting conditions,
- increasing the tax deductibility of health insurance premiums for the self-employed,

- establishing medical savings accounts,

- cracking down on fraud and abuse in Medicare and Medicaid,

- creating tax-qualified long-term care insurance,

- revising the notices for Medicare supplement policies,

- requiring insurers and health care providers to electronically exchange information,

- setting a due date for establishing health information privacy, and

- clarifying the taxation of viatical insurance settlements.

FOCUS QUESTION 1

Name one portability-related and one accountability-related HIPAA provision.

_____

_____

_____

While there is much that could be said about each of these HIPAA provisions, this chapter looks only at the impact of HIPAA on the drafting of long-term care insurance policies. Other HIAA courses consider other aspects of HIPAA's provisions.

HIPAA changed the way LTCI is designed, sold, administered, and used by defining and requiring certain policy provisions and standards. While HIPAA's long-term care provisions codified many of the prevailing policy practices in place at the time, it forever changed the landscape by mandating those provisions and features as standard for a tax-qualified plan and excluding other less prevalent practices from use by tax-qualified plans. The Internal Revenue Service (IRS) has had to clarify some provisions through safe harbor notices. Also, there are many issues regarding administration simplification and the confidentiality of medical records associated with the long-term care insurance product that are still being worked out.

Perhaps the most important outcome of HIPAA was a clear statement of the tax treatment of certain long-term care insurance policies. For the first time, there was a clearly established tax treatment of benefits and premiums for those owning long-term care insurance, whether they purchased it before or after HIPAA's effective date. In exchange for these generous tax incentives, certain clauses are now required in policies. This inadvertently created a situation where companies could still elect to offer policies that did not conform to HIPAA's requirements, but these policies cannot be considered tax-qualified. The controversy between **tax-qualified (TQ) policies** versus **non-tax-qualified (NQ) policies** continues today, but to a lesser extent than when companies first began to introduce their tax-qualified policies. Over time, the perceived initial advantages of the broader design flexibility for NQ policies have diminished in importance. Some still debate whether there are measurable differences in terms of access to benefits, premium cost, and other features or whether the small differences in these areas justify the uncertain tax treatment that NQ policies face.

In this chapter, we will first consider the tax incentives that apply to the consumer, and then we will discuss the policy language that companies must use to ensure that the policy can qualify for those tax benefits.

» Tax Treatment

Taxation of Benefits

Prior to HIPAA's passage, no one was exactly sure how long-term care insurance premiums or benefits should be treated from a tax perspective. Existing IRS rules and regulations simply did not address long-term care insurance. In that vacuum, there were various opinions about how to treat LTCI. Some argued that, logically, health insurance benefits are not included as taxable income, so long-term care insurance should have the same rules. But then again, health insurance payments normally go directly to the care provider for the services provided, and the care lasts a short period of time in the vast majority of cases. So while long-term care has some similarities to health care, there are also some important differences. Also, there is a great deal of long-term care that is not medical in nature. The large component of nonskilled, personal care that makes up long-term care caused some to question whether it could be treated like health care from a tax perspective. Another cause for concern with LTCI benefits was that a certain component of the cost of care in a facility went to housing and meals, not to medical care. Was it appropriate for the government to allow tax-free insurance benefits that were used for expenses the claimants would normally incur without the need for ongoing treatment? Hospitalization covers meals, but that is for short time periods—a couple of days or weeks in most cases. Maybe the right course of action was to apply the same treatment to premiums and benefits that were standard to disability income policies. There were many opinions, but nothing in the Internal Revenue Code that provided the certainty needed to make a definite, absolute determination.

HIPAA changed all this by adding a new section to the IRS Code—Section 7702B. In particular, Section 7702B(a)(1) provided the language for the taxation of benefits. The section states that a "qualified long-term care insurance contract" will enjoy the same tax treatment as an accident and health insurance contract. This means that long-term care insurance benefits are excludable from income. However, as we will see, HIPAA also stated that a policy must meet certain requirements to enjoy these tax advantages.

HIPAA developed a new class of long-term care insurance—federally tax-qualified or TQ plans. Those insurers who wanted to ensure that their insureds would have clarity regarding the taxation of benefits and deductibility of premiums needed to include certain provisions in their policy language. (These requirements are covered later in this chapter.) By default, those companies that held the position that the HIPAA requirements were too onerous for the claimant or for the insurer could issue policies that were not federally tax-qualified (NQ). However, it is not accurate to say that, under an NQ plan, benefit payments one receives are taxable as income and premium payments cannot be tax-deducted. The tax status of these NQ plans is simply uncertain since the HIPAA changes to the IRS code did not address this issue. The industry has asked for, but not yet received, clarification on the tax status of NQ plans.

Long-term care insurance benefits are paid under one of two methods: with regard to the actual cost of care (reimbursement or expense-incurred model) or without regard to the cost of care (indemnity or per diem model). Reimbursing for the cost of care followed the health insurance model under which the government was comfortable providing tax-free benefits. There was concern for the per diem model, since people could theoretically be receiving a cash payment in excess of the costs of care or without incurring any cost of care, so Congress put a limit on the amount of an indemnity payment that could be received on a tax-free basis from policies with this design.

Another concern the government had was that qualified long-term care insurance policies would not keep up with rising costs of care. For this reason, a TQ policy must offer the insured the option of adding inflation protection to the policy. The most frequently used design is to have the daily maximum benefit increase by 5 percent, compounded annually. In other words, the amount payable goes up by 5 percent of the previous year's amount. These increases continue regardless of the insured's age, claim or health status, or even how long they've paid premiums on the policy. While most long-term care policies already offered this plan design, there were some that were not offering inflation protection at all, or not this specific design.

Congress was also concerned with the abuse that might occur when someone not really in need of long-term care used tax-free insurance benefits to pay for room and board expenses. To minimize the potential for this type of abuse, a new disclosure form (IRS Form 8853) included language specifically for per diem long-term care insurance policies. Regardless of which benefit design a claimant's policy follows, the insurance company issues a new reporting form (1099-LTC) to the claimant, with a copy to the Internal Revenue Service. This, in combination with IRS Form 8853, provides assurances to the government that the benefits paid on a long-term care policy go toward paying for care and not just supplementing the insured's retirement income.

FOCUS QUESTION 2

Name some concerns the government had with regard to qualified long-term care insurance policies and what measures were taken to address those concerns.

_____

_____

_____

_____

_____

_____

_____

_____

_____

Policies issued prior to the effective date of HIPAA's long-term care insurance provisions (January 1, 1997) are considered **grandfathered policies**. This means that those who own one of these policies receive the same favorable tax status as those holding a qualified policy, even though their policy might not have all the features and provisions required in a TQ policy. This was done to ensure that wholesale replacement activity that was not in the best interest of insureds would not occur. (When a policy is purchased, the insured locks in a premium price based on their age at the time of purchase, so replacing it some years later would cause the insured to pay the higher premium for comparable coverage, because they are buying that policy at an older attained age. Some refer to this as **age equity**.)

However, grandfathered policies cannot have material changes—that is, changes so substantial that in effect the insurer is issuing a new policy that does not meet HIPAA standards. An example of a material change would be if a new benefit or service that caused a commensurate increase in premiums was added to the policy . An example of a coverage change that would *not* be considered a material change and thus would not jeopardize the policy's grandfathered tax status would be if the insured exercised their right under the policy's future purchase option provision to elect an increase in benefits for an additional attained age premium.

Deductibility of Premiums

Insureds and those completing tax forms did not have a clear picture of how premiums were treated prior to HIPAA's passage. There were no lines on any tax forms to include LTCI premiums as a deduction. Some chose to include them with accident and health insurance premiums, while others made no deduction, deciding not to risk a potential fine as a result of an audit by the IRS.

Before the passage of HIPAA, many questions went unanswered. If premiums were deducted from income, would that affect the taxation of benefits? This is how the IRS Code treats disability income insurance, so why not long-term care insurance? People again argued that long-term care insurance was actually health insurance and should have the same treatment as major medical coverage. Unlike the disability policies that are normally purchased through an employer, individuals paid the premiums for the vast majority of long-term care insurance. Few employers offered the coverage, and most buyers waited until after retirement to make the purchase. What treatment would individuals receive?

HIPAA addressed this issue by clarifying the situations in which individuals and employers can deduct the premiums they pay for long-term care insurance. These tax-deductibility rules for premiums applied to newly issued TQ plans as well as grandfathered policies issued before the effective date of HIPAA. Policies without the required language or provisions that would make them tax-qualified (and without grandfathered status) — the NQ policies — still lack clarification.

Specifically, insured individuals qualify for the premium deduction if they file a tax return with itemized deductions and if their medical expenses (including health and long-term care insurance premiums and any out-of-pocket health or long-term care expenses) exceed 7.5 percent of their adjusted gross income. If they qualify for the premium tax deduction, there are limits on how much of the premiums can be counted. (These figures are adjusted each year for inflation.) The amounts for the 2002 tax year are in Table 4.1.

TABLE 4.1

Maximum Tax Deduction for Qualified LTCI Premiums (2002)

Age of policyholder at close of tax year	Maximum amount of premium that is tax-deductible
40 or younger	$240
41 to 50	$450
51 to 60	$900
61 to 70	$2,390
71 or older	$2,990

In 2002, self-employed individuals can deduct 70 percent of the premiums they pay for a tax-qualified long-term care plan, up to the maximum amount for their age (based on Table 4.1). Beginning in 2003, they will be able to deduct 100 percent, up to the maximums.

Businesses paying the premiums for a qualified policy group these costs with other accident and health plans. Their employees can use their medical savings account to pay premiums, but not on a pre-tax basis through a cafeteria plan or flexible spending arrangement.

» The Making of a Qualified Policy

What constitutes a "qualified long-term care insurance contract"? HIPAA and subsequent clarifications have extensive language that affects many different portions of long-term care insurance contracts and the way an insurance company sells and administers policies. Congress was concerned with the quality of long-term care insurance and how it was sold. The quality issue was addressed with policy provision requirements and consumer protection requirements. The consumer protection portion of HIPAA referenced many sections of the NAIC Model Act and Model Regulation as adopted in January 1993. For the most part, companies were already adhering to those requirements. But few companies used *all* the policy language requirements built into the HIPAA legislation.

Companies that want to design a tax-qualified contract must follow HIPAA's requirements with respect to:

- policy cover page,
- how someone qualifies for benefits,
- which services are reimbursable,
- payments unrelated to care,
- policy exclusions and limitations, and
- renewability provisions.

» The Policy Cover Page

Qualified or Nonqualified?

The policy cover page must clearly indicate whether the policy is one that is federally tax-qualified. This is necessary so that insureds can easily recognize whether the policy they own is qualified.

A qualified policy must have a statement that it is federally tax-qualified, on both the policy cover page and the outline of coverage. Because the federal government is not approving the qualified status of policies, companies need to show their intent to offer a qualified policy. (Policies that do not conform to HIPAA language are normally silent regarding their status. Some states require that companies go beyond the federal government's requirements and identify whether a policy is intended or not intended to qualify.) Companies also have the option to include the language related to qualified status on advertising materials.

An example of a typical statement found on the cover of a policy and in the outline of coverage is as follows: "This policy is intended to be a qualified long-term care insurance contract under Section 7702B(b) of the Internal Revenue Code."

Right to Return

Another requirement for the cover page is the insured's right to return the policy after issuance. When HIPAA was passed, the NAIC Model included a provision to allow an insured 30 days to return the policy after receipt of the policy for a full premium refund. The federal legislation reinforced this consumer protection measure by making it a requirement of a qualified contract.

(As an administrative note, agents are required to deliver a qualified policy within 30 days after the company has issued the policy. This gives the insured additional protection against the unscrupulous business practice of delaying their right to return the policy beyond a reasonable time frame.)

Preexisting Conditions

The policy cover page must also clearly specify the company's procedure for determining the timing and level of benefits stemming from an ailment that was present at the time of application. This preexisting condition limitation is discussed below.

» How Someone Qualifies for Benefits

Chronic Illness

A new term—**chronically ill**—was brought to the long-term care insurance industry in August 1996. Insurers understood and previously used most of the concepts inherent in HIPAA's definition of chronically ill, but that exact term was not found in any company's contract. Now HIPAA requires a qualified policy's benefits to be paid only to those who meet the definition of chronically ill as specified in HIPAA and subsequent clarifications.

This term is used because the drafters of HIPAA wanted to be sure that long-term care insurance did not duplicate other forms of insurance. This was especially important because a qualified policy was to pay tax-free benefits, and most policies offered at the time paid in addition to other insurance coverage—including Medicare. The chronically ill definition is designed to differentiate long-term care insurance from medical reimbursement insurance that pays for someone who has an acute illness. HIPAA also reinforced the NAIC's desire to prohibit companies from requiring as policy benefit triggers prior hospitalization or the arbitrary and ill-defined medical necessity concept—although by 1996, most policies had abandoned either one or both of these concepts.

Essentially, HIPAA requires policies to pay benefits when someone is chronically ill. To be chronically ill as defined by HIPAA, a person must be certified by a licensed health care practitioner as meeting one of these criteria:

- They are unable to perform, without substantial assistance from another person, at least two activities of daily living for a period that is expected to last at least 90 days.

- They require substantial supervision to protect themselves from threats to their health and safety because of a severe cognitive impairment.

- They have a level of disability similar to the level of disability associated with the ADL trigger.

FOCUS QUESTION 3

Describe all three HIPAA criteria used to determine whether someone is chronically ill. (Note, however, that a person needs to fit only one of these to be classified as chronically ill.)

_____

_____

_____

_____

_____

Most insurers were already using ADL loss requiring substantial assistance and cognitive impairment as the basis for benefit eligibility. However, insurers are not comfortable with the last component of the chronically ill definition regarding the level of disability option since this is yet to be defined. Most companies do not include that additional option in their policies, but some states have taken the position that including the exact HIPAA language, including the third option, is required. One thing that HIPAA did bring to insurers was a new standardized term defining the level of chronic illness needed before benefits would be payable under a qualified long-term care insurance contract. Prior to HIPAA, there was more variation in this regard, even among carriers that were using ADL and cognitive loss as benefit triggers.

A **licensed health care practitioner (LHCP)** must determine if the insured is chronically ill as defined in the policy. A licensed health care practitioner can be a physician, registered nurse, licensed social worker, or other individual who meets such requirements as may be prescribed by the Secretary of the Treasury. Most companies access a vendor's network of LHCPs or use the services available in care facilities rather than having their own employees perform benefit assessments. Companies generally prefer to designate their own LHCP, rather than allowing or requiring the insured to use any physician, nurse, or social worker. It is important to the carrier that the LHCP have the necessary training, tools, and objectivity to make the determination as to whether someone is chronically ill. The insurer also has a responsibility to its insureds to see that this determination is made equitably and consistently across insureds.

The legislation identifies the six basic activities of daily living—eating, toileting, transferring, bathing, dressing, and continence. A qualified plan must use a minimum of five of these six. Benefits are not payable unless substantial assistance is needed with at least two of the ADLs used in the policy. Companies can choose to add other ADLs but must then trigger benefits on more than just two ADLs. As an example, a company can add ambulating or walking to the other six, and require impairment with three of those seven ADLs to qualify for benefits.

Substantial Assistance

The original HIPAA legislation left certain essential terms undefined. The insurance industry asked for further clarification to ensure that the policies insurers intended to meet the qualified guidelines did in fact meet them. The Internal Revenue Service put forth safe-harbor definitions through interim guidance (IRS Notice 97-31) to aid insurers in defining these terms. One such term was "substantial assistance."

Substantial assistance could mean many different things to many different people. Prior to HIPAA, one company might require more help in performing an ADL than another company, yet both could claim that they used the minimum allowed. Researchers did not provide a standard definition, although many considered levels of necessary assistance in their measurements. The IRS provided the consistent measure. Substantial assistance includes either hands-on assistance or standby assistance, both of which were also defined in Notice 97-31.

■→ Notice 97-31 defines **hands-on assistance** as "the physical assistance of another person without which the individual would be unable to perform
■→ the ADL." And **standby assistance** means "the presence of another person within arm's reach of the individual that is necessary to prevent, by physical intervention, injury to the individual while the individual is performing the ADL." An example of standby assistance was given in the notice: ". . . such as being ready to catch the individual if the individual falls while getting into or out of the bathtub or shower as part of bathing. . ."

FOCUS QUESTION 4

Provide definitions for "substantial," "hands-on," and "standby" assistance, showing how they differ.

_____

_____

_____

_____

_____

_____

_____

_____

_____

There was concern that this new term was more stringent than contracts companies previously offered. The IRS clarified the fact that companies offering long-term care insurance before the January 1, 1997 effective date of HIPAA were not required to make their determination of ADL impairment any different for their new qualified contracts. In essence, defining substantial assistance caused companies to include language alluding to the breakpoint language for benefit qualification in their policy while the administration manual did not change. Companies entering the market after 1997 are not held at a competitive disadvantage with more stringent requirements that go beyond those in the business before them.

Ninety-Day Certification

The requirement that the chronic illness be expected to last at least 90 days is intended to ensure that the need truly represents a long-term care situation, rather than a short-term or acute care need. The claimant must have an inability to perform at least two activities of daily living without substantial assistance for a period of time expected to last at least 90 days.

The **90-day certification requirement** was cause for concern. Did this mean that all policies needed a 90-day elimination period? Would the company withhold all benefits payments until 90 days after a claim was submitted? The IRS clarified the fact that the 90-day requirement was not a waiting period. There is an expectation of how long the impairment would last that is independent from the number of days in the elimination period. As long as the LHCP certifies that the impairment is expected to last 90 days, benefits can begin on day one, if the insured has elected a zero-day elimination period. However, if the impairment does not last for 90 days, even though it was expected to, the insured would not have satisfied the chronically ill definition and benefits are not payable.

The licensed health care practitioner needs to certify that the condition is likely to continue for 90 days owing to a loss of functional capacity before qualified benefits are payable. The intent is to avoid duplicating Medicare or a major medical insurance policy's payment for care because of an acute condition. Ninety days is considered a fair length of time to ensure that the condition is chronic in nature, and in fact 90 days is an accepted delineation in the health care field when determining whether a condition needs short-term or long-term care.

In practice, the 90-day criterion is not an impediment to gaining access to benefits. If someone has arthritis or Alzheimer's disease, they are not going to get better in 90 days. People don't recover from either of these chronic conditions—there are lots of treatments but no cures for them.

On the other hand, someone with a hip replacement normally gets better within a month or two. Medicare would cover this individual's rehabilitation. But if complications arise and physical therapy continues for six months, Medicare would likely stop payments to a facility after 100 days. A qualified long-term care insurance contract could pay benefits as soon as the licensed health care practitioner certified that the care was expected to last 90 days. This certification is pretty easy to grant for the practitioner after care has already been delivered for 100 days—actually, this could have happened before Medicare stopped payments. In this situation, most insurers would honor the original elimination period and pay benefits back to the day it was satisfied.

Cognitive Impairment

Clinical researchers have known for a long time that there are many people who need long-term care but have no ADL impairments—they have cognitive impairments. The IRS also recognized this and made the cognitive impairment trigger separate from the physical impairment trigger. This is another area in which HIPAA instituted language that was somewhat new to long-term care insurers.

While most insurers had separate benefit triggers for cognitive impairment, the definitions they used in their contracts differed from the HIPAA-required definition. Also, while the underlying approach to measuring cognitive impairment was not expected to be different under HIPAA language from what most carriers were using previously, HIPAA added the word "severe" to describe cognitive impairment. Insurers were less comfortable with the HIPAA language that included the words "severe" and "substantial" because of the vagueness of these terms.

The IRS's safe harbor definitions put insurers at ease regarding these terms. Substantial supervision was comparable to the ADL definition of substantial assistance. With a cognitive impairment, this means regular supervision by another person. The other person may provide cueing by means of words, actions, or other techniques to ensure the chronically ill person is safe.

People with cognitive impairments tend to lose a sense of safety awareness. They may leave burners on until a fire starts. Some are unable to remember the importance of maintaining a clean home, thus creating physical and health-related hazards throughout their home. They may walk away from their residence. This is cause for concern when they are not aware of oncoming automobile traffic or the dangers of staying outside all night in the cold. Once they begin wandering outside their protected area, they normally are unable to find their way back to their residence. For caregivers of people with Alzheimer's disease, substantial supervision is a way of life.

The IRS provided identifiable areas to assess an individual's condition for a **severe cognitive impairment**. The safe harbor definition included the intent to utilize existing tools to determine a loss of one's:

- memory (short-term and long-term),
- orientation (people, places, or time), and
- reasoning (deductive or abstract).

A qualified contract uses these clinically proven measures to identify a chronic loss of intellectual capacity — one from which recovery is not likely. Alzheimer's disease and many forms of dementia and senility result in a permanent and continuous loss for which no cure is available. This loss of memory, orientation, and reasoning is independent of an ADL impairment, and HIPAA allows for independence between the two when measuring for a chronic illness.

FOCUS QUESTION 5

What are the three areas of loss in severe cognitive impairment?

_____

_____

_____

The IRS recognized the potential conflict between grandfathered plans (those long-term care insurance policies issued before January 1, 1997) and qualified contracts. Because companies did not define in their contracts the measurement tools or breakpoints for cognitive impairments, there was no way to determine differences between the new and old ways of doing business. Nor did the IRS want companies to tighten up on their claims adjudication and administration process. Just as with the ADL standards, the IRS allowed companies to use the same standards used prior to the effective date of HIPAA in defining when an individual requires substantial supervision resulting from a severe cognitive impairment.

Integrating the terms "substantial" and "severe" was an attempt to bring the breakpoints used by the insurer into the contract language without getting too specific. If the exact breakpoint was spelled out in the contract, the insured could simply exhibit that level of impairment at the time of assessment in order to qualify for benefits. These terms do show the claimant that a minor impairment, such as forgetting where they placed their car keys, is insufficient to qualify for benefits. Companies decided not to tinker with the HIPAA language that included "substantial" and "severe" for fear that it might jeopardize the tax status of the policy.

Recertification

Both cognitive and physical impairments must be recertified every 12 months. A licensed health care practitioner is regularly asked on the claim assessment form how long they think the impairment will last. There is no cure for chronic conditions, so services are needed in most situations for the rest of the insured's life. But there are times when someone with a physical impairment receives necessary therapy and proper nutrition and hydration while in a facility. These individuals can bounce back and no longer show deficiencies in their daily abilities. The federal government wants assurances that they are not receiving tax-free benefit payments when they really don't show signs of the chronic illness any longer. And certainly the insurance company does not want to maintain benefit payments for someone who no longer meets the benefit eligibility criteria.

Summary of Benefit Eligibility

Long-term care insurance companies offering a qualified contract don't assess the condition that caused the loss of independence. That's left up to Medicare and major medical insurance. Rather, they look at the end result of that condition. Does the condition limit the claimant's ability to perform a certain number of ADLs? Do they get assistance with those ADLs? Is that expected to last at least three months? The passage of HIPAA ensured a separation between qualified long-term care insurance and other forms of health insurance.

» Determining Which Services Are Reimbursable

Long-term care insurers have traditionally paid benefits when the claimant shows a loss of physical or cognitive independence and moves to a facility or has someone come to their home. Who provided the care was just as important as documentation of the loss that necessitated long-term care.

Congress was concerned about the potential abuse of the tax-free benefits coming from insurance to pay for room and board type expenses when someone was not really in need of care or services. For this reason, HIPAA requires that there be impairment (as described above) and that the services received be related to that impairment.

Rather than naming the specific services allowed in a qualified contract, HIPAA lists what the services are designed to do. Any service meeting the HIPAA requirement is considered a **qualified long-term care service**. This is described as any "necessary diagnostic, preventive, therapeutic, curing, treating, mitigating, and rehabilitative services, and maintenance or personal care services."

These terms do not stifle coverage for evolving care providers or limit creative service or provider alternatives the insurers may want to integrate into their contract. Dictating nursing homes or home care agencies as a requirement to receive benefits would have been woefully inadequate in this dynamic care provider environment. Fortunately, the broad parameters of HIPAA allow insurers to recognize a wide array of options without paying benefits inappropriately.

The services received under a qualified contract need to be tied to the need for assistance resulting from the chronic illness. If someone is impaired in their ability to take a bath and get dressed, the qualified services they receive should provide assistance with at least bathing and dressing. Someone with a cognitive impairment might need ongoing assistance throughout the day for safety reasons, or help with when and how to complete ADLs. This only makes sense for someone who is not trying to game the system.

Plan of Care

Physicians, discharge planners at hospitals, and registered nurses map out an organized schedule of treatment for each patient. This is referred to as a **plan of care** and is another requirement of HIPAA's definition of qualified services. These plans look at the underlying cause of the need for services, the types of services available in the area, and the patient's personal health situation. If the patient's condition is acute, the plan will focus on rehabilitation services, utilizing therapies and health care providers. If it is chronic in nature, the plan will look to maintain the patient's well-being and attempt to maximize their desire for independence.

The idea behind a plan of care is to help individuals in need identify and gain access to services that will best help them. It is not about how best to manage care or reduce costs. Rather, many people, in conjunction with their family, are unaware of the extent of their impairments and unaware of the types of services various providers make available. They may have a preference for home care but might not be aware of the full range of options available from the different agencies.

A plan of care helps the claimant and claimant's informal caregivers sift through the myriad of options available to identify the best services for the situation. Many people do not investigate long-term care providers until they need the services. The plan helps with their research. A discussion with the person who develops the plan of care will identify specific providers in a community that will best serve the claimant's needs.

Care providers have used plans of care for years. The plan helps to ensure that the care they provide is appropriate using the professional's input along with the provider's experience. Providers working through Medicare reimbursement policies have found the plans helpful. They list specific therapies, nutritional concerns, medical treatments, prescribed medications, and other related tasks that will help the person seeking services. In today's litigious environment, they provide a level of protection for the provider.

These plans are updated frequently. As the person's condition changes, different services become more effective or more appropriate. Physical therapy may help people who have undergone a hip replacement, but over time the formal services may no longer be beneficial. The patients get better and integrate back into their normal daily routine without the limitations encountered soon after surgery. They can continue with an exercise program as needed to regain or maintain their functional capabilities without a provider's oversight. Someone with arthritis might find that occupational therapy helps with difficult tasks that were once done without a conscious effort. These plans of care are flexible over time to accurately reflect the needs of the care recipient.

HIPAA requires a licensed health care practitioner to develop the plan of care before an insurer reimburses for qualified services. Again, HIPAA doesn't identify which specific services are qualified services and thus reimbursable with a qualified plan. It just requires that the services received are part of the plan of care and related to the care needs resulting from the chronic illness. Some insurers already had included a plan of care as a tool to help the claimant prior to this HIPAA requirement. So for many carriers, this requirement did not mean a significant change in procedure or language.

FOCUS QUESTION 6

What are some of the pieces of information that may appear as part of a plan of care?

_____

_____

_____

_____

_____

_____

_____

» Payments Unrelated to Care

The options allowed under HIPAA when payments unrelated to care are made are quite limited, although a policy can have dividends or nonforfeiture values, assuming they conform to the specifications for such nonforfeiture.

Congress has frequently considered the idea of taxing the internal build-up of cash values in life insurance policies. The feeling is that the money is available to the insured much like interest payments are available to owners of bonds or dividend payments to stockholders. So why not tax life insurance cash values? Many people understand that accumulating cash values in life insurance policies is done to maintain affordable premiums in later years of owning the policy. Thus the policy will remain in force at a time when benefits are needed, and the cash values are only used to stabilize premiums.

The same design is available to long-term care insurance companies. After all, insureds hold on to their LTCI policies into their later years of life, when affordability may become an issue for some. The idea is to have level premiums as long as the insured continues paying premiums on the policy. This results in a pricing design in which the insured pays a higher premium than the actual risk assumed in the early years of the contract and underpays the premium in later years. Creating internal policy values, the easiest of which is cash values, helps to maintain those level premiums. As a result of HIPAA's passage, the insurer maintains the "extra" payment with other insureds' payments in reserve for future use. Under normal circumstances, an insured does not have access to these reserves.

HIPAA clearly states that a qualified long-term care insurance policy cannot contain cash surrender values or other monetary worth available to a lender as collateral. It cannot contain values accessible to the insured as a loan. Withdrawing cash values is simply not allowed with qualified long-term care insurance, so cash values are not accumulated. To maintain affordable premiums in the insured's later years, the company establishes reserves on which to draw to pay claims in later years. But insureds do not have access to those policy values other than for the receipt of benefits.

If dividends are paid from a policy, they are available only to reduce future premiums or increase future benefits. Refunding a portion of the premium payment is not available with a qualified plan because of the deductibility of premiums. A tax shelter is created when an insured pays and deducts an annual premium and then the company turns around and pays a dividend in cash to the insured. This is essentially a situation where the insured reduces their taxable income and then gets an unreported refund on the expense that creates the tax reduction. To avoid creating a tax shelter, HIPAA limited the use of dividends to reducing future premiums or increasing future benefits. It is permitted to apply the dividend to the premiums paid for the following year's coverage, thus reducing the net cost to the insured. It is also permitted to add to the maximum daily benefit, reduce the elimination period, or extend the policy maximum. In other words, the benefits of dividends can only enhance the policy and cannot be used for other purposes.

(However, policies are allowed to refund unearned premiums—for example, if an insured paid an annual premium in advance and then died or cancelled the policy after only six months, the portion of premium that was prepaid but has not yet been "earned" can be returned. The responsibility at tax time, therefore, would be for the insured to deduct the amount of premium actually paid and not returned as unearned.)

Nonforfeiture

Nonforfeiture return of premium payments up to the amount of premiums paid are possible with a qualified plan if the policy is no longer needed by the insured. This is available to those who decide to discontinue their coverage either with a complete surrender or cancellation of the contract, such as to the insured's estate when the insured dies. This is called a **nonforfeiture benefit** because it is part of the payment that the premium payer does not give up—or forfeit—when the policy is no longer needed. Another term for it is a **surrender value** because it is a policy value paid out when the policy is surrendered or no longer needed .

HIPAA did not eliminate the potential for these types of values; it simply put guidelines around the design. For example, the full premium is available to the insured at lapse or death in a qualified long-term care insurance contract. However, paying more than the aggregate premium is not allowed with a qualified plan, and policy refunds are considered regular income to the extent the insured deducted premiums from their taxes. Certain consumers still believe they should get something back from their years of premium payments, so insurers have come up with creative alternatives to this clause.

Refunding the full premium is available from some companies. Others have found that phasing in the premium refund based on the number of years the insured owns the policy is a less expensive alternative for the insured to paying back the full premium. (Each return of premium feature costs the insurer something, so there is an additional charge when purchasing one.) As an example, refunding half the premium in the first year and then adding 10 percent each year thereafter is less expensive to the consumer than returning the full premium when the policy terminates.

Without getting too prescriptive regarding actual designs, HIPAA requires insurers to offer at least one of the following nonforfeiture riders:

- a shortened benefit period,

- reduced paid-up insurance,

- extended term insurance, or

- another similar offering.

In the NAIC Model Regulation, all companies offering a qualified contract must offer one particular nonforfeiture benefit—the shortened benefit period. This design provides for the continuation of the policy, but on a limited basis, without further premium payments. Typically, the total dollar amount available for claims or the length of time the claim payments are available is reduced under a nonforfeiture benefit. The nonforfeiture benefit is only available if the policy stayed in force prior to lapse for at least three years. All contract terms remain in place, including the benefit qualification criteria and the elimination period. Most policies also "freeze" the daily benefits amounts at the level they are at the time of lapse, even if the insured had an inflation feature with their coverage. Some carriers will allow the inflation feature to continue within the nonforfeiture benefit, but this is less common because it is more expensive for the insured. The reduced benefit maximum in the nonforfeiture benefit typically is the greater of (a) the aggregate amount of premiums paid over the life of the contract or (b) 30 times the daily benefit. Premiums are no longer due after lapse if the insured includes this feature at the time of purchase. The policy does not lapse until the new reduced benefit amount is exhausted or the insured dies.

The other allowed nonforfeiture benefits are rarely seen in today's LTCI marketplace. The **reduced paid-up design** creates a policy in which the maximum daily benefit is decreased (hence "reduced") and no future premiums are due (hence "paid-up"). The issuing company creates a formula for reducing the maximum daily benefit based on the original maximum daily benefit, the insured's age when the policy was issued, and the number of years the policy was in premium paying status.

The **extended term insurance design** is based on a common life insurance option. When the policy lapses, the coverage does not change, and premiums are no longer due while the policy remains in force for a limited period of time. If a claim occurs during this "extended term," it is payable as if premiums were paid until the insured entered claim status—the claim can continue beyond the extended term. The policy will lapse at the end of the extended term.

FOCUS QUESTION 7

What are some of the nonforfeiture riders offered by insurers to satisfy consumer feeling that years of premium payments should result in some sort of tangible benefit in the event the policy proves unnecessary?

_____

_____

_____

_____

_____

_____

» Exclusions and Limitations

The drafters of HIPAA wanted to limit an insurer's ability to add policy exclusions and limitations. Companies and regulators had pretty much standardized the allowable language, and HIPAA for the most part simply reinforced the NAIC's efforts in this regard. It did, however, add a few twists.

Medicare Coordination

Policies that reimburse the insured for services need to take into consideration whether Medicare pays benefits. Again, the idea was to differentiate long-term care insurance from medical insurance and not allow for tax-free benefit payments for duplicate services. So HIPAA requires that a qualified contract not pay benefits to the extent that Medicare pays benefits for the same service.

If a company wants to get away from Medicare coordination, another option is available — offering a per diem or indemnity policy. These policies pay a predetermined dollar amount directly to the claimant (or an assigned entity) regardless of the actual cost of care. One design of the indemnity-type policy pays only when covered services are received. The other method pays benefits after the existence of a chronic illness is determined without regard to the types of services received. Either way, this design is allowed in a qualified policy.

Preexisting Conditions

Another policy provision that was a cause of concern was a company's preexisting condition provision. This language is common to almost all personal insurance related to one's health. It is protection for the insurance company to ensure that the company receives complete and accurate information when it makes an underwriting decision to issue the policy.

With long-term care insurance, a **preexisting condition** is one for which the insured received treatment or was advised to receive treatment no more than six months before the policy became effective. If such a condition is identified no later than six months after the policy's effective date, care resulting from that condition need not be covered by the insurer. This creates a waiting period for both the insured and insurer in regard to an applicant's known health history.

While common initially, a growing number of long-term care insurance policies no longer include a limitation or exclusion on coverage for a preexisting condition. Many insurers feel that the concept is ill defined and poorly applied to long-term care as it is often difficult to link one's subsequent functional or cognitive loss to any one specific previously existing diagnosis or condition. Preexisting condition clauses are particularly rare in individual LTCI policies—instead, insurers do extensive underwriting.

A company's right to use a preexisting condition exclusion is limited when the policy it issues replaces another company's policy. The new insurer reduces the limited length of time to the extent similar exclusions were satisfied under the first policy. This is designed so that the insured is not penalized for buying what they feel is better coverage.

The option to utilize a preexisting condition limitation does not prohibit an insurer from investigating an applicant's medical records. In fact, insurers are required to use an application form designed to obtain an applicant's health history. Applicants are to list the medications physicians have prescribed. Companies also request the right to obtain information from the applicant's primary physician or health care specialist before making a decision on whether to issue the policy.

One thing companies are not allowed to do, as reinforced in HIPAA, is engage in **post-claim underwriting**. This refers to the practice of accepting someone for insurance and then, at time of claim, finding some reason to rescind or cancel their coverage based on information they neglected to provide at the time of underwriting. Furthermore, if the applicant discloses on the application that they are taking a medication that is a known treatment for a condition the insurance company would normally deny coverage for, the company cannot claim ignorance that the insured did not disclose that they had a declinable health history. The company cannot rescind the policy, or exclude, limit, or reduce benefits based on that preexisting condition.

Insurers do have the right to rescind, or take back, a policy from the insured. The insurer can do this when it discovers at claim time that the insured withheld information pertinent to the acceptance of coverage. If this is detected within the first six months of issuing the policy, the company must show that the applicant misrepresented their health history in a way that was material to the acceptance of coverage given the insurer's underwriting standards. Between six months and two years, the proof must show both that the condition was material to the acceptance of coverage and that the condition misrepresented led to needing services. After two years, the company must show the applicant (now insured and claimant) knowingly and intentionally misrepresented their health history for the purpose of obtaining insurance coverage. This final standard indicates a level of fraud on the part of the insured and has no time limit on its use.

If in fact the company paid benefits to the claimant of a rescinded policy, those payments are gone forever. The insurer cannot recover those benefit payments.

FOCUS QUESTION 8

Present a brief scenario in which an insurer would not be allowed to cancel an insured's coverage at the time a claim is filed. Present another scenario in which the insurer does have the right to rescind the policy.

_____

_____

_____

_____

_____

_____

_____

_____

_____

» Renewability Provisions

HIPAA referenced the NAIC model regulation in determining appropriate renewability provisions. The two renewability options are guaranteed renewable and noncancelable.

A policy is **guaranteed renewable** when the insured is the only one who can cancel the policy. The easiest and most common way the insured does that is to simply stop paying premiums. The company cannot unilaterally change any provision of the contract while it remains in force. The only change allowed is an adjustment in premiums. The insurer must identify a class of insureds that needs the premium adjustment—not an individual insured. The class can be as narrow as, for example, all those between ages 62 and 70 with a nursing-home-only plan with a three-year maximum who were issued with a 30 percent rating. Or it can be as broad as everyone with a nursing home and home care (comprehensive) policy. Under a guaranteed renewable policy, the insurance company cannot cancel the coverage except for nonpayment of premium as due or because all benefits under the policy have been used up.

A **noncancelable** policy goes further in consumer protection by not only providing a guaranteed renewable contract, but by also guaranteeing that premium rates will never change. The thought of guaranteeing premiums for the life of the contract has caused companies to reexamine the pricing data available, the administrative and assessment tools that are utilized, and the possible future changes in the provider community. The general conclusion is that the additional risk of guaranteeing premiums forever goes beyond the company's ability to successfully market the adequately priced product.

Some companies are experimenting with the notion of locking in rates to create a noncancelable policy. They add an extra load into their premium to account for the loss of ability to adjust rates later. But the industry is a long way from other insurance products (namely some forms of life insurance) that provide rates that will not and cannot change.

While the premium for a guaranteed renewable contract is designed to remain level over the life of the policy, the insurer does have the right to adjust rates on a class basis. Therefore, insurers cannot describe their products as having "**level premiums**" unless that contract is noncancelable. This is in spite of the fact that companies offering guaranteed renewable contracts price their product to have the same premiums for the life of the contract while maintaining the right to adjust premiums in the future. This isn't like term life insurance, where the premium goes up each year or after a predetermined number of years. Experience from various companies indicates, however, that rates have been lowered and raised after the policy was issued—with the majority of adjustments being upward. The term "level premiums" has the potential to mislead consumers into believing rates will never change.

If an LTCI premium is not paid within 30 days after its due date, the policy is no longer in force—it will lapse or terminate. HIPAA integrated the unintentional lapse provision designed by the drafters of the NAIC Models. This states that if the insured was chronically ill when the premium was due, putting the policy back in force without proving insurability is an option for the insured. This option is available for up to five months after the policy has lapsed. The insurer may have a standard for physical or cognitive assessments for the reinstatement that is no more stringent than that used for benefit qualification. The insured pays back due premiums to reinstate the policy.

» HIPAA's Integration with the NAIC Models

The drafters of HIPAA were keenly aware of the provisions contained in both the NAIC Model Act and Model Regulation. There are sections of HIPAA, especially in Part II (Consumer Protection Provisions), that simply reference the NAIC's January 1993 model provisions. At the same time, many of HIPAA's terms were new to the long-term care insurance industry when it was passed in 1996. There were no state regulations to coincide with this new federal legislation, thus creating challenges for state regulators when they received new product filings from companies that wanted to offer a qualified long-term care insurance contract. In addition, the companies needed state approval before HIPAA's effective date of January 1, 1997.

States took the position that they were not going to determine whether a product design met HIPAA's requirements for a qualified contract. Rather, they would assess the contract language under its previously stated mission of balancing consumer and industry needs. States took varying approaches to these newfangled terms—some embraced qualified plans while others required insurers to file policies that met their previous regulations alongside HIPAA's rules. Some states had to scramble to change their regulations to allow approval of qualified plans while other states required a legislative fix.

The NAIC recognized the challenge that lay ahead. Although NAIC's models were recognized as providing a resource for approving qualified plans, changes were necessary. Today, both the NAIC Model Act and Model Regulation have integrated HIPAA's language. At the same time, the Models recognize that a qualified contract is not the only policy for all companies to offer or for every consumer to purchase. There is no requirement that all contracts need be qualified contracts.

Many states have adopted the new models to help facilitate the approval of qualified contracts. The last remaining state that required companies to offer nonqualified policies alongside their qualified contracts has let that legislation sunset. The market for both types of contracts is now well established. Many companies have decided to only offer tax-qualified policies, so that they don't have to issue warnings about the possible future tax consequences of an NQ policy. Some companies still like the flexibility of having both TQ and NQ policies, so they continue to offer both.

» Summary

HIPAA laid a foundation of minimum standards for a qualified long-term care insurance policy. These standards changed the way some policies were written but not necessarily how they were administered. Clarifications made after HIPAA was originally issued have provided companies the confidence that their prior business practices were and are acceptable to making long-term care insurance available to the buying public.

Companies and regulators have taken steps to ensure that these policies are available. Insurers that offer the qualified policies have redrafted their policy using the new language. State insurance departments and the NAIC have integrated the HIPAA language into the way they do business. All parties worked diligently together after HIPAA's passage to have their product available for the buying public once it became effective.

Some companies have elected to build their product without adhering to HIPAA standards. These companies are of the opinion that consumers are better off without terms such as "substantial" and "severe" in their policy language. This is an option all companies have, although the majority of long-term care insurance policies purchased today are intended to be qualified long-term care insurance policies.

Most companies have accepted the new standards and even found nuances within the HIPAA guidelines to offer innovations that were not considered prior to the passage of the act. Rather than stifling competition, HIPAA has laid a foundation from which companies are able to move the products forward in this rapidly changing industry.

The jury is still out on HIPAA's effectiveness. Insurers are still gaining experience with it. It is one thing to write a policy and develop procedure manuals to administer it. It is another to have enough experience with claims to thoroughly document HIPAA's success or failure. What is determined is that everyone going into claim status with a qualified long-term care insurance policy appreciates the clarification of income tax-free benefits. In addition, the many people who receive an income tax reduction because they include their premium with unreimbursed medical expenses find a value-added benefit in owning these policies.

Key Terms 🔑

Age equity

Chronically ill

Extended term insurance design

Grandfathered policy

Guaranteed renewable

Hands-on assistance

Health Insurance Portability and Accountability Act (HIPAA)

Level premiums

Licensed health care practitioner (LHCP)

Ninety-day certification requirement

Noncancelable

Nonforfeiture benefit

Non-tax-qualified (NQ) policy

Plan of care

Post-claim underwriting

Preexisting condition

Qualified long-term care service

Reduced paid-up design

Severe cognitive impairment

Standby assistance

Substantial assistance

Surrender value

Tax-qualified (TQ) policy

» Review Questions

1. What does HIPAA stand for? What is its primary focus?

2. What was the most important tax consequence of HIPAA for long-term care insurance?

3. What was the intent of "grandfathering" insurance policies that had been issued before HIPAA's LTCI provisions went into effect?

4. Where does a long-term care insurance policy need to state whether it is intended to be federally tax qualified? Why is the placement important?

5. Who qualifies as a licensed health care practitioner?

6. What are the HIPAA requirements designed to ensure that a short-term or acute care need is not classified as a long-term care situation?

7. How often do cognitive and physical impairments need to be re-certified?

8. What is the definition of a preexisting condition in the context of long-term care insurance?

9. What is post-claim underwriting?

10. What is a guaranteed renewable policy? What is a noncancelable policy?

» Answers

1. The Health Insurance Portability and Accountability Act. The act's primary focus is to ensure that people have access to major medical insurance without proving evidence of insurability.

2. HIPAA established that long-term care insurance benefits were excludable from income (as long as the policy met certain requirements).

3. Grandfathering meant that individuals owning a pre-HIPAA policy would receive the same favorable tax status as those holding a qualified policy, even though their policy might not have all the features and provisions required in a TQ policy. (However, grandfathered policies cannot have material changes—that is, changes so substantial that in effect the insurer is issuing a new policy that does not meet HIPAA standards.)

4. A qualified policy must have a statement that it is intended to be federally tax-qualified on both the policy cover page and the outline of coverage. This way, insureds can easily recognize whether the policy they own is a qualified policy.

5. A licensed health care practitioner can be a physician, registered nurse, licensed social worker, or other individual who meets such requirements as may be prescribed by the Secretary of the Treasury.

6. The claimant must have an inability to perform at least two activities of daily living without substantial assistance for a period of time expected to last at least 90 days.

7. Every 12 months.

8. A preexisting condition is one for which the insured received treatment or was advised to receive treatment no more than six months before the policy became effective.

9. This is defined as the practice of accepting someone for insurance and then, at the time a claim is filed, coming up with a reason to rescind or cancel that person's coverage based on information the person neglected to provide at the time of underwriting. HIPAA forbids the practice.

10. A guaranteed renewable policy is one that can be canceled only by the insured. A noncancelable policy is guaranteed renewable and further, its premium rates cannot be changed.

5

Long-Term Care Services

» Overview

After confirming that a claimant's impairment meets the policy's benefit qualification criteria, the next thing an insurer looks at before paying benefits is which services the claimant is receiving and who is providing those services. This chapter looks at the various services commonly provided in a long-term care setting, while the next chapter covers the potential providers of care.

» Levels of Care

During the beginnings of the long-term care insurance industry, services were classified into one of three categories of care: skilled, intermediate, or custodial care. This followed level-of-care distinctions that, at one time, were used in facility licensure. While these levels-of-care distinctions and terminology are no longer used, it is still useful to define and differentiate them. **Skilled care** is daily, restorative care, provided by skilled personnel under the direction of a physician. Generally, when someone receives skilled care, there is an expectation for improvement. Once the individual's condition stabilizes and progress toward recovery is no longer evident, skilled care ends under the classic definition. Receiving skilled care was and is a requirement of receiving Medicare's reimbursement. Medicare still describes the type of care it covers as skilled care, although officials actually scrutinize the types of services received. Many of these are described below.

Intermediate care is considered one step down in intensity from skilled care. Just like skilled care, it is restorative in nature, delivered by skilled personnel (such as nurses) with a physician overseeing the care. The difference is that the care is delivered less frequently than daily—it is intermittent. Medicare traditionally defined daily care as care delivered at least five days a week. Intermediate care is simply care delivered four or fewer days a week. This level of care may be appropriate as people want to maintain their abilities during their recovery but no longer benefit from the more intense regimen.

Custodial care is completely different. Custodial care focuses on providing assistance when someone needs help with ADLs or IADLs. There is no requirement for frequency, who provides the care, or who orders the care. People in need of skilled or intermediate care normally need some custodial care—it is not exclusive of the other levels of care. Frequently, when chronic conditions set in, family and friends are the ones who recognize the need for assistance and act as the initial providers of custodial care. Professionals provide assistance when informal caregivers aren't available or when informal caregivers need help because of emotional or physical strain or because of other demands on their time.

Although the skilled, intermediate, and custodial terminology is still heard from time to time, the provider community steers clear of it today. It is rarely used in today's LTCI contracts, and regulators find the terms too vague. These terms are too simplistic for the types of care provided using today's advances in treatments and technology. However, understanding them is essential to understanding the origins of long-term care insurance.

FOCUS QUESTION 1

Define skilled, intermediate, and custodial care.

_____

_____

_____

_____

_____

_____

_____

_____

» Long-Term Care Services

Defining Services

A qualified LTCI contract includes a listing of the services that are covered by the policy. The choices spelled out in HIPAA are "diagnostic, preventive, therapeutic, curing, treating, mitigating, and rehabilitative services, and maintenance or personal care services." None of these were defined in the legislation or subsequent clarifications. They were left up to the insurers and regulators to interpret.

There is no listing of the possible services that fall under each of these categories. There are, however, many lists of services available in the health care community. The term that refers to these lists is **universal code sets**. These code sets are used throughout the world, but unfortunately more than one set is utilized. Private insurers, Medicare, Medicaid, and other payers of care use these in the reimbursement of medical care. Researchers use them to analyze the success of various treatments of conditions.

In comparison to the medical community code sets, the list is somewhat limited for long-term care services. Even so, there are too many to cover them all in this chapter. Instead, some of the more common services are discussed.

Available Services

A registered nurse (RN) or licensed practical nurse (LPN) provides **skilled nursing services**. The services are normally provided under the orders of a physician or as part of a plan of care developed by a physician. The services provided by an RN or LPN can include administering prescription medications, supervising a dietary regime, changing bandages, or providing therapies. This care is provided in short increments — mostly less than two hours in the home or facility.

Under the skilled nursing service umbrella are a variety of services.[1] Therapies provided include physical therapy, speech therapy, respiratory therapy, and occupational therapy. Chemotherapy, injections, catheter care, oxygen, and tube feeding are other available services. Nurses, audiologists, or therapists provide these services. Paramedics receive special training so they're able to provide some of these services also.

Less skilled personnel can also provide important long-term care services. Companion services or elder sitters simply help many people maintain a safe environment. Personal care or attendant care services focus on the ADL needs of the patients. Someone in need of long-term care might need assistance with personal hygiene services such as cleaning body and hair. Homemaker services provide help with necessary IADLs such as light housekeeping, money management, meal preparation, dishwashing, and shopping. Sometimes laundry services are differentiated from homemaker services.

Chore services include household maintenance beyond daily homemaker services such as landscape maintenance, painting, and minor repairs. These are different from home modification services that make structural changes, such as installing grab bars, widening doorways, or assembling wheelchair ramps.

A dietician assesses one's nutritional needs and then maps out a plan for appropriate food to eat. There are services that deliver meals to one's home, provide congregate meals, or even provide a restaurant meal allowance. Family members benefit from caregiver training or teaching and demonstration services, which teach family members how to safely and appropriately provide a variety of personal care services, such as moving someone from a bed to a chair or helping them dress. Respite care services provide short-term, overnight relief for caregivers by providing paid providers to take over caregiving temporarily while the informal caregivers take some time off.

A **personal emergency response system** is a service designed to provide an impaired person with access to assistance in the event of a medical, physical, emotional, or environmental crisis.

Hospice services provide caring and compassion to the terminally ill and their family members. When a cure for a person's condition is no longer possible, treatment changes to pain management, spiritual assistance, reassurance interventions, volunteer support, and bereavement and grief counseling.

Case management or **care coordination** services assist with the development and implementation of the plan of care, help people identify appropriate services, and help make arrangements to receive care, if desired. The plan of care is developed based on a comprehensive assessment of the individual's physical and cognitive needs, social situation, health condition, and other factors. The plan of care also takes into account the individual's and family's preferences about services and what is available in their community that best meets their needs. The case manager oversees the other services received through coordination and monitoring. Periodic reassessment is needed as the health status of the person in need of care improves or declines.

Transportation services are available from various sources. Many communities have vans or coach services to help people in need because of handicaps or impairments. Taxis, volunteers, and buses help people move about so they can remain in a community-based setting. An ambulance service to obtain medical care is an option. Many adult day centers have their own transportation network. Some suppliers, such as pharmacies, offer delivery services to minimize the need for transportation by the person in need of care.

Many people with impairments need medical equipment and supplies. Equipment includes hospital beds, wheelchairs, walkers, or toilets designed to help people in need. It is typically available for rent or purchase. The supplies are needed to treat medical conditions. This can include ointments, bandages, and other disposable items.

All these services can fit under HIPAA's definition of qualified services— "diagnostic, preventive, therapeutic, curing, treating, mitigating, and rehabilitative services, and maintenance or personal care services." Imagine the length and the difficulty in drafting the legislation if all of the services above were listed and defined. Imagine the number of pages in an insurance policy if all these services were included. And this is not an exhaustive list of services and doesn't include the availability of new services under development today or in the future. One reason HIPAA was immediately embraced by the long-term care insurance community is that it allows for this level of flexibility in services.

» The Development of a Plan of Care

Under a qualified LTCI policy, a plan of care is developed for each claimant. A licensed health care practitioner (usually a nurse or social worker) designs the plan of care, in consultation with the claimant, the primary caregiver, other family members, and therapists.

Generally, a long-term care plan of care is designed to provide comfort and assistance for the insured's current condition. These plans focus on care providers appropriate for the person's physical and environmental needs. Some people who receive an aggressive plan of care opt not to follow it because of advanced age or multiple chronic conditions. They do not want to have invasive testing or therapies performed.

Most plans of care include a nutritional assessment. The claimant's weight is taken and diet assessed to determine whether a weight loss or a weight gain program would be appropriate. The individual's ability to prepare a meal and feed themselves is evaluated. Prescription medications that can affect the individual's eating habits are evaluated. Modifications to existing eating practices are recommended as needed.

Additional testing is frequently seen in a plan of care. When someone is suspected of having a cognitive impairment, time-tested evaluation tools are used to gain a better understanding of the level and potential cause of the impairment. Other age-related evaluations are made, such as tests for diabetes, thyroid disease, prostate or breast cancer, and extensive blood tests. All prescription medications are scrutinized to ensure that the original reason for taking the medication is still present. Also, combining multiple medications can lead to toxicity or an unnatural deterioration of memory or reasoning abilities, both of which are reversible with careful treatment.

Some people have a plan of care with an end-of-life focus. These include recommendation for advance directives and hospice-oriented care. Physicians and their patients reach an agreement on general treatment and philosophies to help them avoid the need to make critical decisions in a time of crisis.

FOCUS QUESTION 2

What might be included in a long-term care plan of care?

_____

_____

_____

_____

_____

_____

_____

_____

The People Who Develop the Plan of Care

There are people who thoroughly understand plans of care, each of the services included in them, and the appropriate use of those services. HIPAA refers to these people as licensed health care practitioners, which includes physicians, professional nurses, and Master's-trained social workers. The best ones for long-term care services have a gerontology background and training in the care of the elderly. These people are found in:

- hospitals (including discharge planners),
- nursing homes and other facilities that provide assistance care,
- home care agencies,
- insurance company home office staff, and
- independent care management service agencies.

These licensed health care practitioners are specially trained to be able to assess an individual's need for care. They combine a person's health history with a functional assessment of ADLs and standardized tests of cognitive capabilities, using standardized tools and techniques. They also take into consideration the person's age and abilities before they became impaired. Potential outcomes or patient desires are also considered.

These professionals know which services are most appropriate to fit the patient's needs and personal situation. They normally recommend a combination of services that will provide the greatest opportunity for either rehabilitative or maintenance care, or services that provide the least restrictive setting of care. The frequency of services needed is also part of the recommendation. Measuring the units of frequency depends on the service. Options include the number of hours per day, the number of days per week or specific days, the number of visits, per month, per meal, or per job. Adjustments are made as the impairment gets better or worse or if the patient's personal or social situation changes.

These care planning professionals are familiar with the provider options in a community. They know which providers offer multiple services, so they can minimize the number of places the impaired person must go or minimize the number of people coming in the home. The most experienced care planners know each provider's strengths and weaknesses and which ones provide the highest quality service. They know how much each provider charges and the insurance arrangements it accepts.

They also take into consideration the impaired person's ability to pay for the services. Good planners look into utilizing government funding (such as Medicare or Medicaid), private health insurance (including major medical, Medicare supplement, or long-term care insurance), and personal funds (assets or income). They will know of any grant programs that are available in a community or state that are made available for certain conditions. There might be a special study or research project that provides innovative, experimental services without charge for those willing to participate. They maximize the use of free or low-cost subsidized services available in many communities.

All this analysis is part of the plan of care required by HIPAA and reviewed by insurers before paying qualified LTCI benefits. Traditionally, nurses and social workers have often developed the plan of care after consultation with the physician or medical specialist. These plans spell out the types and frequency of services appropriate for the individual's condition. The plan will recommend frequency of services—such as "physical therapy three days a week"—and might include a duration—such as "for the next six weeks." The provider records the services by units—such as per hour, per visit, per day, per week, or per month.

The plan of care remains flexible as positive or negative changes to the patient's condition warrant a change in the plan. For acute conditions, changes are frequent as people rehabilitate and need fewer services. For cognitive impairments, changes to the plan of care often reflect a worsening condition. HIPAA requires an update to the plan of care annually to ensure benefits continue only to those who continue to exhibit a functional impairment requiring care services. Most insurers reserve the right to update the plan of care as needed but not more frequently than every 30 days.

FOCUS QUESTION 3

Describe some of the individuals (in terms of their affiliations or qualifications) who might be involved in putting together a plan of care.

_____

_____

_____

_____

_____

_____

_____

» Payment for Services

Not all long-term care insurance companies have the same approach to paying for long-term care services. In this regard, there are essentially three types of LTCI policies:

- disability,
- indemnity, and
- reimbursement.

The Disability Model

There are a few companies that have designed their policies without consideration of specific covered services. These policies follow the **disability model**. They pay a flat dollar amount when the appropriate level of impairment exists without consideration of the services received or who provides the services. Provider's bills are not required. Payments are normally made on a monthly basis based on the number of days in the month on which the insured met the disability triggers in the policy. The benefit is paid without regard to whether services are received or which services are received.

This design is possible with either a qualified or nonqualified policy. HIPAA requires companies to reimburse for qualified services but makes an allowance for these types of "cash payment disability" policies. In other words, consideration of which services are received isn't important to HIPAA unless payments are made for those services. These contracts can, but are not required to, coordinate benefits with Medicare as the private insurance takes a back seat as the secondary payer.

The challenge with this design is the level of certainty in the assessment of the claimant's physical and cognitive abilities. The company trusts that the licensed health care practitioner is honest and fair in the measurement of the insured's impairment. This is the most consumer-friendly policy design in that there is no limit on the types of providers or services covered. However, it is also often more expensive than the other policy types. For the insurance company, there are added costs in administering these policies because insureds have a greater incentive to request benefit (cash) payments even if they do not meet the disability requirements. So the insurer needs to spend more time and money assessing and verifying disability on an ongoing basis. However, there are also administrative simplicities in this model for the insurance company, since the insurer does not need to review and verify the accuracy of provider bills and verify that the provider or service meets the requirements to be covered under the policy.

The Indemnity Model

Another approach is the **indemnity model**, which considers the frequency of services and whether or not the provider or service meets the policy definitions of a covered service, but does not reimburse for actual charges.

Some refer to this design as a **per diem policy** because the payments are like a daily fee or allowance. These policies are like the disability model in that they pay a flat dollar amount regardless of the actual cost of care, but the two differ in that the insured is required to receive paid care and only defined covered providers or services are eligible for the indemnity payment.

The advantage for consumers is that they can use the benefit payment amount in excess of their care costs to pay for items that might not be covered, such as private duty nursing, convenience items in the nursing home, etc. The claimant manages the pool of funds available to them. Sometimes there are charges for noncovered services or unpaid hidden costs (such as a family caregiver having to shift from full-time to part-time employment to continue providing care to their loved one). Some believe that claims are processed faster when the disability or indemnity model is utilized. There isn't a need to analyze the actual charges from the provider or wait to hear whether Medicare paid a portion of the bill (unless the company did include a Medicare coordination clause), although the insurer still needs to verify that the provider or service is covered under the policy.

The Reimbursement Model

The third type of LTCI design is the **reimbursement model**. Under this model, the actual bill received is considered. The insurer looks at which services are provided, who is providing the service, and how much the provider charged for the service. The reimbursement model pays benefits only for the actual charges. If expenses exceed the daily or monthly benefit limit, the insured receives benefits up to that limit and must pay any excess charges on their own. Assuming the policy has a pool of money, if charges are less than the daily or monthly maximum of the policy, the excess remains in the pool of money.

This design is fair to the consumer and minimizes the risk to the insurer. Consumers are reimbursed for their out-of-pocket costs—which is as much as they should expect from any form of accident and health insurance. This is the design of most types of insurance—medical expense insurance pays the provider directly, while automobile insurance will provide a check payable to the insured and provider of the repair after reviewing an estimate of the cost to make the repair. If the actual charges are in excess of the daily benefit maximum, this difference remains in the policy's overall maximum.

This design provides a check and balance to the quality of the functional assessment. The company takes on less risk for fraud and abuse by monitoring the services received through the provider's billing statement and making sure the services provided are consistent with the plan of care. They are paying for only the services the claimant receives. Reviewing service use also helps the insurance company identify whether the insured's condition is improving or declining, such that a revised plan of care may be appropriate.

A reimbursement policy that is a qualified contract will pay benefits after Medicare. The insurance is the secondary payer while Medicare is the primary.

FOCUS QUESTION 4

Briefly describe the advantages of the reimbursement model—for consumers as well as for insurers.

_____

_____

_____

_____

_____

_____

» Summary

The original long-term care insurance contracts used skilled, intermediate, and custodial levels of care to determine the appropriateness of benefits paid. Eventually, there was a recognition in the provider and insurance communities that these terms were inadequate to accurately describe the care people receive—they were vague and difficult to use because of the duplication and blending of the levels of care. The fine line between skilled and intermediate care frequently overlapped in practice, and almost all care recipients received at least some custodial care.

HIPAA provided new terms for insurers to use. These were more descriptive but not specific to the actual services provided. The new terms are now used in most qualified long-term care insurance policies, and insurers' claim administration manuals consider the specific services performed by the long-term care provider community.

Key Terms 🔑

Care coordination	Personal emergency response system
Case management	Reimbursement model
Custodial care	Skilled care
Disability model	Skilled nursing services
Indemnity model	Universal code sets
Intermediate care	
Per diem policy	

» Review Questions

1. Why are the terms "skilled," "intermediate," and "custodial" care not usually encountered in long-term care insurance contracts today?

2. Who usually provides skilled nursing services?

3. Name some of the therapies administered under the term "skilled nursing services."

4. Name some important long-term care services provided by individuals who are less skilled than nurses.

5. What is the preferred educational background for professionals providing long-term care?

6. Why is flexibility important for a plan of care?

7. How often does HIPAA mandate an update to plans of care? How often do insurers update their plans in actual practice?

8. In terms of payment of benefits for services, what are the three common types of long-term care insurance policies?

9. From the consumer's perspective, what makes a disability LTCI policy attractive? What is its downside?

10. What is another name for the indemnity model of long-term care insurance policy?

» Answers

1. Regulators find these terms, once very common, too vague. They are considered too simplistic for the types of care provided using today's advances in treatments and technology.

2. A registered nurse (RN) or licensed practical nurse (LPN)—under the orders of a physician or as part of a plan of care developed by a physician. In some cases audiologists, therapists, and paramedics may also provide these services.

3. Physical therapy, speech therapy, respiratory therapy, occupational therapy, chemotherapy, injections, catheter care, oxygen, tube feeding, and so on.

4. These include companion services, personal care or attendant care services, personal hygiene services, homemaker services, laundry services, chore services, and home modification services.

5. Gerontology.

6. The plan of care should be able to react to positive and negative changes in the patient's condition.

7. Once a year. Insurers may update their plans as frequently as every 30 days.

8. Disability, indemnity, and reimbursement.

9. There is no limit on the types of providers or services covered. On the flip side, it is often more expensive than the other policy types (indemnity and reimbursement).

10. This model is also known as a per diem policy because the payments are in the form of a daily fee or allowance.

NOTE

1 For definitions of many of the terms used here, refer to http://aspe.hhs.gov/daltcp/ diction.htm.

 **6**

Long-Term Care Providers

» Overview

In the not too distant past, long-term care providers consisted primarily of family members, neighbors, or fellow members of a church, synagogue, or other religious congregation. Multigenerational households were common, so when someone needed care, there were family members available to help out. Paid professionals usually weren't needed because communities and family support networks were strong. This began to change as the economy moved from an agricultural to an industrial base. Large families were no longer a necessity, and younger generations began to establish separate households for their families.

Those in need of services today still receive most of their assistance from family members and friends. These people are considered **informal caregivers** because they do it out of a sense of love or duty rather than as a profession. Seldom do they receive monetary compensation for their efforts. They are considered the **primary caregivers**. Not only do they roll up their sleeves to provide the bulk of care, they also act as a case manager by researching, obtaining, coordinating, and monitoring the secondary providers of care services when additional paid care providers are needed.

These **secondary providers**, or **formal care providers**, are qualified by training and/or experience to provide long-term care. They are professionals in the sense that they provide long-term care services for a living and have some type of training or experience, although they may not be "professionals" in the sense that one usually thinks of (such as a skilled nurse, therapist, or physician). The professionals or formal caregivers are called in when there is no primary informal caregiver, or when the primary caregiver experiences stress or exhaustion of a physical or emotional nature, or when care needs exceed the capabilities of informal caregivers, or when the primary caregiver cannot give sufficient time to care. The formal caregivers have broadened and expanded the services they offer to adapt to the changing needs of care recipients and informal primary caregivers.

The secondary or formal care provider usually takes on the primary caregiver role when the care recipient lives in a care facility. This alleviates the family member's need for physical interventions and allows them to act as the overseer of care to ensure that appropriate care is delivered. Having 24 hours of care provided by a paid provider in one's home is expensive, a luxury unaffordable to most Americans.

Long-term care insurance has traditionally been based on services provided in a care facility. In the last two decades, it has expanded to encompass a wide array of formal care providers that supplement or substitute for the care provided by family members. There exists today a large number of options for people who need long-term care services. Insurers are responding to rapidly changing care provider options with expanded policy language and/or administrative procedures to accommodate claimants' needs.

FOCUS QUESTION 1

Provide examples of people who are informal caregivers and others who are formal caregivers.

» The Care Continuum

One can think of available long-term care options as a **care continuum**. The continuum shown in Figure 6.1 is a simple summary of the options available today. This has seen considerable expansion since the time when long-term care insurance was originally introduced, as the provider community has changed and continues to evolve.

The continuum generally ranges from the most impaired person to the least impaired person. The least impaired person is on the left. Few services are needed by this person, and those providing the services usually do not require a great deal of education. The most impaired person is on the right. This person probably needs more skilled services or even multiple services.

People with chronic conditions generally move from left to right along the continuum. Independence is maintained at home as long as possible. Informal primary caregivers are called upon to provide the necessary assistance. As informal caregivers need help, or if they are not readily available, paid in-home caregivers or community-based services are the next option people typically seek. As the chronic condition worsens, the impaired person may have paid providers help with homemaker services, personal care at home, or health care brought into the home. Adult day services vary greatly and are available while residing in the community.

When an informal caregiver is experiencing too much stress, or the needed care is beyond their abilities, or in-home and community-based paid care

FIGURE 6.1

The Care Continuum

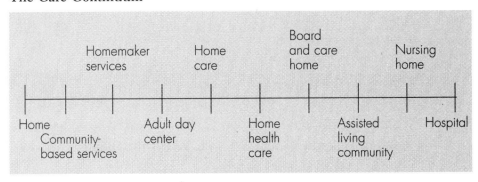

options become expensive because of a higher level of care needs, facilities may become the most appropriate option. People with mild chronic conditions might find board and care homes adequate. Those in need of assistance with a few ADLs can often receive their care in assisted living communities. Those with the most needs will find that nursing homes (skilled nursing facilities) offer the broadest array of services available from the most highly trained people. Only the most extreme chronic or acute conditions (or complications from those conditions) result in the need for hospitalization.

People with acute conditions move from right to left across the care continuum. Their acute episode often places them in the hospital for surgery or initial treatment. The nursing facility may then be used for rehabilitation after the risk of complications is reduced to an acceptable level. An assisted living community or board and care home provides a less expensive alternative to the nursing home as they begin to regain their independence, although many people who have a home to return to and needs that can be cost-effectively met at home are likely to prefer to move directly to care at home. If they choose to remain in the lower-level care facility, a qualified home care agency might provide the types of services needed if they are not available from the staff on site.

If there is qualified, informal caregiver support at home and the residence is a clean environment, bypassing facilities is an option for those recovering from an acute condition. The majority of treatments available in a nursing home are now available from a home health care agency with properly trained nurses and therapists on staff. As recovery continues, personal assistance from less trained personnel may be used for personal home care. Adult day services or community-based services can be used to supplement the informal caregiver's needs and abilities or to minimize the need for paid in-home care.

» Nursing Homes

Nursing homes have traditionally been covered by long-term care insurance—this is where it all began in 1965 with policies covering Medicare-certified skilled nursing facilities.

Traditionally, nursing homes were thought of as the place where people go to die. Many people still enter a nursing home as a final setting for care, but more are using nursing homes for shorter-term rehabilitation from a hospitalization. This short stay is frequently a result of conditions such as broken bones caused by falls, heart attacks, strokes, or cancer. Some enter the facility for closer monitoring of prescription medications and nutritional needs. Many of these people recover quickly as a result of treatment and therapy and then receive care in less restrictive settings, moving from right to left along the care continuum. Terminal illnesses and rehabilitation account for most of the short stays (three months or less) in nursing homes, which make up about a quarter of the nursing home population.

Chronic illnesses—either physical or cognitive impairments—account for those people who have longer stays in nursing homes. These people have probably moved from left to right along the care continuum, although some may enter a nursing home directly from a hospital following a disabling accident or illness. They may need the services available in a nursing home because of dementia or Alzheimer's disease or because of severe physical limitations due to heart disease, stroke, diabetes, or arthritis. They may have become disruptive in their previous setting or simply lost the ability to perform more ADLs. Individuals with cognitive impairments may have special needs other facilities may not be able to accommodate, or they may become too burdensome for family members to continue with informal care. The broadest array of services—from therapies to post-acute medical services—are available in nursing homes. Nursing homes are also designed to provide supervision and necessary assistance with all ADLs, while the other type of facilities normally provide assistance with only a limited number of ADLs.

A snapshot of the people in nursing homes today shows that the vast majority of residents are impaired in their ability to perform ADLs or suffer from a cognitive impairment. Few have no physical or mental impairments.[1]

Moreover, data suggest that a privately insured population (that is, those who have purchased long-term care insurance) presents a different profile.

Generally, an insured population shows higher levels of impairment in the nursing home, compared with the general population of nursing home residents.[2] An insured population tends to be younger, better educated, and more affluent, which might lead to a reduction in the use of facility care, with only the more impaired individuals relying on that option. Also, someone with insurance is more likely to have more options about where to receive care, again minimizing the reliance on facility care.

Licensing

There is concern among insurers about whether appropriate care and quality care are provided when an insurer pays for services. Insurers could find themselves liable if care does not meet an insured's expectations. Using broad criteria for acceptable providers helps insurance companies point claimants in the direction of appropriate and quality care.

Nursing homes are relatively easy to define because states license them and the government specifies criteria the facility has to meet before receiving reimbursement for Medicare or Medicaid residents. The licensing process varies by state, but all states scrutinize the facilities. This is done when the facility opens, and ongoing assessment is required to maintain a state license. Nursing homes that don't meet the state's expectations lose their license to operate. Some states license nursing homes that offer specialized care, such as Alzheimer's facilities. Insurers recognize the licensing process as going beyond their facility assessment capabilities and have always required that a facility be licensed.

Long-term care insurers may specify additional requirements for a nursing home to be covered under a policy, beyond state licensure. The insurer's criteria may pertain more to staffing and service requirements, while state licensure requirements typically focus on physical plant and safety issues.

Insurer experience with nursing homes is extensive. It is the other, newer provider types that are more challenging for insurers to incorporate into policy language. Lack of uniform standards or licensure procedures for these newer provider types is an important source of the challenge they pose for insurers concerned with offering a consistent policy across jurisdictions.

FOCUS QUESTION 2

How do states and insurers differ in their approval criteria for nursing homes?

_____

_____

_____

_____

_____

» Assisted Living

To meet the demand of an aging population for long-term care facilities, an alternative to nursing homes emerged. The idea was to provide mostly personal care services to those who were losing their independence but didn't require medical attention or therapies. **Assisted living** communities began to spring up in the 1980s and gained widespread acceptance in the early 1990s.

Assisting living sought to provide a home-like alternative to nursing homes that many people wanted. The cost of building a facility was less than for a nursing home because therapy facilities weren't a requirement and medical treatment (such as access to oxygen) wasn't a necessity. Operating costs were also lower because the skill level of personnel was less and because assisted living communities could operate without the burden of government oversight and the overhead costs associated with reporting requirements. Financing was easy to obtain because the facilities filled up with residents as quickly as they were built.

At first, assisted living providers seemed like rebels in their resistance to regulation and government reimbursement for services. They felt they could self-regulate, and they didn't want the paperwork burdens involved in getting reimbursement from the government. Few government programs recognized assisted living communities, but consumers flocked to them.

Eventually, insurers found that claims were being submitted for assisted living on their nursing-home-only policies. The original intent was to cover only nursing homes with those policies. Early on, these claims were categorically denied—it was not care in a licensed nursing home. Even the early comprehensive policies did not recognize assisted living as a covered provider and struggled with whether benefits were payable for claimants in these newly emerging facilities.

Many claimants wanted their existing insurance coverage to expand and cover services in these assisted living facilities. Assisted living provided a more home-like and lower-cost alternative to nursing homes—averaging between half and three-quarters of the costs of nursing home care. This saved money both for the claimant and the insurer.

FOCUS QUESTION 3

What are some of the advantages of assisted living communities over nursing homes?

_____

_____

_____

_____

_____

_____

_____

_____

_____

_____

_____

Initial Concerns

Insurers initially struggled with how to best cover assisted living communities. There were many unanswered questions insurers needed to address before they could design and price policies that included assisted living coverage, such as:

■ Were people really receiving long-term care in these communities, or was it a living arrangement for people unable or unwilling to maintain their own household?

■ Was there enough consistency in the types of care provided to adequately adjudicate claims?

■ Was the setting too comfortable to provide the same disincentive to entering the facility that nursing homes provided?

■ Was the state licensing of assisted living communities adequate to ensure that quality care was actually provided?

■ Would care in an assisted living community be a substitute for nursing home care or for at-home care, or would it simply add a level of care to the range of services covered by the insurance?

The first question was answered as companies learned more about the assisted living industry. They learned that the types of care these communities provide vary from facility to facility, but that they all provide at least some level of personal care beyond meeting basic housing needs. Each community carefully evaluates the type of resident it wants to attract and offers the types of services appropriate for those people. The cost of care in the facility can vary in the number or types of services one receives but is most always less than in a comparable nursing home. Once the person needs a service beyond the type of care that the assisted living community can provide, the administrators at the community counsel them and/or their family regarding a different living arrangement such as a nursing home.

Research on the level of impairment of assisted living community residents indicates that they, for the most part, have care needs, although they are a less disabled population than one sees in a nursing home.[3] This suggests that assisted living communities are viewed as a care alternative, in addition to being a living alternative. In part, the assisted living community has a less disabled resident profile than nursing homes because state law or facility policy stipulates that persons with high degrees of physical or mental impairment cannot continue to reside in an assisted living community. When that occurs, the resident would typically transfer to a higher level of care such as a nursing home.

This research provided assurance to long-term care insurers that assisted living communities were providing an appropriate type of long-term care that could be covered by insurance. But there were concerns with the wide range of prices and amenities that these facilities provide. Also, insurers worried about whether having a more home-like environment might increase overall utilization of services, since these facilities are more desirable and attractive than the typical nursing home. Would these services be a less costly substitute to nursing home care, or an additional service to be covered?

Licensing

The regulatory environment for assisted living began to mature during the 1990s. Insurers traditionally preferred to utilize the licensing process as a method of verifying the quality of a facility. The thinking goes that if a facility is able to obtain a license, at least one group of people recognized that the quality of care and level of services provided were above some minimum. Some states have a Medicaid waiver program that allows for Medicaid coverage for assisted living communities. This puts additional pressure on the states to have strict licensing policies.

Thus, obtaining a state license became essential for an assisted living community. Not always did a facility receive what is typically referred to as an assisted living license, because not all states issue a license under that term. Insurers worked with their consultants to better understand the regulatory environment for this new provider facility. Typically, if a state licenses an assisted living facility, the insurer will set that as the benchmark for the facility's being a covered provider. In the absence of state licensure, an insurer might specify the staffing, service, and medical records requirements that a facility must meet in order to be considered an eligible assisted living facility provider under its policy.

Long-term care insurers needed to develop definitions for assisted living facilities. Some found using the term **alternate living facility** was better than assisted living as the category of facility. Using this term gave the insurer more flexibility in determining what the right type of facility was. Many companies established a minimum number of beds under the facility's roof to differentiate care in an assisted living community from care provided in one's home. They also wanted someone who was trained in providing care available around the clock and a physician available on site or on call.

The Impact of Assisted Living Benefits

For long-term care insurers, the results of covering assisted living have been excellent in many ways. Although the disincentive to enter an assisted living community is not as strong as that of a nursing home, it still exists. Anytime someone moves from familiar surroundings a stressful situation is created. Research shows that those claiming assisted living benefits under their LTCI policy do have a need for care.[4]

Some companies have found that adding an assisted living benefit option to an existing nursing-home-only policy creates valuable goodwill with insureds while creating the potential for reducing claims costs and helping insureds stretch the value of their insurance dollar. These policies are then thought of as **facility care plans** rather than as nursing home plans. Adding assisted living facilities to policies covering nursing home and home care creates a truly comprehensive policy. Some state insurance departments have asked companies that have nursing-home-only policies in force to give consideration to adding assisted living to those policies. This new benefit has pricing implications for some policy types, so those companies do not automatically comply with this request. However, most insurers have developed and now offer policies specifically designed to pay for care in assisted living communities as well as nursing homes and at-home care.

» Board and Care Homes

If assisted living was the innovative long-term care provider of the 1990s, **board and care homes** are likely to fill that role in this decade. There is extensive research and experimentation related to this type of facility provider, which provides even less care than assisted living. This rapidly evolving portion of the care continuum has regulators and long-term care insurers watching it closely. Consumer acceptance is sporadic.

Board and care homes go under many names. These names are sometimes used as a substitute for assisted living communities, but, generally speaking, they all provide less personal care and supervision than is typically found in assisted living facilities. Some of the options include:

- adult care homes,
- adult foster care homes,
- adult family homes,
- personal care operations,
- sheltered care homes,
- community-based residential care facilities, and
- independent living facilities.

Board and care homes target individuals who are unable or who choose not to live alone but who do not require nursing care and may require only limited personal care. Residents do not have direct access to doctors and nurses at the facility. The focus is on personal care rather than medical care. The intent is to encourage residents to make as many choices as possible about their daily life and health care while providing a home-like setting.

Residents might need help with scheduled personal activities, such as assistance with bathing and dressing, but normally do not receive help with the ADLs that require continual supervision, such as toileting or transferring. Some of these facilities specialize in caring for older individuals with mild or moderate cognitive impairments or younger people with disabilities or behavioral problems. Just as with assisted living communities, board and care homes have limits on the types of residents they can or will accept and retain. When someone's condition goes beyond those limits, they are counseled into a facility designed to better accommodate their needs.

Board and care facilities are normally smaller than nursing homes and assisted living communities, frequently averaging between two and 10 residents. They are typically owned and operated by families or individuals who have modified a home in a residential neighborhood or a small commercial setting to accommodate living arrangements for multiple impaired people. The owner might live in the home so that they are available to residents 24 hours a day.

Usually, everyone in a board and care home will have a personal bedroom and will likely share a bathroom with at least one other resident. Residents are free to decorate their rooms and are allowed to bring personal belongings for their room or to share with the other members of the household. Normally there is a shared living area including space for social interaction, cooking, and eating.

There is a wide variety of options with regard to available services in board and care homes. Besides the typical meals and housekeeping services, these homes might provide recreational activities, opportunities for flower or vegetable gardening, cable television (possibly in individual rooms), laundry services, reminders of when to take prescription medications, and/ or regularly delivered newspapers and magazines. Therapies or management of medication found in nursing homes or assisted living facilities are generally not found in board and care homes. (Arrangements with a home care agency might provide those services.) Transportation to shopping centers, the movies, religious services, or other outings is an option at some. (Nearby family members, friends, community-based vans, or taxis are more likely to provide individualized transportation services such as to medical appointments.) Access to emergency services is a requirement.

FOCUS QUESTION 4

List some benefits that a resident of a board and care facility may expect.

_____

_____

_____

_____

_____

_____

_____

_____

_____

_____

_____

A board and care home can specialize in the needs of individuals experiencing cognitive impairments due to Alzheimer's disease or other forms of dementia. Some might help out with younger people who have developmental disabilities. These facilities face the same architecture and staffing challenges in providing care to these people as nursing homes and assisted living facilities. They must keep the residents active in small work areas while maintaining a secure home that does not allow residents to wander away. A low staff to resident ratio will play a role in determining whether the facility is able to adequately care for these residents.

Given the unstructured network of board and care homes, there is not an abundance of data on the residents. There is no trade organization that gives organized support to board and care homes that would commission studies. The demographic profile of residents and their level of impairment vary greatly.

Some states license these types of facilities while other states do not. The licensing criteria take into consideration the same checkpoints as assisted living, but lower standards may be applied to board and care homes. In some states there are specific licensing requirements when caring for dementia sufferers.

Because of care and licensing inconsistencies, some long-term care insurers are reluctant to provide benefits specifically for board and care homes. There is little regulatory oversight that provides assurance to insurers that the benefit dollars provided are appropriately paid out for quality care. Companies that offer a broad contractual or administrative definition of assisted living or use the term alternate living facilities might analyze each individual claimant's board and care home with an eye toward fitting it in that category. In situations where board and care homes are not specifically included as a covered provider in the policy, benefits paid to someone in one of these facilities is made on a case-by-case or exception basis.

Insurance companies that include board and care homes in their contract language have strict requirements surrounding how the facility is defined. Such requirements can include a state license in states that license such facilities, a minimum number of beds, availability of personal care services, maintenance of a daily log of the different types of care provided, staff available around the clock, and access to medical personnel. These types of requirements place a burden of facility oversight on the claimant and the insurer, oversight that is provided by state licensing authorities for nursing homes and assisted living facilities.

There are some states with strong board and care lobbying groups that get state insurance departments to require long-term care insurance to specifically cover their facilities. Oregon residents get adult foster care homes in their policy, while those in California get residential care facilities for the elderly.

» Bed Reservation Benefit

There are times when a resident at any of the facilities listed above would like or needs a break from the facility. For example, the resident may be able to participate in a family reunion or holiday activity. More frequently, though, the absence from the care facility is a result of an acute condition requiring medical attention in a hospital. In fact, about one-quarter of the people leaving a nursing home go to a hospital.[5]

These short-term absences from a facility are disruptive to the operation of the facility. There are ongoing administrative requirements, and staffing levels are difficult to change based on a temporary situation. Facilities incur costs anytime there is turnover of their residents.

Facilities also want to maximize the number of people they care for and thus their revenue. When a facility has a waiting list, they have the luxury of maintaining the optimum efficiency of having all the beds occupied. As soon as one person leaves the facility, someone else is ready to gain admittance. Finding an empty bed in one of these facilities is not likely.

For these reasons, facilities have found they are able to continue charging the resident a fee when they vacate their room even when it is for just a couple days. Even Medicaid pays the fee for a week or two when a Medicaid recipient needs hospitalization. Insurers began seeing charges on invoices for "bed reservation" without a clear understanding of the expense. It was determined this was an appropriate expense when they called the facility to investigate the matter. This was the beginning of the **bed reservation benefit (BRB)**.

For most insurers, it is now standard to specifically include a bed reservation benefit as a covered expense in an LTCI contract. The criteria to qualify for payment under the BRB vary from company to company. One of the standard requirements is that the claimant must have satisfied the elimination period and thus qualified for facility benefits. The BRB days are not used as a credit against the elimination period.

The nature of a person's absence from a facility is another variable used by companies. Some require hospitalization, while others simply require that the absence from the facility be temporary. Companies can limit the number of BRB days to ensure that the claimant is not able to abuse the short-term intent of the benefit.

A long-term care policy based on the reimbursement design will require a charge that is made by the facility to reserve the bed. There is no reimbursement when there isn't a charge.

Although this benefit is not utilized frequently, it does provide the insured the peace of mind of knowing they have access to benefits in these situations. And the assurance they are able to return to the same room after a short absence is quite comforting during the times of uncertainty inherent when someone requires assistance because of an illness.

List ways in which an insurance company may mandate conditions for a BRB-qualifying absence so that the benefit is not abused.

_____

_____

_____

_____

_____

_____

» Home Care

Consumers have stated loud and clear a strong preference for receiving care at home. Both the provider community and long-term care insurers have responded with meaningful home care options. In the continuum of care (see Figure 6.1), there are three different types of care available at home: home health care, home care, and homemaker services, as defined below.

- **Home health care** is the receipt of care or services from skilled personnel — nurses and therapists — under the direction of a physician. This includes services such as administering prescription and intravenous medications, monitoring blood levels, wound care, diabetic care, incontinence management, and injections. Therapists provide rehabilitation therapies such as physical therapy, occupational therapy, and speech therapy.

- **Home care** is thought of as personal care services provided by trained but not skilled personnel. A physician is not likely involved in the development of the plan of care for someone receiving home or personal care. These services focus on tasks healthy people take for granted, such as ADLs, grooming, personal hygiene, and management of medications. The assistance is delivered with the caregiver actually helping the recipient perform the task (hands-on assistance), being within arm's reach while the task is performed (standby assistance), or giving verbal reminders or cueing on how to complete the task.

⌗ **Homemaker services** focus on managing the household when a chronically ill person is unable to do so. This may include light housekeeping (changing bed linens, vacuuming, and dusting), laundry, meal planning and preparation, grocery shopping, and washing dishes. Outdoor landscape maintenance or paying of bills is sometimes included in homemaker services. Heavy lifting, improvements to the home, or durable medical equipment are not normally included. Homemaker services are available from homemakers or personal care attendants who may not have had a post-high school education (unlike a registered nurse, who receives extensive education) but are trained by the agency that hired them to provide these services. In some states they take a course lasting several months and are accredited by the state.

Not all long-term care insurers cover all these services provided in the home. Some question whether providing benefits for homemaker services is an insurable event. There is no definite determination that all homemaker services are part of HIPAA's definition of qualified long-term care services. After all, almost everyone would like a clean home without having to do the work—whether they are impaired or not.

Home care is another situation where the checks and balances of monitoring for impairments and the use of services provide assurance to the insurance company that benefits are paid in an appropriate situation. Insurers were initially reluctant to provide benefit to someone needing home care. In the early 1980s, companies started out covering home care only as a post-confinement benefit. Home care benefits were only available after a claimant received benefits while confined in a nursing home. The length of time that benefits were payable was typically equal to the number of days benefits were paid in a nursing home. As an example, someone qualified for 20 days of home care benefits if they were in a nursing home for 50 days—they met their 30-day elimination period and received insurance benefits in the nursing home for an additional 20 days. This was really designed for recovery from an acute condition.

Insurance companies began to liberalize the criteria for receiving home care in the late 1980s and early 1990s. Some insurers offered optional home care riders to their nursing home policies while others integrated both provider options into one policy. Some combined policy maximums, while others put shorter limits on the home care.

There was a reluctance to provide extensive home care benefits for a medically necessary condition. Too much ambiguity existed. Giving a physician the final say on whether care was needed did not provide the consistency or objectivity insurers needed to feel comfortable providing benefits in a setting where someone wanted to receive care. But once insurers gained a comfort level with ADLs and cognitive impairment as the way someone qualified for benefits, home care options in LTCI expanded significantly.

People receiving home care have fewer ADL impairments than those receiving care in a facility.[6] This is in part because it is easier to get care at home—from family or paid providers—when the individual has a lower level of disability.

FOCUS QUESTION 6

Provide simple definitions for the three different kinds of home care, showing how they differ.

_____

_____

_____

_____

_____

_____

_____

_____

_____

_____

_____

_____

Licensing

Defining a home care agency in the early days presented the same sort of challenges faced with assisted living—state licensing requirements were inconsistent. There were even a few states that did not offer home care agency licensing. One approach insurers considered was to use the same definition of a home care agency that Medicare used. This had the potential for consumer backlash, however, when the home care agency of their choice decided not to participate in the Medicare reimbursement program. There are many agencies that elect not to participate in the Medicare program because of the paperwork involved in getting reimbursed for the services provided. Companies found that Medicare certification was too stringent a requirement and too limiting since many agencies do not seek Medicare-certification but are still appropriate to provide care at home in long-term care situations.

On the other end of the spectrum were requirements that were too lenient. If the home care agency only provided homemaker services, insurers felt this could allow for abuse in receiving benefits. Everyone would want meals prepared and their home cleaned. Insurers simply cannot price a risk-based product where people want the benefits regardless of whether or not they need the benefits. In essence, providing benefits only for homemaker services would look much like an annuity that did not make sense for long-term care insurance.

A middle ground on home care agency requirements has evolved from experience—on both the selling of the product and the administration of claims. States are doing a better job of licensing home care agencies. They needed better requirements because there were some unscrupulous agencies opening operations and some employees who were hired were not qualified to provide care or were not trustworthy based on their criminal background history.

Some companies have experimented with providing benefits when an unlicensed provider delivers the home care. These people might have the right credentials but have found working for an agency to be too confining. They want to be their own boss. Some states now register or certify home care providers. However, this registry does not guarantee quality of care or provide safeguards to ensure that crimes are not committed.

Companies have found these independent providers to be an excellent choice for claimants in some situations, while at other times people have found that their expectations were not met. The potential for fraud is higher because these people generally are not bonded and are subject to no oversight other than that of the care recipient. Insurers have difficulty monitoring for quality of services and may require that someone else double-check the appropriateness of the services provided and the accuracy of the billing. The companies allowing family members to act as the unlicensed provider are subjecting themselves to scrutiny from other family members, regulators, and other insureds.

The Impact of Home Care Benefits

Consumers embrace the various types of home care available in their long-term care policies. They like the thought of not having to leave familiar surroundings when they become impaired. Today there are many more options for the availability of services from home care agencies. Long-term care insurers have remained open-minded to this evolution and have adjusted their policy language to accommodate their insureds' desires while maintaining the integrity of their risk-based insurance policy.

» Hospice Care

Hospice care does not appear on the care continuum that introduced this chapter because people receiving hospice care have varying needs for care and support. Also, many people question whether hospice care is appropriate to include within the purview of long-term care.

By its nature, hospice care is designed to ease the pain associated with dying during the final stages of life for someone who is terminally ill, and to help the family with the grieving process. Hospice addresses the physical, psychological, social, and spiritual needs of those experiencing the loss, grief, and bereavement that come with a terminal illness.

Hospice care focuses on providing comfort and support rather than providing treatments designed to improve or cure the terminal illness. Hospice care patients receive pain relief, counseling, and spiritual guidance rather than surgery and medical interventions. The goal is no longer to recover from an illness but rather gain the highest quality of life for the remaining days. **Comfort care** or **palliative care** is used to describe hospice care more often than long-term care. Hospice care might last a couple days, weeks, or months, while long-term care by definition lasts more than 90 days. And care in the form of grief counseling is provided to family members as well as the terminally ill person.

An interdisciplinary team of physicians, specialists, nurses, social workers, psychologists, spiritual advisors, therapists, pharmacists, home health aides, and volunteers administers hospice care. These team members are professionals who have received special training in hospice or palliative care. The physicians and nurses strive to minimize the pain while maximizing the comfort. The social worker acts as a case manager by arranging many of the requested services and counseling the family on financial, insurance, and legal issues. Therapists go beyond traditional therapy by integrating music, art, pet, and massage programs into the plan of care. Bereavement counselors help the patient and the patient's loved ones close out their lives together.

Hospice care is provided in multiple settings. Hospitals, nursing homes, hospice-specific facilities, or at home. By having access to this care in multiple settings, the people who find themselves in a terminal situation are not forced to leave familiar surroundings. Most people receive hospice care while remaining at home from a home care agency or in a hospice care facility.

Individuals who do not have an informal caregiver available normally choose freestanding hospice facilities. They provide a home-like setting with round-the-clock visitation. Much like board and care facilities, a private sleeping room is available, and there are usually common living areas, kitchen, and eating areas. They normally have rooms for spiritual reflection and family counseling. Pet visitation or finding pets on site is common. Larger facilities have nurses on staff and regular visits from members of the interdisciplinary team.

FOCUS QUESTION 7

Name some ways in which hospice care may differ from long-term care.

_____

_____

_____

_____

_____

_____

_____

_____

_____

Hospice and LTCI

Historically, Medicare has provided the majority of the financial reimbursement for hospice care—including the cost of prescription medications—when someone forgoes standard medical treatment. Including hospice care with a long-term care insurance policy was considered a duplication of Medicare services. But things are changing.

Medicare is limiting the amount of time hospice care is payable. The rule was always that someone needed to have a life expectancy of less than six months to qualify for Medicare's hospice benefit. For those who lived longer than expected but still had a six-month prognosis, benefits continued until death. The six-month life expectancy standard is now more strictly enforced so that benefits regularly cease after six months. It is quite difficult for a physician to give a prognosis that is always perfectly accurate—there are too many variables that physicians neither control nor understand that keep people alive longer than predicted or cause the person to die sooner than expected. Yet Medicare has tighter scrutiny of the life expectancy rules than ever before.

Long-term care insurers now look at this type of end-of-life care as a potential long-term care service that can be covered by their policies. The types of care provided in a hospice setting fit under HIPAA's scope of a qualified long-term care service. The location of hospice care fits under most insurers' covered providers—a nursing home, as part of home care, or in an alternate care facility. Furthermore, hospice care is what many consumers perceive when they think of long-term care. Having a loved one using hospice service might be a consumer's only personal experience with long-term care.

Insurers either specifically cover hospice care under the basic terms of an LTCI policy or make a decision on a case-by-case basis. They will require that the provider be appropriately licensed and that it keep records of the care it provides the claimant. Requiring Medicare certification of the hospice provider goes beyond the expectation of most consumers and agents when considering a company's contract. Some insurers require that hospice care be delivered by a nurse. Some limit benefits to services delivered to the claimant and do not pay for services received by family members.

Under most policies, to qualify for hospice care benefits, the insured must satisfy the requirement for hospice care (a physician's determination that they are terminally ill), and they must also meet the policy's long-term care benefit triggers (typically inability to perform a certain number of ADLs or having a cognitive impairment). If someone has a terminal illness but is able to function independently, they are not eligible for hospice care benefits under a long-term care policy.

Another challenge for insurers is ensuring that benefits are paid only for services received by the insured. Bereavement counseling for family members is normally part of a hospice care plan of care. However, HIPAA requires that services be delivered to a chronically ill person, making it questionable whether counseling for a family member is a qualified long-term care service. Also, providing long-term care insurance benefit to family members is difficult to design, price, and administer.

Still another challenge is the fact that Medicare still pays for the majority of the cost of hospice care. Long-term care insurance that coordinates with Medicare might not pay for hospice care. In light of this, some view hospice care as an illusionary benefit, while it is really a safeguard against the inevitable changes to Medicare's payment structure. For insureds not eligible for Medicare, a hospice care benefit within a long-term care policy can be an important component of coverage. While some private health insurance plans cover hospice care similarly to Medicare, some policies do not do so.

Hospice care is not a traditional long-term care service. It is normally provided to terminally ill people for short periods of time—from a couple days to a couple months. The goal of hospice care is to give comfort and support to the care recipient and family members. Many consumers have experienced the benefits of hospice care when a loved one died and want it included in their policy. Many companies are providing this valuable benefit as part of the long-term care insurance policy they offer.

» Adult Day Centers

Adult day centers serve an important role for impaired adults who frequently need assistance during the day but who may not have informal caregivers available to them during the day (as when family members must work). Without this option, some people ended up in facilities earlier than necessary.

The model for adult day centers was based on psychiatric day hospital experiments. The concept gained momentum in the early 1970s and has continued to grow to the present day. Many centers are operated in affiliation with other providers of care—nursing homes, home care agencies, hospitals, and senior centers—sometimes on a nonprofit basis. Some churches and other religious congregations find providing adult day services an excellent use of their excess building capacity that fits in with their mission to provide services to church members and the community.

These providers initially referred to themselves as "adult day care." In doing research, it was found that "day care" had the connotation of caring for children. This gave potential recipients an inaccurate stereotype of what was provided in the center, even with the term "adult" preceding it. The industry and its trade organizations have attempted to provide a better brand to the industry by changing the classification of provider to an "adult day center" that provides "adult day services." Not all centers have accepted this change. Many insurers and most insurance regulators still use the old term in describing this provider.

Adult day centers provide important services for the impaired population. These services are designed for personal needs, socialization, or health-related care. Some services and activities are designed to help promote self-esteem, restore or maintain self-care skills, stimulate memory and reasoning, encourage learning new information or skills, stay current with world events, or improve physical function, including flexibility, strength, and coordination.

The informal caregiver also benefits from adult day services. There is support and encouragement from people who understand their plight. This break during the day provides an opportunity for the caregiver to pursue other activities (job or family) or simply recharge their energy for the demanding task of caring for someone around the clock. The caregiver can clean the house, do grocery shopping, reactivate an exercise routine, or resume social interaction with friends and family. For caregivers who continue working, adult day centers provide the peace of mind of knowing that their loved one is properly cared for while they tend to professional responsibilities.

Some centers have developed a specialty in caring for people with Alzheimer's disease or other forms of dementia. One survey of people using adult day centers found that half of the people showed signs of a cognitive impairment.[7] These programs provide activities meaningful to the person in need of care. The center might offer in adjacent rooms counseling and peer interaction programs for the caregivers. This gives caregivers the much-needed support to help them through the stress and strain of living with someone requiring full-time care.

More often, the people accessing services at an adult day center are experiencing physical impairments. Almost 60 percent of participants require assistance with two or more ADLs, and 41 percent require assistance with three or more.[8] In addition help with physical and cognitive impairments, some need physical activity, nutrition assistance, socialization with peers, or are not yet ready for round-the-clock care in a facility.

The exercise programs available are much different from those found in a health club. The focus is on increasing mobility, with exercises designed to put the major muscle groups through the full range of motion. When there is difficulty in exercising, passive exercise is done to encourage even the smallest of efforts that can lead to increased independence. Even walking (with or without a device for assistance) or stretching helps.

Adult day centers provide a lunch and snacks as part of their nutrition programs. These do more than just provide the impaired person with a well-balanced meal once a day. The individuals are encouraged to select foods outside of the center that promote a healthy lifestyle given their personal health condition. They receive tips on methods of preparation that maximize their abilities and minimize their impairments. Some centers will inquire about nutrition intake and maintain dietary records.

The fee structure for adult day centers varies considerably. Because the vast majority are nonprofit operations, they normally will accept anyone into the program. Some centers receive funding from governmental agencies, organizations such as the United Way, philanthropic bequests, or gifts in kind from property owners—such as free rent in a hard-to-rent storefront of a small shopping center. Centers might structure their costs by the half-day—either beginning or ending with lunch—or the full day. Most centers are open from the morning (between 6 and 8 AM) to the late afternoon or early evening (5 or 6 PM). Some are open Monday through Friday, others are open a couple days a week, while others offer weekend hours of operation in addition to the normal workweek hours. Many have a sliding fee scale to enable people of all incomes to afford care.

Adult day centers are normally staffed with a director of operations, registered nurse, activity coordinator, social worker, and volunteers. These people have an appreciation for older adults, empathy for their situation, patience and flexibility when working with the participants, enthusiasm when things go well, and calmness when they don't. They need creativity to maintain the energy level at the center that in turn provides encouragement for participants to join in the activities.

FOCUS QUESTION 8

Name some individuals who may work as caregivers at an adult day center.

_____

_____

_____

_____

_____

One challenge a long-term care insurer faces is with how a center is defined in the insurance policy. Many states now regulate or license the centers based on staff to participant ratios, staff education or professional designations, service availability, facility size, and management structure. Utilization and training of volunteers can contribute to staff-to-participant ratios.

Many centers offer transportation services. This can entail a coach or van bringing people to and from the center and home. Expanded transportation includes trips for shopping or for medical appointments. Insurers struggle with providing reimbursement for transportation, given its gray area within HIPAA's standards for qualified long-term care services.

Adult day centers fill a niche in the long-term care provider community. They help participants maintain an active lifestyle and enhance dignity by encouraging self-care. Through the services available, informal caregivers receive a respite, and the quality of life for the person in need of care and the caregivers is enhanced. Insurers have embraced adult day centers as a key component of insurance products designed to provide the widest variety of long-term care provider choices.

» Alternate Plan of Care

What will long-term care insurance policies cover 20 years from now? What new providers will emerge? What services will consumers want? No one is certain. But long-term care insurers have a clause available that will accommodate the changes.

Insurers recognized early on that flexibility within the confines of policy design was the key to serving their insureds. There were new types of facilities cropping up, home care agencies were providing more services, and provider options were expanding. Hence, the birth of the concept of an **alternate plan of care**.

An alternate plan of care allows the company to pay benefits for providers or services not listed in the policy language. This feature came in handy for owners of grandfathered policies who requested an expansion of providers. If the alternate plan of care was in the policy, modifications that might jeopardize the favorable tax status of the policy are not needed. As an example, the popularity of assisted living facilities dramatically increased during the 1990s. The policies issued early in the decade generally did not have the assisted living benefit, while those issued in the latter part did have them included. To add the benefit to a policy issued before 1997 would likely disqualify that policy. But administering the assisting living benefit within the alternate plan of care is acceptable under HIPAA.

To ensure that it is in the best interest of the insured, three stakeholders must agree to the alternate plan of care—the insured, the insured's physician, and the insurance company. A different plan is sought if any one of the three objects to the proposed plan of care. One factor the insurer takes into consideration with a qualified policy is whether the alternate plan of care recommends services that fit within HIPAA's brief description of qualified long-term care services. If it doesn't, the insurer will likely object to the proposed changes.

FOCUS QUESTION 9

Name the three stakeholders that need to agree for an alternate plan of care to be implemented.

_____

_____

_____

As effective as this feature is, potential exists for misunderstanding by any of the three interested parties. There are many claim situations where the claimant asserts that the agent explained the feature differently from how the policy language reads. Many situations exist where the owner of a nursing-facility-only policy files a home care claim under the alternate plan of care benefit. This goes against the intent and the language of the policy. Each company handles these situations based on the merits of the case.

The alternate plan of care is one of the most consumer-friendly features of a long-term care insurance policy. It allows for the policy to remain current even after someone has paid premiums for 20 or more years. The older policies didn't have this feature, so insureds had to replace their coverage to gain access to the expanded benefit choices. Policies with the alternate plan of care are able to accommodate changes in the provider community without the necessity of amending or replacing the policy.

» Summary

The long-term care provider community is diverse and evolving. Many providers initially developed in the years following World War II and expanded rapidly only relatively recently. Assisted living, adult day centers, and board and care homes were unknowns when long-term care insurance was in its infancy, and now those providers enjoy mainstream consumer acceptance. Even the oldest providers — nursing homes and home care agencies — have seen dramatic changes during the last decade in the types of services they provide.

The insurance industry has done an excellent job developing policies that address the providers that consumers want to access. Insurers have expanded the choices available—sometimes amending existing policies to meet the demand for new providers. As a result, claimants are benefiting from the wider array of choices than ever.

Key Terms 🔑

Adult day centers	Formal care provider
Alternate living facility	Home care
Alternate plan of care	Home health care
Assisting living	Homemaker services
Bed reservation benefit (BRB)	Hospice care
Board and care homes	Informal caregiver
Care continuum	Palliative care
Comfort care	Primary caregiver
Facility care plans	Secondary providers

» Review Questions

1. To what can we attribute the societal shift that brought about a new or increased necessity for professional caregivers?

2. Define continuum of care.

3. Name the category of long-term care institution that emerged as an alternative to nursing homes in the 1980s.

4. In what way do board and care homes differ from assisted living communities?

5. What is the term used to define insurance reimbursement for facility charges during short periods one spends away from a long-term care facility?

6. List home health care services that are provided by skilled personnel.

7. What is the level of education and training that people providing homemaker services generally have? How do some states ensure that this education is supplemented?

8. What is the maximum length of time Medicare will pay for hospice care?

9. What is an alternate plan of care, and why is it important?

10. Review the care continuum by listing the different types of care included in it.

» Answers

1. As the economy moved from an agricultural to an industrial base, multigenerational households and strong communities—traditionally a supply of primary caregivers—gave way to more disjointed, separate households.

2. The range of long-term care options available to individuals.

3. Assisted living communities.

4. They usually provide less personal care and supervision than is generally found in assisted living communities.

5. Bed reservation benefit (BRB).

6. Administering prescription and intravenous medications, monitoring blood levels, wound care, diabetic care, incontinence management, injections, and rehabilitation therapies such as physical therapy, occupational therapy, and speech therapy.

7. In most cases, high school, augmented by agency training. In some states these individuals take a course that lasts several months and are accredited by the state.

8. Six months.

9. An alternate plan of care allows an insurance company to pay benefits for providers or services not listed in the policy language. This enables the coverage to deal with forms of care that are not yet in existence but may come into being within the life of the policy.

10. Home, community-based services, homemaker services, adult day services, home care, home health care, board and care home, assisted living community, nursing home, hospital.

NOTES

1 http://www.cdc.gov/nchs/data/ad/ad312.pdf and http://www.rti.org/publications/RAI_gerontologist.cfm.

2 http://aspe.hhs.gov/daltcp/reports/nhalfuse.htm.

3 http://research.aarp.org/il/fs62r — assisted.html.

4 http://aspe.hhs.gov/daltcp/reports/nhalfuse.htm.

5 http://www.cdc.gov/nchs/data/ad/ad312.pdf, (page 9).

6 http://www.ahca.org/brief/bg-hc.htm.

7 http://www.ncoa.org/nadsa/ADS — factsheet.htm.

8 Ibid.

When Are Benefits Paid?

» Overview

The previous chapters focused on qualifications and criteria for receiving benefits. The criteria for LTCI policies are similar to those of other insurance products—there is a loss or "insured event," there are "repairs" that can be applied to that loss (for example, fixing the dented fender or obtaining in-home help for bathing and dressing), and there is financial compensation for the "repair." When long-term care insurance claimants meet these requirements, benefits are payable.

Once a claimant qualifies for benefits, there are three primary concerns:

- When are the benefits paid?
- How much is paid?
- For how long are benefits paid?

How these questions are answered depends on the product design options selected by the insured. When benefits are paid depends on the services covered by the policy and the elimination period. "How much" is determined by the daily or monthly benefit amount and any inflation protection options chosen. "How long" is based on the lifetime policy maximum.

These options are selected at the time of purchase. The purchaser's choices, along with their age at purchase and, in some cases, their health status (for a preferred or substandard rate adjustment), form the basis for determining the premium they will pay.

Some coverage changes can be made after a policy becomes effective, but many cannot or are subject to additional underwriting. This is designed to prevent someone from buying the least expensive coverage they can but then deciding to buy very comprehensive coverage once they begin to need long-term care.

This chapter discusses in detail the specifics of when benefits are paid, focusing on meeting the requirements for the service covered or the provider of care and the elimination period.

» Identifying Covered Services and Providers

Once the insured is eligible for benefits based on the nature and degree of their loss, the first consideration in determining whether benefits are payable is whether the care is delivered by a service or provider that is specifically covered in the policy. Insurers offer three types of LTCI policies today: a facility-care-only policy, a home-care-only policy, and a comprehensive policy. There are variances even within these three primary categories.

FOCUS QUESTION 1

What are the three types of long-term care insurance policies offered by companies?

_____

_____

_____

Facility-Care-Only Policies

A **facility-care-only policy** may cover just nursing home care or may include other types of care facilities. The traditional nursing facility policies covered just nursing homes. These were the original LTCI policies. The only provider that was covered under these older policies was a state-licensed nursing home. Companies had other requirements that normally duplicated the criteria for licensure, such as a number of beds, a registered nurse on staff, and a physician on call. Fortunately, things have changed, and these very limited care policies are now very rare.

Today, most facility-care-only policies provide benefits for more than just nursing homes. These policies are likely to cover care in an assisted living facility and may also include board and care homes. Some companies initially included alternate (assisted) living communities as part of their home care benefit, not as a type of facility care/nursing home benefit. That meant that care in an alternate care facility would only be covered in comprehensive or home-care-only policies. It also typically meant that care in an assisted living community was covered at the same daily maximum as other in-home care services were paid. That is not as common today as it once was. As the options for care in a long-term care facility have expanded, LTCI companies have broadened the definition of a "facility" or "nursing home," defining a nursing home benefit to include a variety of long-term care facilities, including assisted living communities, board and care homes, personal care homes, alternative care facilities, hospice care facilities, and others.

Home-Care-Only Policies

Most people prefer to receive care in their own home if that is feasible. Even if it means incurring larger expenses for round-the-clock in-home care, many consumers would rather receive their care at home than move to a care facility. Long-term care insurers developed **home-care-only policies** for these people. These home care policies encompass home health care, home care, adult day centers, and some homemaker services (the left side of the care continuum—see Chapter Six), but they do not cover care in any type of facility. These policies tend to be less expensive, because they don't cover all possible settings for care. The consumer runs the risk, however, that they may eventually be unable to meet their care needs at home and need facility care. Under a home-care-only policy, such facility care would not be covered. Consumers who buy these types of policies are often willing to "take their chances" and pay on their own for care if they do end up needing care that they simply cannot obtain in their home.

Comprehensive Policies

Insurers have found that the most desirable model for both consumers and insurers is a **comprehensive policy**, which covers both facility-based and home-based care. With these comprehensive policies, the consumer doesn't have to guess in advance the type and setting of care they will need. And when an insured does need care, they have broader choices—they don't have to overextend their stay in a home setting, nor do they have to enter a facility unnecessarily early. They can receive care in the most appropriate setting and are not limited by which care settings are covered and which are not.

Policy Type and the Elimination Period

The type of policy also determines when and how the elimination period can be satisfied. In order for services to count toward satisfying the elimination period as discussed below, the provider delivering the care must be covered in the policy. As an example, days on which the insured receives home health care would not apply to the elimination period for a facility-care-only policy. Likewise, nursing facility care does not count in meeting the elimination period when the insured owns a home-care-only policy.

» The Elimination Period

The Concept of a Deductible

Most types of insurance have some form of **deductible**, by which the insured pays the initial portion of the cost of making a repair or receiving a service for their loss. The deductible helps make premiums more affordable and is also designed to minimize the frequency of small claims. Homeowners', automobile, and many medical insurance plans use a dollar-amount deductible. Long-term care insurance is different in that the deductible normally takes the form of an **elimination period** (as it is typically called), which is generally based on a number of days, not a dollar amount.

Insurers incur fixed administrative expenses each time a claim is filed. Spreading those fixed costs across a sizable claim is more efficient than spreading them across a small claim. As an example, when a claim is filed for a dent in a car door that is repaired for $200, it may cost the insurer $150 to establish a claim file and issue a payment. The potential for fraud and abuse exists with small claims because the insurer is not likely to adjudicate them (review them for validity and accuracy), since this would add even more to the cost of administering the small claim.

As a result, insurance is more expensive when the deductible is smaller. Paying for smaller claims is more expensive for the insurer, and those higher costs are passed on to those buying those policies. Also, the likelihood of paying a claim is increased if the deductible is smaller, because even a small loss will result in some benefits being paid. (For example, if it cost $200 to repair your car dent, and you have a $50 deductible, the policy will pay the balance of $150 in benefits. But if you have a $500 deductible, there would be no benefits paid out.)

The concept of a deductible is used by insurers offering long-term care insurance. In LTCI, the deductible is referred to as an elimination period, and it normally is based on a number of days rather than a dollar amount. It is easier for some to think of the elimination period as a waiting period before benefits are payable, although it is important to note that during the waiting period, certain requirements with respect to having a loss and sometimes with respect to receiving a certain type of covered service also apply. It is not a waiting period strictly in terms of the passage of time.

The Evolution of the LTCI Elimination Period

The original developers of LTCI policies were concerned with administering small claims, specifically claims for short nursing home stays. Insurers first considered Medicare's requirements for benefit qualification. If someone qualifies for Medicare payments (it should be noted that most people needing long-term care do not), Medicare will pay the first 20 days of skilled nursing care in a Medicare-certified facility following a hospital stay. After that, Medicare pays the balance of nursing home costs for the next 80 days, after the insured has paid a daily copayment ($102.50 in 2002). The early developers of LTCI policies thought a deductible period of 20 days or 100 days would fit best with Medicare policies. The 20-day deductible reflects the period of time that Medicare would pay in full, and the 100-day deductible would cover the period of time during which Medicare would make partial payments.

Companies with disability income insurance experience or those that wanted to differentiate themselves in the marketplace were more likely to offer different options—zero-day, 30-day, 45-day, 60-day, or 90-day options were common. Companies working with individuals with higher net worth or offering life insurance policies with long-term care riders offered longer elimination policies—180 days, 365 days, and even 730 days—on the theory that insureds could afford to self-insure for the initial six months to two years, thus making possible a lower premium for a longer-duration policy.

Many consumers, on the other hand, were seeking shorter elimination periods. Many wanted their LTCI policy to provide **first dollar coverage**, or a zero-day elimination period. A zero-day period adds significantly to a company's administrative costs, and this additional expense was factored into the cost of the insurance. But despite the higher premium cost for a plan with a zero-day deductible, some consumers still bought it. And agents liked selling a plan with a zero-day deductible because they could promise that the insured would pay no out-of-pocket costs during the initial portion of their long-term care needs. With a 30- or 90-day elimination period, the insured takes the chance of having to pay some out-of-pocket costs.

FOCUS QUESTION 2

Explain the potential appeal of long and short elimination periods for different types of purchasers.

_____

_____

_____

_____

_____

_____

_____

_____

_____

_____

_____

HIPAA's Impact on the Elimination Period

In order for an insured to qualify for benefits under HIPAA, there must be an expectation that the inability to perform ADLs will last for at least 90 days. (There is no such length-of-time requirement for the cognitive impairment benefit trigger since most cognitive impairment is not reversible or temporary.) This requirement was intended to avoid potential duplication of benefits with Medicare's acute care benefit structure and to ensure that the services being covered are truly long-term care and not acute, short-term care. The length-of-time expectation is a part of the claimant's written plan of care and is usually determined at the time they first become eligible for benefits. Clinicians are skilled at assessing whether the loss the person has is one that can reasonably be expected to continue for 90 days or is likely to be more short term.

Some interpreted this requirement to mean that a 90-day elimination period was the shortest available with a qualified policy. The federal government clarified this issue in Notice 97-31 with the following statement: "This 90-day requirement does not establish a waiting period before which benefits may be paid or before which services may constitute qualified long-term care services."

This clarification established beyond a doubt that an elimination period of less than 90 days is possible with a tax-qualified LTCI policy. The 90-day requirement of HIPAA does mean, however, that if an impairment is expected to last for less than 90 days, benefits cannot be paid, regardless of what elimination period the policy has.

Thus, counting days toward satisfying the elimination period of a qualified policy does not begin unless the impairment is expected to last at least 90 days. If at time of claim the person had a condition for which normal recovery would take longer than three months, days are counted right away. This is the case with chronic conditions such as osteoporosis or arthritis, and some acute conditions such as a stroke. On the other hand, days are not counted toward the elimination period when the claimant has an acute condition for which the normal recovery is less than 90 days. An example of such a condition is a broken bone or joint replacement surgery.

Benefits are paid retroactively to the end of the elimination period if complications arise during recovery, prolonging care beyond the 90th day, even if the initial expectation was that the loss would not last 90 days. As an example, consider the following situation: Someone has an LTCI policy with a 20-day elimination period. They have a simple hip fracture, which has a normal recovery time of 60 days. The initial benefit determination is to deny the claim, because the loss is not expected to last 90 days. If, however, complications arise resulting in care continuing beyond 90 days, the insurer would pay for care received from the 21st day until the claimant no longer qualifies for benefits.

Days do count toward the elimination period when the plan of care states that recovery is expected after the 90th day, even if it actually occurs sooner. This can happen when someone has complicated heart surgery but has a strong will to resume normal activities. They engage themselves in physical therapy, take the appropriate medications, and closely follow the doctor's orders and the plan of care. The LTCI policy will count the days of care toward the elimination period when the condition is expected to last more than 90 days, regardless of how long it actually lasts. For example, if the policy has a short elimination period where benefits are payable in 20 days and no care is needed after the 50th day, the claimant is still able to keep the benefits paid. The qualified status of the services is not under question as long as, when the initial claim assessment was made, there was an expectation based on the professional judgment of a licensed health care practitioner that the care would last more than 90 days.

The HIPAA 90-day requirement works in conjunction with the insurer's elimination period but does not raise the minimum number of days allowed for an elimination period. Once the 90-day expectation of impairment exists, days start counting toward satisfying the elimination period.

FOCUS QUESTION 3

Explain how a claimant might be paid benefits under a qualified LTCI policy even if their care ends up not lasting 90 days.

_____

_____

_____

_____

_____

_____

» Which Days to Count

Consecutive Days vs. Accumulating Days

In the earliest LTCI policies, each consecutive day on which the insured received any covered service counted toward satisfying the elimination period. The original nursing home insurance policies had an easy time of counting days. Almost everyone stayed in the nursing home for consecutive days—there were few intermittent days of care back then. Each day the insured was in the nursing home counted toward one day of meeting their elimination period. But once companies started including home care benefits and other services, they needed to reevaluate how they counted days to satisfy the elimination period, since home care is not typically received in terms of consecutive days.

Home care is not always delivered every day. Daily care might happen as someone recovers from an acute condition at home rather than in a nursing home. These people normally require services from a registered nurse (to change bandages or administer medications) or a therapist (to enhance range of motion or bring back speech and hearing skills) for short periods. They may receive these services daily, or they might receive them every other day or less frequently. The people receiving daily care are likely to begin showing signs of recovery (or reaching a functional plateau) and may start receiving care in the home on a less frequent basis.

More often, people receive home care services a few days a week, rather than daily, because the services are supplementing care delivered by the informal, primary caregiver. The informal caregiver can easily learn to perform many of the tasks that a paid home care provider delivers. A family member can help someone bathe or dress, change bandages, administer medications, and assist with light exercises or movement activities on days that the home care agency isn't there. The home care agency monitors the recovery progress and the in-home situation, including the availability of family caregivers, and it may adjust the care plans and therapies accordingly. Their supervision simply is not needed every day when an informal caregiver is willing and able to provide the needed assistance. (It is important to note that informal caregivers are not required to provide care. The plan of care reflects the care needs of the individual as well as their preferences regarding the mix of paid care and informal care. Someone who has family living nearby may not want to burden them with the responsibility of providing any care. Their plan of care would not require them to do so.)

This non-daily character of home care created a problem for long-term care insurance companies. They knew that if they only counted consecutive days of care toward satisfying the elimination period, few people would qualify for benefits, or it would take much longer to qualify.

Therefore, insurers decided to count any day on which professionals delivered home care services, allowing these days to occur on an intermittent basis and accumulate. Under this system, for someone receiving home care three days a week, satisfying a 20-day elimination period takes about seven weeks. Counting intermittent days of care makes sense from the insurer's perspective. After all, insurance is designed to pay benefits when there is a financial loss. When someone receives support from an informal caregiver, no charge in incurred. Counting the days that a professional home care agency was actually providing care seemed appropriate.

The Accumulation Period

The next question was how long an insured should be given to accumulate the number of days of care needed to satisfy the elimination period—that is, how long would the **accumulation period** be. If this period was too long, the insurer and claimant might lose track of the days. Also, the appropriateness of counting care delivered over several years prior to filing a claim was questioned. On the other hand, if the period was too short, the consumer would not have the opportunity to start and stop the professional services as appropriate or receive the minimal assistance spelled out in their plan of care. Insurers first looked to Medicare for insights into how to define an "episode of care" over which to accumulate days of care.

Medicare uses the concept of a **benefit period**. If inpatient care is delivered in a nursing home or hospital within a period of 60 consecutive days, Medicare considers that the same illness was the cause of the need for services. A new benefit period is established only when someone receives no care for 60 consecutive days.

Some companies use Medicare's concept of a fixed number of days, but normally the time limit is longer than 60 days. The claimant might have 90, 180, 365, or 730 days over which to accumulate enough days of care to satisfy the elimination period. Insurers are less concerned with related illnesses that cause a need for care than Medicare. This extended time gives the claimant freedom to use care as appropriate for their condition.

Other long-term care insurers use a multiple of the elimination period, such as two, three, or five times the elimination period. Under this system, if the claimant has a 20-day elimination period, they would have 40, 60, or 100 days to accumulate enough days of care to satisfy the elimination period. An insured with a 100-day elimination period would have 200, 300, or 500 days. If the insured did not accumulate the required number of days of care over that time period, the elimination period would not be met, and if care resumed at a later date, care received previously would not be counted toward satisfying the elimination period.

There are two ways of administering an accumulation period. One approach is similar to Medicare's benefit period concept—all days of care accumulate until the elimination period is satisfied or until no care is received for a specified length of time, in which case the accumulation period ends. If after one accumulation period has ended, care is again received, a new accumulation period begins.

The other method is to have a moving window of time over which to accumulate the days of care. The insurer looks back to the previous number of days to see if an adequate number of care days are present. The days are not carried forward beyond the length of time allowed in the moving window of the accumulation period.

A relatively recent approach is to have no defined time limit over which days of care can accumulate—they can accumulate indefinitely until the elimination period is satisfied. This is sometimes called a **lifetime accumulation period**. The challenge with this approach is maintaining documentation as to when care was delivered and the level of impairment that existed at the time of receiving care. Insureds may tend to submit more claims to the insurer, expecting insurer personnel to keep track of the days of care. Alternatively, there may be a scramble later on to document when care was received. However, this is the most consumer-friendly method of administering an elimination period.

FOCUS QUESTION 4

Outline the three approaches to administering an accumulation period.

_____

_____

_____

_____

_____

_____

_____

_____

Service Days vs. Calendar Days

Although the ability to accumulate days of care over a period of time is a great improvement over an elimination period that only counts consecutive days of care, some consumers didn't like the concept that only days on which they received paid care would count toward the elimination period (the **service day design**). An insured with a 100-day elimination period often felt that they should begin to receive benefits as soon as 100 days of impairment had elapsed, even if they did not receive 100 days of paid care. Sometimes this would cause problems at time of claim, since insureds believed their policy worked in one way (that is, benefits were paid after 100 days of impairment), when in fact it worked in another (they were not eligible for benefits until they had received 100 days of care within a defined accumulation period).

To address this consumer confusion and concern, some insurers altered the elimination period to match claimants' expectations. In this model, there is a **calendar day** or **disability day design**—that is, every day the insured is impaired counts toward the elimination period, even if formal care services are not provided. Since this approach makes it easier to qualify for benefits more quickly, there is also an impact on the premium that the insurer must charge.

This design raised a number of questions: How much additional premium would the company need to charge? How would it administer claims? (If an insurer does not require that insureds receive a paid service on a given day, it becomes more difficult for the insurer to validate that the individual continued to be impaired on that day. It does not have information from paid care providers to help verify the nature and degree of disability.) Would consumers pay the additional cost for this type of elimination period? Would agents recognize the value and offer the product? Would regulators approve the new method of counting days?

Some companies decided to continue counting only days of care. They felt the purpose of insurance is to offset a financial loss caused by an unforeseen event. Counting days when no payment for services was made goes against this basic concept.

Other companies decided to offer the calendar day design. Consumers liked the notion of counting calendar days (on which the person is impaired) rather than counting only days of paid care. Some insurers started counting days from the first day of impairment, even if no paid services had been provided. Others started counting only with the first day on which the individual was both impaired and received one day of covered care. But paid care was not required to be provided in order to continue to count calendar days toward the elimination period. That is, days began counting from the day when the impairment first existed and paid services were first delivered and continued to count until the elimination period was satisfied, whether paid care was received or not. In this way, a 30-day elimination period could be satisfied a month after the first home care visit, regardless of how many visits were made during that time.

Insurers saw the potential for consumers to game this concept. An insured could receive one day of paid home care simply to commence the elimination period, receive no more paid care until the elimination period was satisfied, and then receive paid care five days a week once benefits began and the insurance company was reimbursing for the services. This went against the basics of insurance requiring the insured to have compensatory out-of-pocket expenses before the benefits begin. An alternative to pure calendar days, triggered by a single day of service, was sought.

In working with consultants and home care providers, some long-term care insurers concluded they could count a week's worth of care if the insured received care two or three days a week. The rationale was that these people were receiving informal care the other days, so they needed care that whole week. And the claimant would likely require care in a facility that costs more than a few days of home care if they didn't have the informal caregiver present on the days the agency didn't come.

Some companies today count seven days of home care against the elimination period when the claimant receives only one, two or three days of care. This hybrid approach counts service days, but also gives "credit" and counts disability days when no services are received, as long as they fall within the same calendar week as when a service was provided. This approach costs more than the pure service day elimination period, but less than the pure disability or calendar day elimination period, making it an attractive middle option. It is, however, a little more difficult for consumers to understand than the approach that simply counts disability or calendar days.

TABLE 7.1

The Impact on Premium Cost of Alternative Elimination Period Designs

Elimination period design	Pricing factor
Consecutive service days	1.0
Service days accumulating over 90 calendar days	1.2
Calendar days from first day of service	1.5
Calendar days with no initial service day required	1.7
Service days, but each week in which service received counts as seven days	1.3

(Pricing factors assume a 30-day elimination period and a 90-day accumulation period where applicable.)

Per Episode vs. Once per Lifetime

The earliest LTCI policies required that a new elimination period be satisfied each time the claimant stopped receiving care. This was called a **per episode design**. For each episode of care, a new deductible period had to be met. This seemed like an adequate design until it was put into practice with actual claims. Consumers did not appreciate having to pay out of pocket for their care during the elimination period more than once over their lifetime.

Now, most insurers offer a **once per lifetime design**. If the insured satisfies the elimination period, qualifies for and begins to receive benefits, but then recovers, they never have to meet the elimination period requirement again. That is, if they ever need care again, they get first dollar coverage. While most people who need long-term care do not have multiple episodes of care in their lifetime (that is, they do not receive benefits, then recover, and subsequently require benefits at a future date), it is still viewed by many consumers as a plus to have this once per lifetime feature. It adds only minimally to the cost of the policy, and consumers like it since it has great conceptual appeal and helps them better predict possible out-of-pocket expenses.

Outline the once per lifetime design of determining coverage based on the elimination period.

_____

_____

_____

_____

_____

_____

What Counts as a Day of Care?

Under the service-day design, insurers also had to consider whether to count a day of home care the same as a day on which the individual received nursing home care. While "a day is a day," typically the home care day is less costly, in terms of out-of-pocket costs, than a day of care in a nursing home. There was a perceived conflict if someone satisfied their long-term care insurance elimination period with home care benefits and then entered a nursing facility—the claimant's out-of-pocket expenses would be less per day during the elimination period than the insurance company's benefit payments after the elimination period was satisfied.

Initially, companies responded to this problem in one of two ways. Some had separate elimination periods for home care and facility care. These separate elimination periods acted independently of one another. Some insurers designed their policies to have the benefit days paid under one provider counted against the elimination period of the other provider. A consumer could even select separate elimination periods for the different providers—a shorter one for home care and a longer one for facility care was common. Some policies had a single combined elimination period for all services, but only counted a day of home care as half a day toward meeting the elimination period.

Today, most comprehensive policies have a single elimination period that applies toward any covered service, and one day of home care and one day of nursing facility care both count as one day toward satisfying the elimination period.

» Alternatives to Counting Days

New developments are seen every year in the design of the elimination period for long-term care insurance. One innovation is to use a dollar-amount maximum instead of counting days. Another approach is to waive the elimination period requirement completely either for specific benefits (e.g., hospice care or equipment) or when an insurance company care advisor is used from the first day of impairment.

Dollar Deductible

Some LTCI agents present the elimination period to prospects like a deductible on automobile insurance. For instance, they explain that a 90-day elimination period with an average cost of care of $200 per day would result in the insured paying $18,000 in out-of-pocket costs before the insurance benefits kick in. It is easier for some consumers to grasp paying a dollar amount than paying for a number of days. However, this can be misleading, as many consumers will have out-of-pocket costs far less than the potential maximum during the elimination period since they might not require the most costly type of care or might not require paid care every day.

Some LTCI policies do actually have a **dollar deductible**. It works in this way: The claimant submits bills for the expenses incurred. When the expenses reach the amount of the deductible, the insurer begins to pay benefits. This results in counting expenses at claim time rather than counting days of care. Presumably, to be attractive to the consumer, the dollar deductible approach would have to be either less expensive (in terms of premium cost) or less costly in terms of likely out-of-pocket expenses than any of the other elimination period designs described above.

In an inflationary environment, the dollar deductible can become more valuable over time. It will always take 30 days to satisfy a 30-day elimination period, no matter how much long-term care costs rise. But years from now it will take many fewer days to satisfy a $20,000 deductible than it does today, because each day of care will cost much more. In fact, with a dollar deductible, the longer the insured owns the policy, the fewer days it will take to satisfy the deductible (assuming inflation continues).

The dollar deductible is rare in the LTCI industry. The projected claim costs for this design are significantly higher than for an elimination period that counts days of care.

Care Management

Another novel approach to the elimination period involves the use of **care management** services provided by the insurance company. The company may have licensed health care practitioners under contract with its network of assessors (not company employees) that develop the plan of care. This plan might try to maximize the use of community-based providers that are available free of charge or government-reimbursed home care services. The idea is to have the claimant receive a like level of care at a lower cost.

Companies utilizing this design have a higher level of trust that the person developing the plan of care is objective and not affiliated with a provider of services. Therefore, to encourage the use of care management services, some companies have developed policies that waive the elimination period when care management services are used. To further minimize the potential for fraud and abuse, the insurer has the option of having the claimant pay a portion of the ongoing cost when using this service. As an example, the insurance company might pay 80 percent of the cost, while the claimant pays the remaining 20 percent. This is an alternative to paying the entire cost of care during the elimination period.

» Summary

People buying insurance are concerned with the payment of benefits. Some are not concerned until they file a claim, when it may be too late to understand their policy features. The three components to payment of benefits were introduced in this chapter—when, how much, and for how long.

Satisfaction of the elimination period is one of the cornerstones of receiving benefits from an LTCI policy. The intent of an elimination period is to lower the premium charge and to have the insured pay a portion of the cost of services—much as other types of insurance have deductibles or copayments. There are two choices for consumers: the services and providers that are covered and the length of time they must wait until benefits are paid.

The insurer has several different options for how to design and administer the elimination period. They can count days or count dollars. They can allow the days to accumulate or require consecutive days. They can have a long accumulation period or a short one—or no accumulation period. They can count service days or disability/calendar days. HIPAA allows for all these variations in elimination period design. The prevailing design is a once per lifetime elimination period that either allows service days to accumulate or uses disability/calendar days in whole or in part.

The following chapters discuss the other two components to receiving benefits—how much is paid and for how long.

Accumulation period	Elimination period
Benefit period	Facility-care-only policy
Calendar day design	First dollar coverage
Care management	Home-care-only policy
Comprehensive policy	Lifetime accumulation period
Deductible	Once per lifetime design
Disability day design	Per episode design
Dollar deductible	Service day design

Key Terms &—

» Review Questions

1. Do facility-care-only policies cover only state-licensed nursing homes?

2. Which LTCI policy model does not limit care settings?

3. What is the LTCI equivalent of a deductible?

4. What are HIPAA duration requirements for cognitive impairment and physical impairment benefit triggers?

5. Can an LTCI policy offer a period of elimination that is under 90 days and still be tax-qualified?

6. How did home care complicate the practice of counting days for the elimination period?

7. In the context of the question above, what is an accumulation period?

8. Why did the per episode design result in consumer complaints, and what was the alternative designed by the insurance industry?

9. What is the common trend today in counting home care days and facility care days? How does it differ from past practice?

10. Name the two methods developed as alternatives to counting elimination period days.

» Answers

1. No. This was the case with early LTCI policies, but the requirement has been relaxed to cover other qualified facilities—such as assisted living communities and board and care homes.

2. The comprehensive model.

3. The elimination period.

4. Zero and 90 days, respectively.

5. Yes. The 90-day requirement of HIPAA does mean, however, that if an impairment is expected to last for less than 90 days, benefits cannot be paid, regardless of what elimination period the policy has. Therefore, counting days toward satisfying the elimination period of a qualified policy does not begin unless the impairment is expected to last at least 90 days.

6. Home care is not always delivered on consecutive days, so counting days becomes more difficult compared to keeping track of how many

days someone spends in a nursing home. In response to this problem, insurance companies decided to accumulate days on which professional caregivers provided care.

7. The accumulation period is the maximum length of time an insured can take to accumulate the number of days specified in their policy's elimination period.

8. The per episode design specifies that for each episode of care, a new elimination period has to be satisfied. This seemed like an adequate design in theory, but when put into practice, consumers complained that they were having to pay out of pocket for their care during the elimination period more than once over their lifetime. To address this complaint, most insurers now offer a once per lifetime design.

9. In the past, companies experimented with various methods to keep separate tallies of days spent in home care and nursing facility care. Today, however, most comprehensive policies have a single elimination period that applies toward any covered service, and both one day of home care and one day of nursing facility care count as one day toward satisfying the elimination period.

10. Dollar deductible and care management.

8

How Much Is Paid in Benefits?

» Overview

How much money is available to pay benefits is normally a consumer's primary concern when they enter claim status. This is the time they realize that the actual cost of care will affect their budget and potentially their retirement nest egg. They want funds available to help offset the expenses they will incur for the services they will require.

All insurance has a limit on how much is paid in benefits. Homeowners' insurance, for example, has replacement cost, depreciated cost, or cost at purchase. Automobile insurance will "total" a car when the cost to repair it exceeds the cost to replace it with a like car. Long-term care insurance uses a maximum amount of money on a daily, weekly, or monthly basis. There are two choices consumers make regarding how much money they'll receive—an initial amount and whether and how their benefits will keep pace with inflation.

» Selecting an Initial Benefit Amount

The benefit amount to be paid for daily (or weekly or monthly) expenses is chosen at the time of purchase. Companies offer a range of choices, with a minimum and a maximum amount they will offer. The minimum is frequently dictated by state regulations or a level the company feels is appropriate for its clientele. The maximum is normally significantly higher than the average cost of care in an area. This accommodates someone who desires going to a better-than-average facility or someone who lives in a higher-cost area—frequently in or near a metropolitan area where costs are higher. A typical range of choice might be $50 to $350, where the individual can elect any amount they desire in $10 increments between these amounts.

The benefit amount is usually expressed in either a daily, weekly, or monthly benefit amount. Traditional long-term care insurance used the daily amount because that is the method used by Medicare's skilled nursing facility benefit. Most nursing homes set their charges on a daily amount because of the varying number of days per month. Most home care agencies express their cost in terms of visit or hour—the common measure for how care is delivered at home.

This daily amount is the maximum payable for each day the insured receives services. This is the limit on how much is payable for each day services are received even if the individual receives multiple services or incurs multiple costs on a given day. Some policies limit the type of expenses that can be paid on the same day—for example, the insured can't receive both home care and nursing home care on the same day. But typically one can receive care from a home care agency and adult day center on a single day, with those expenses being covered, up to the daily maximum the individual has selected. Often people who receive care at home receive varying amounts of services each day—possibly getting several services one day and maybe few or no services on days when family or friends are available to provide care. Companies with a weekly maximum allowance multiply the daily limit by seven to create the weekly amount. This weekly maximum allows for reimbursement of more expenses when more than one provider delivers care on a single day and some days no care is received. The monthly maximum benefit works in much the same way as the weekly limit, with 30 as the multiple. The monthly maximum provides even greater flexibility for "stacking" multiple services on certain days or during certain weeks of the month.

Some companies will vary the amount payable during a claim based on who provides the care. The nursing home amount is the primary driver for determining the maximum, with a percentage of this amount paid for the other providers. As an example, a nursing home benefit is the maximum of 100 percent while assisted living might be 75 percent and home care might be 50 percent of the nursing home amount. Conceptually, this makes sense because the other providers are normally less expensive than the nursing home. But it can cause confusion at the time of claim if the insured didn't understand that some services are paid based on a percentage of the daily benefit amount they selected.

Companies can vary the daily maximum for the various providers by allowing the insured to select the appropriate amount for each provider. For instance, insurers can design a policy that pays $175 per day for nursing home care, $150 for assisted living, and $100 for home care. It was common to find separate choices for nursing home and home care benefit amounts in the mid-1990s. Normally companies will require that the highest daily limit be for the nursing home benefit. The problem with this much flexibility is that consumers and agents tend to find themselves over-whelmed with choices on an already complicated product. Therefore, some companies specify how much they will pay for services other than nursing home care, specifying this as a percentage of the nursing home daily benefit. Often, insureds will have a choice of 50, 75, or 100 percent for home care. Assisted living facility care is usually paid at the same amount as nursing home care, or the insured might have a choice of 75 percent or 100 percent.

Another method of determining the benefit amount that is payable uses a copayment, as is common with major medical insurance. The insurance pays a certain percentage of the expenses and the claimant pays the balance of the cost. An 80-20 copayment means the insurance company pays 80 percent of actual charges while the claimant pays the remaining 20 percent. (There are two approaches—the insurer can pay 80 percent of charges up to the daily benefit amount or 80 percent of all covered expenses with no maximum.) The copayment approach can be an alternative to using an elimination period—the claimant pays a small portion of the ongoing out-of-pocket expenses rather than the entire expense before qualifying for benefits. However, this is not common for LTCI.

Many companies now have a single daily maximum for all services on their LTCI policies. This design is easier to understand. It requires the agent and the insured to make just one choice on how much money is paid at the time of claim. If the daily maximum benefit is $150 per day, the amount available during a claim is $150 per day regardless of who is providing the care or the type of service provided. The disadvantage of this approach is that it is more costly than one where there are lower daily benefit amounts for less expensive services like home care. One variation on this approach that some companies provide is an option with a reduced amount for home care based on a percentage of the nursing home amount—normally 50 percent or 75 percent. This helps make premiums more affordable and tracks well with the costs of home care, which are typically (but not always) less than nursing home costs.

FOCUS QUESTION 1

Briefly outline different approaches used by insurance companies in determining benefit allocation for different kinds of long-term care.

_____

_____

_____

_____

_____

_____

_____

_____

_____

_____

_____

Some consumers decide to select a benefit amount less than the cost of care in their area. In doing so, they are deciding to accept some of the risk themselves. There is nothing wrong with this choice as long as the consumer recognizes that the policy they are designing will require them to pay for some of the costs of care. The agent should help the consumer analyze their financial situation and determine what portion of their care they could afford to pay, and whether it would be in their interest to take this approach.

In contrast, some consumers select a benefit amount that is in excess of costs in their area so that they have some hedge against rising costs, rather than choosing an inflation protection option.

Finally, it is important to note that policies have two approaches to how much they pay. Some policies pay actual incurred expenses, up to this daily (or monthly or weekly) benefit amount selected, while others pay the actual daily benefit amount selected, regardless of the actual amount of expense incurred. This is discussed below.

» LTC Cost Increases

The costs of long-term care services have risen consistently over the last 20 years. Nursing homes in 1980 cost about $18,000 per year, and now they average over $50,000 per year. (People in metropolitan areas will find average costs higher, and those in rural areas will find average costs lower.) This trend of rising costs is likely to continue along with other cost increases in our economy.

The increase in nursing home costs over the last 20 years is higher than the general inflation rate for a number of reasons. The types of services nursing homes provide are much different today from those of 20 years ago. There are many more discharges from hospitals to nursing homes, which now are designed to complete the recovery process. This requires nursing homes to have more advanced technology and therapy equipment available for the residents. Nursing facilities also must be built to accommodate the extra space needed for the new services, which adds to the cost of developing a facility.

Staffing a nursing home is much different today than 20 years ago. The types of services delivered require someone with more of a medical background or experience with one of the various therapies. These people can command higher salaries than less skilled workers. The shortage of nurses throughout the medical community has made it more difficult for long-term care providers to attract and retain the right employees. Even the aides in a facility are better paid than in the past because nursing homes are competing with other employers for entry-level employees. Furthermore, more people are needed to file the paperwork required to receive government reimbursement and the associated certification requirements. All these changes add to the cost of long-term care services.

FOCUS QUESTION 2

Explain why the rise in nursing home costs over the last 20 years is higher than the general inflation rate.

_____

_____

_____

_____

_____

_____

_____

_____

_____

_____

While the above trends are important, it is also true that the cost of long-term care services has not risen as sharply as the costs of other types of health and medical care. That's because long-term care is "high touch" (meaning it is very people-intensive) where health care and hospital care are rapidly becoming extremely "high tech," driving costs up more quickly.

The overall payments to nursing homes and home care providers have been tracked for many years. The Health Care Financing Administration (HCFA) monitors total payments to nursing homes and home health care agencies and whether the payments came from public or private funds.[1] This data goes back to 1960 for nursing homes and 1992 for home care. The tables show the increasing amounts of money that go to the formal providers of these services and provide the most comprehensive analysis of who pays for the care. What they do not accurately reflect is an inflation rate of the cost of care. It reflects a mixture of changes in the number of people needing care, the type and intensity of care provided, and changes in the costs of care.

The Bureau of Labor Statistics (BLS) now tracks the cost of nursing home and home care as a separate price index from other types of health care costs. The nursing home data include nursing home care, convalescent and rehabilitation care, and adult day services. The indexes are found on the BLS website.[2]

The nursing home index is made up of skilled and intermediate care facility costs. Before 1997, these costs were tracked as part of the hospital index. Facilities that provide more custodial care, such as board and care homes and assisted living facilities, are not included in the index. The home care index is made up of skilled nursing or medical care provided in the home under the supervision of a physician. This includes home health care services and visiting nurse associations but not homemaker or personal care services.

» LTCI Inflation Protection

In the early years of the LTCI industry, insurers, regulators, and consumer advocates recognized the impact of inflation on the purchasing power of LTCI benefits. Insurers were able to price an optional inflation rider to LTCI policies but found that it added significantly to cost. There was no consistency in the way companies designed their inflation protection. Consumer advocates warned that LTCI coverage without some sort of inflation protection would not provide meaningful benefits years after the policy was purchased, which is when most insureds file claims. As an example, if LTC costs rise an average of 5 percent annually, costs double every 15 years, and the purchasing power of benefits is halved in that time.

Automatic Options

There was much discussion within the industry and among interested parties on how to handle the inflation issue. Some wanted **automatic inflation protection** to be part of the mandatory requirements of long-term care insurance policies. Others wanted the choice to be left to consumers. The compromise was to make it mandatory to offer consumers the option of automatic inflation protection. This approach alerts the consumer to the importance of having some type of inflation protection and makes sure they have the opportunity to have it, but it lets each consumer select the method that best meets their needs and financial means.

There was also discussion of whether the automatic inflation increases should be of a fixed amount each year, or whether they should be variable, based on the actual rates of inflation. Until recently, however, an index for inflation specific to long-term care was not available, so using a fixed annual percentage was the preferred approach. Also, a variable increase is extremely difficult to price from the insurer perspective because of the uncertainty of future increases. This could lead to undercharging (and the need for future premium increases) or overcharging (and the potential for premium decreases or excess company profits). A fixed rate provided better stability to the premium, which was a concern of all involved. The drawback of having a fixed increase is that it may understate or overstate the actual increase in the cost of care. The likelihood of each is about equal. The consensus was to use fixed increases.

Determining the right rate of increase was difficult. The general feeling was that offering a high rate of inflation was too expensive and might overstate the actual increases. A low rate of inflation was more affordable but didn't provide meaningful protection for even conservative estimates of the potential increasing costs. The rate that seemed to satisfy everyone was a fixed 5 percent of the daily benefit. In fact, this figure is approximately how much nursing home costs have been increasing over the past 20 years.

Discussion then focused on whether simple or compounded increases were best. Many companies offer a simple increase option—which means the increases are based on the original issue amount. For example, if someone owns a $100-per-day plan with 5 percent simple increases, each year the daily benefit increases by five dollars. Compounded increases are based on the previous year's daily benefit. The first year there is no difference between the two designs, but in subsequent years there is, and the difference grows over time. In fact, a simple increase option doubles the daily benefit every 20 years, while the compounded increases take just 15 years to double. Given the fact that the cost of care increases at compounded rates and the intent of inflation protection is to provide an offset that is close to the rising costs of care, the preferred approach is to use a 5 percent compounded increase. Some policies, however, offer a choice of a simple or compound inflation increase, providing a lower-cost option for those who want it.

FOCUS QUESTION 3

Summarize the concerns involved in deciding on the specifics of an inflation protection option.

_____

_____

_____

_____

_____

_____

_____

_____

_____

_____

_____

_____

_____

Most policies continue the inflation protection increases for the life of the policy, but some "cap" the inflation increases at a specific age (for example, 80 or 85) or once the daily benefit amount has doubled. A policy with a **capped inflation increase** is obviously less expensive than one that continues for the life of the coverage, but it also provides less complete protection.

With automatic inflation protection, all the coverage amounts increase by 5 percent compounded annually. That means that the daily benefit amount as well as the lifetime maximum increase at this defined rate. Without an increase in the lifetime maximum, an increasing daily benefit amount would simply penalize the claimant by having more funds available for a shorter period of time than they originally had available at the time of purchase. In order for the policy to maintain its value, the increases to the policy maximum need to mirror the 5 percent increases found in the daily maximum.

Inflation Protection and the Premium

How to price for these automatic coverage increases was the final hurdle for insurers. Some insisted on prefunding the increases in the early policy years while others preferred a "pay-as-you-go" arrangement. With the **prefunded level-premium design**, the initial premium is higher than with the pay-as-you-go approach. But this premium is designed to remain the same through the life of the policy, even though benefits are increasing with inflation. In other words, the insured overpays for coverage in the beginning and underpays in the later years, which results in a level premium. It also means that the policy is more cost-effective the longer someone owns it.

In the **pay-as-you-go design**, premiums are based on the benefit amount at the current age of the insured—that is, premiums increase during the life of the policy, as benefits increase with inflation and the age of the insured increases. In this design, the premium eventually grows to the point of unaffordability for many insureds—just as they are approaching an age when they need the benefits. Buying additional coverage at the more expensive attained age rates becomes financially burdensome for people in their seventies or eighties living on a fixed retirement income. People beginning to experience chronic health problems are not able to

FIGURE 8.1

Comparing Premium Designs

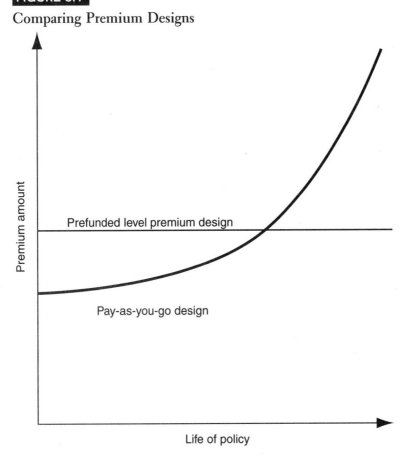

obtain coverage elsewhere, and their disposable income is earmarked for receiving medical care, not paying long-term care insurance premiums. This scenario would have insureds either lapsing their policy or not receiving further increases when they need the increases the most.

The prefunded level-premium design is in many ways in the interests of consumers. The premiums are higher in the younger years, when people are normally healthier and have more disposable income. The later years of the insurance policy will reflect the benefit of this prepayment with rates that are significantly lower than the insured would have paid based on benefit amounts and age. Prudent insureds purchase the coverage while still working so that initial payments are made while receiving a paycheck and affordability is even less of an issue.

After extensive negotiation, the NAIC regulations for inflation protection were written in such a way as to not stifle innovation. The option all insurers must offer is a prefunded level-premium automatic 5 percent increase, on a compounded basis, that lasts for the life of the policy. The regulations require the insured to sign a waiver if they do not choose this type of inflation protection. But insurers are free to offer other methods as well, and many companies do.

One of the more common automatic inflation options offered today is a simple increase instead of a compound increase. This lowers the cost of the inflation feature while not significantly reducing benefit increases in the initial years. (It takes about 10 years before a sizable difference between the two options is recognized.) The simple increase is often appropriate for purchasers who expect to need benefits in just a few years, such as the elderly. (Note that not all states allow a simple increase.)

Purchase Options

Another common inflation option is a **purchase option**—the insured has the option of increasing the daily and lifetime benefit maximums at regular intervals. Insureds exercising this option need not apply for the additional coverage and go through underwriting again. They simply state that they want additional coverage, which is offered in an amount determined in advance by the carrier. The insurance company will then recalculate the premium by adding to the existing premium (based on the insured's original issue age) the premium for the increased amount of coverage (based on the insured's age at the time they purchase the increased coverage).

Some companies design their purchase options with an annual increase, while others make the increase offer every other year or every third year. The insured then has a choice on those option dates whether to accept the offer of increased coverage or leave their coverage at the current levels.

With most companies that offer purchase options, the insured must accept the increase—that is, the insured needs to say that they want the increase. A less common approach is to automatically increase the benefit and the premium for the increased amount of benefit and give the insured the right to opt out of the increase. This design requires insureds to say that they don't want the increase. If they don't decline the offer for the increase, it is put into effect.

Companies usually place a limit on how often an insured can decline an optional increase and still continue to receive the periodic offers. Some will use a number or frequency of rejected options. This can vary from one rejection to many rejections. Companies can either use consecutive choices or cumulative choices. As an example, a company can cease making additional offers if an insured doesn't accept two consecutive purchase options. Another approach is to cease making additional offers once the insured declines any two or three prior offers, but allows them to decline consecutive offers.

Another variable in the purchase option design is the amount of the increase. The more that is offered, the greater the risk of **anti-selection** (when someone who is becoming impaired buys more coverage for a claim that only they know will occur soon). Some long-term care insurers use a predetermined amount while others use an index. The predetermined amount is normally expressed as a percentage—for instance, 5 percent per year. Under this system, an insurer that is offering the periodic increase every three years would offer a 15 percent increase. In another design, the predetermined amount is a dollar amount—five or 10 dollars a day. Some carriers will allow the insured to "make up" in a subsequent offer the amount they decline from a prior offer, but many companies offer the additional amount for that period only. If the insured declined the prior offer, they are not able to "make it up" in a subsequent offer.

Some companies link the periodic increase amount to an index such as the Consumer Price Index (CPI). Indexing the increases is tricky, since this will result in high benefit amounts during times of high inflation, such as the late 1970s, but low amounts in the current low-inflation environment. Prior to the Department of Labor's new indexes for nursing home and home health care costs, long-term care insurers might use the general Consumer Price Index. History shows that this slightly understated the actual amount of increases in the long-term care provider community.

Some companies now can use the more precise measures when designing their indexing purchase options.

Some insurers allow insureds to exercise the full option, or insureds can choose to elect a smaller portion of it. As an example, suppose the option is for 20 percent of the original amount every two years and the original amount is $200 per day. The option would allow the insured to increase the daily benefit by an additional $40 per day every two years. If the company allowed the purchase of less than the full amount, the insured could accept $20 per day. This choice might affect future increases depending on how the policy is designed.

Normally, increase options are made available only to those insureds not currently on claim. But a company can design the options to continue even while the insured is receiving benefits. Since most policies have a waiver of premium feature, this means the insured will receive the increase even though they are not paying premiums for the increases during a claim. An insurer that does not allow the increase offers to be made or exercised during claim can resume the options after the insured is no longer on claim status.

When an insured has exercised their purchase option to increase the daily benefit, the company will recalculate the lifetime maximum at claim time. This new lifetime maximum will reflect the new daily maximum in order not to reduce the length of time benefits are payable.

It should be noted that most companies also allow an insured to request an increase in coverage (that is, increase the daily benefit amount and/or the lifetime maximum) at any time, but they require that the insured apply for the increase and pass underwriting. Obviously, someone in benefit or whose health status has declined would not be approved for the increase. The premium charged for the increase usually reflects a blended rate based on the premium for the original coverage at the original purchase age and the cost of the additional coverage at the insured's age when they make the increase.

FOCUS QUESTION 4

Name some common methods or designs used in establishing an inflation protection option.

_____

_____

_____

_____

_____

_____

_____

_____

_____

_____

_____

_____

_____

_____

_____

_____

_____

» How Benefits Are Paid

The payment of LTCI benefits is done under one of two general methods: the **indemnity** or **per diem model**, which pays the full daily maximum for any day on which covered services are received, regardless of the actual cost of those services; or the **reimbursement model**, which pays expenses for the actual cost of the service up to the daily benefit maximum specified in the policy.

The Indemnity Model

The earliest LTCI policies paid a flat dollar amount regardless of the actual cost of care. The amount paid was the daily benefit amount.

This design is referred to as an indemnity or per diem model. (The **disability model** discussed in an earlier chapter will pay benefits in much the same way as an indemnity model. The primary difference is that the disability model does not consider which services were received and does not require that any services be received or any expense be incurred. The disability model simply provides a cash payment for each day on which the insured meets the policy's definition of impairment, regardless of service use.)

Under the indemnity model, the insurer normally pays benefits once a month after services are received. It is generally assumed that when someone is in a facility they will receive care every day during the month. The claim representative calls the facility to confirm the claimant is still a resident of that facility and then processes the payment. Or the insured might be required to submit a continuing claim form with documentation of expenses. Under the indemnity benefit approach, the payment is equal to the daily benefit times the number of days in the month. For home care or adult day services, the insurer might require an invoice to determine the number of days on which care was delivered. Payments are in the amount of the daily benefit for that provider multiplied by the number of days on which care was received.

If multiple providers were present on a single day, the per diem payment is still paid, although there may be some services that the policy defines as not being covered on the same day (for example, nursing home care and in-home care). For policies with a weekly or monthly benefit amount, the policy will pay benefits equal to the full weekly or monthly benefit, or, if the insured was not disabled for the entire week or month being covered, on a pro-rata basis.

As an example of the difference between a daily and a weekly benefit amount, consider someone with a daily benefit of $100 versus someone with a policy that pays a weekly benefit of $700. With a $100 daily benefit, if the insured receives home care services on Monday, Wednesday, and Friday and adult day services Monday through Friday, this person would receive $500 per week because care was delivered just five days during that week. With the weekly maximum, the person receives the full $700 as long as they were disabled during the entire seven days of the week, even though they did not receive care every day of the week. The weekly benefit design gives insureds more flexibility to "stack services" on days when family or informal care may not be available.

HIPAA and the Indemnity Model

HIPAA gave a special allowance for indemnity policies. Under this design, the insurer need not coordinate benefits with Medicare or pay benefits only for qualified long-term care services. This gives insurers maximum flexibility in designing a qualified long-term care insurance indemnity policy.

HIPAA does have a mechanism to ensure that people are not getting rich with their long-term care insurance when benefits are paid without regard to the actual charges. The aggregate amount paid from the policy is reported to the IRS each year on Form 1099-LTC. Those with an indemnity design (which includes the disability model) have a maximum amount of tax-free benefit available. For 2002, this is $210 per day. (There are annual adjustments made to this figure based on inflation.) When actual charges are proven to exceed this amount, this cap is functionally raised to the actual charges for the year. When benefits paid are above the actual charges and $210 per day, the overage is considered ordinary income. This analysis is done on IRS Form 8853.

Advantages and Disadvantages of the Indemnity Model

The indemnity design is easier to understand for everyone involved in the process. Benefits are paid quickly and efficiently by a claim staff that does not require specialized training in monitoring provider billings or government reimbursement policies and procedures. (However, the claim staff must still verify that the insured received service from a provider that meets the policy's definition of a covered provider, that expenses were incurred, and that the insured met the impairment definition of the policy.) The claimant knows how much they will receive each month based on the number of days in the month on which they received care. If care costs less than the daily benefit amount they receive, they can save those dollars and put them toward other uses. And it is easy for the agent to explain at the time of sale exactly how much benefit will be paid each day when someone needs care.

One problem with the indemnity design is that the insured could actually make money on the insurance company during a claim. Insurance is designed to protect the insured from financial catastrophe when an unexpected event occurs. People buying an indemnity LTCI policy have the potential of overinsuring. At the time of claim, they could receive a benefit that exceeds the cost of care. This leads to the potential for fraud and abuse. Because the daily benefit is always paid out at the maximum amount under the indemnity model, this approach also has a higher premium cost than a policy using the reimbursement approach. The cost differential is greater between these two models at the higher daily benefit amounts.

On the other hand, many people in a chronically ill situation have ongoing, ancillary expenses associated with receiving care that are not covered under the policy (such as prescription drugs and equipment costs). There may also be uninsured costs incurred when an adult child who is caring for the claimant takes a reduction in the number of hours that they work in order to provide the care. The extra cash paid in benefits in the indemnity model can be used for these purposes.

FOCUS QUESTION 5

Summarize the pros and cons of the indemnity model.

_____

_____

_____

_____

_____

_____

_____

_____

_____

_____

_____

_____

_____

_____

_____

_____

The Reimbursement Model

The reimbursement model is different from the indemnity model in that the insured is reimbursed for the actual cost of the services received, up to the daily benefit amount specified in the policy. The person handling the insured's financial matters submits receipts, invoices, or bills from the care providers utilized by the insured. The insurer's claim representative analyzes the billing to determine which expenses are for qualified services that are covered under the policy. The claim representative then evaluates the billings and the potential for other third-party payers (such as Medicare) to determine the amount payable. A check to ensure that this amount is below the policy's maximum payable benefit is made just before the payment amount is finalized.

Advantages and Disadvantages of the Reimbursement Model

The reimbursement model addresses the insurer's cause for concern regarding overinsurance. When paying only for covered services after reviewing the actual billing statement, there is a level of assurance that the insured is only receiving money to pay the actual bills. There are no excess funds paid, as could potentially be the case with an indemnity plan. And the claimant receives payment for their actual out-of-pocket expenses.

The lifetime maximum pool of benefit dollars also can last longer under this model, since the insured is only "drawing down" from that lifetime pool the amount needed to actually cover costs. If the costs of care are less than the daily benefit amount allowed, the difference stays in the insured's lifetime pool of dollars and can be used to extend the period of time over which benefits will be paid.

Finally, this approach has a lower premium cost because the insurer anticipates some "salvage." This refers to the difference between the full daily benefit maximum and the actual costs of care. The amount paid in benefits each day is on average less than the full daily benefit amount, especially at the higher daily benefit amounts. Insurers factor this into their pricing so that this approach usually costs a little less in premiums than does the indemnity model.

FOCUS QUESTION 6

Summarize the pros and cons of the reimbursement model.

_____

_____

_____

_____

_____

_____

_____

_____

_____

_____

HIPAA and the Reimbursement Model

The reimbursement model is a HIPAA-friendly design because the benefits paid from a qualified contract are always considered free from income taxation. The aggregate payments of benefits will not exceed the cost of care when the claims department pays for only the actual charges of the covered services.

HIPAA has a special clause for reimbursement plans—a coordination of benefits requirement for qualified policies. When a policy pays for services that are reimbursable under Medicare, the insurance policy becomes the secondary payer. This is in place so as to avoid duplication of payments by Medicare and the long-term care policy, which would in effect provide the insured with a tax-free income stream from the LTCI policy.

This clause does mean that the person processing a claim must determine which expenses Medicare covers and adjust payments as per the policy's Medicare coordination language. However, this step is often not necessary as most long-term care events do not qualify for Medicare coverage at all.

» The Taxation of Benefits

Another consideration in determining the amount received from an LTCI policy is to calculate the net after-tax proceeds. HIPAA clearly states that the claimant receives benefits free from income taxation when paid from a qualified long-term care insurance policy. A few wrinkles are included to ensure that individuals do not take advantage of the tax code. (There is no language in the tax code regarding long-term care insurance policies that do not meet HIPAA's definition of a qualified plan.)

All long-term care insurance claimants receive Form 1099-LTC at the beginning of the calendar year following their receipt of benefits. This form provides information to the claimant and the Internal Revenue Service regarding the total dollar amount of benefits paid in the preceding calendar year. The claimant then uses this information to complete IRS Form 8853.

The taxation of benefits under the reimbursement model is easy to understand. Because the insurance company administers the policy to pay only for qualified long-term care services, HIPAA allows all benefits to go to the claimant tax-free. There is no room in the benefit structure for the claimant to find loopholes that will provide them with excess tax-free income.

The HIPAA legislation included special provisions for indemnity policies. If the daily benefit amount paid during the year is less than a certain amount, the receipt of all benefits paid is income tax-free. This amount is $210 in 2002. It is reset every year by the IRS based on inflation. If the amount paid exceeds the IRS's limit, then consideration is given to the cost of care received. Form 8853 is used to determine the difference between the amount of benefits received and the cost of qualified long-term care services. If the cost of care was equal to or exceeded the indemnity long-term care insurance benefits paid, the benefits are tax-free. If the benefits exceed the cost of care, the excess income is taxable.

Form 8853 considers the total cost of care and the total benefits received in the tax year; it does not record the daily cost of care and the daily benefits received. Therefore, there is no consideration of the fact the insured might have paid for care during the insurance policy's elimination period when making these calculations.

The treatment of a nonqualified long-term care insurance policy is uncertain. IRS Form 8853 instructions directs the person receiving benefits from a policy other than a qualified policy to record the benefits under line 19—"Gross LTC payments received on a per diem or other periodic basis"—and to justify why the taxpayer thinks the benefits should be tax-free.

» Waiver of Premium

An insured's financial situation at claim time is a function not only of the amount the insurer pays them in benefits, but also of whether or not they are required to continue paying the premium. Consider the saving to the claimant if their premium is $1,800 per year and they no longer have to pay that amount while they are receiving benefits. Not only do they receive reimbursement or a fixed payment to offset their long-term care costs, but they are also relieved of an expense of $1,800. Most companies include a waiver of premium clause, either as a standard policy provision or an optional benefit rider for an additional cost.

The waiver of premium provision benefits both the claimant and the insurer. The claimant receives a monetary benefit by not having to continue with the expense of paying premiums. The cost of waiving premiums during time of claim is calculated in advance when the insurance company establishes its premium charges. The claimant also has the peace of mind of knowing that their policy will remain in force during a claim and will not lapse as a result of nonpayment of premium. The insurer benefits by avoiding the concern of canceling a policy of someone in claim status because premiums were not paid in time. And it doesn't make sense to have checks crossing in the mail—one for the insured's claim and another from the insured for the premium. This becomes an administrative nightmare.

When the Waiver Begins

Policies have different approaches to the waiver of premium provision. The waiver can begin based on when the impairment and the need for services begin, or based on when benefits begin (that is, when the elimination period ends). Which approach is taken can make a significant difference to insureds with a long elimination period.

For companies that begin the premium waiver when benefits begin, some waive premiums on the first day of benefits, while others waive premiums after a certain number of days of benefit (such as 30 or 90 days). Some companies don't count short-term benefits like hospice care, respite care, or care advisory services as the basis for triggering a premium waiver.

Companies that base the beginning of the waiver on when the insured begins to need care generally require 90 days of impairment and LTC services to pass before premiums are waived. Thus, if the insured has a 90-day elimination period, the premium waiver would begin on the first day of benefits. But if they have a shorter elimination period (for example, 30 days), the premium waiver would not begin until the 91st day, so they would have received 60 days of benefits before the premium waiver began.

Insurers may count either days of service or calendar days when determining the effective date of the waiver of premium. This becomes significant in a home care situation when someone receives covered services on an intermittent basis. As an example, suppose an insured receives care three days a week and has a policy that requires 90 service days before premiums are no longer due. Counting service days will result in premiums still due after six months. Most consumers would expect satisfaction of the 90 days after about three months—they think in terms of calendar days.

Normally, the waiver of premium ends when the insured is no longer eligible for benefits. One reason for this is that, under HIPAA, the waiver of premium is considered a benefit and qualified long-term care insurance benefits are available only to chronically ill individuals. The other is that the concern regarding checks crossing in the mail no longer exists—there is no longer a need for the benefit. Also, it would increase premiums significantly if premiums were waived for the life of the coverage once someone had triggered the premium waiver with an initial claim event.

The earliest LTCI policies only provided a waiver of premium when the insured needed facility care. Premiums were still payable when the claimant received home care. This was due in large part to the cost of the waiver benefit when added to the home care portion of a policy. However, although it does add to the cost of the policy, many insurers now include all covered providers in the waiver of premium benefit because of the advantages to the consumer.

A variation on the waiver of premium is a **spousal premium waiver**. This feature is usually offered as an additional optional benefit rider to the policy. This variation provides a premium waiver for both husband and wife when either one enters a claim situation that qualifies for the premium waiver. Either linking two separate policies together or putting both insureds on a single policy accomplishes the concept of a dual waiver of premium.

The waiver of premium is a valuable benefit for both the insurance company and the insured. Fortunately all companies include it in their policy in one form or another.

» Summary

There are two components in determining the amount of money an insured receives when they become a claimant of any long-term care insurance policy: the original daily (or monthly) benefit amount and the inflation protection feature used to increase that amount. Both are choices made by the insured at the time of application.

Inflation protection can take different forms. All tax-qualified long-term care policies are required to offer as an option a automatic 5 percent, annually compounded prefunded level-premium increase that lasts for the life of the policy. This is likely to provide meaningful benefits and cost-effective premiums over the long run. There are many different alternatives to this that many companies also offer, but every company must offer this one.

How benefits are paid affects how much an insured receives at the time of claim. Benefits can be paid as an indemnity, where a set dollar amount is paid regardless of the cost of care, or as a reimbursement that pays for the actual expenses only up to the daily benefit limit specified in the policy. These designs are treated differently under HIPAA, but generally speaking, both designs in a qualified long-term care insurance policy will pay tax-free benefits.

The waiver of premium benefit is a valuable feature that contributes to reducing a claimant's expenses (rather than increasing their income as the other benefits do).

Key Terms 🔑

Anti-selection	Per diem model
Automatic inflation protection	Prefunded level-premium design
Capped inflation increase	
Disability model	Purchase option
Indemnity model	Reimbursement model
Pay-as-you-go design	Spousal premium waiver

» Review Questions

1. Describe the trend in nursing home costs in the last two decades.

2. Why is the average cost increase in the general medical care field over the last 20 years higher than the increase in the long-term care industry?

3. Name two sources from which statistics on nursing home costs are available.

4. Are long-term care insurers required to include inflation protection in their policies?

5. What is the primary reason the prefunded level-premium design is preferable to the pay-as-you-go design?

6. Name the three LTCI benefit payment models.

7. Under the indemnity model, how does HIPAA ensure that people are not turning long-term care benefits into a for-profit enterprise when their plan pays benefits regardless of actual charges?

8. What is the primary difference between the indemnity and reimbursement models?

9. When is the payment of one's long-term care insurance premium often waived?

10. How does a spousal premium waiver work?

» Answers

1. The annual cost has gone up from about $18,000 in 1980 to over $50,000 currently.

2. While cost increases in health care and hospital care are largely attributable to high technology, long-term care's cost increase is due largely to the compensation of more highly skilled personnel. The former drives costs up more quickly than the latter.

3. The Health Care Financing Administration (HCFA) and the Bureau of Labor Statistics (BLS).

4. No, but it is mandatory to offer consumers the option of inflation protection. The choice is then left to the consumer.

5. In pay-as-you-go, the premium eventually grows to the point of unaffordability for many individuals, just as they are approaching an age when they need the benefits. Whereas for the prefunded level-premium design, the premiums are higher in the insureds' younger years—when they are normally healthier and have more disposable income.

6. The disability model, the indemnity (or per diem) model, and the reimbursement model.

7. HIPAA caps the amount of long-term care benefits that are considered tax-free. The total amount paid from a policy is reported to the IRS, and benefits in excess of the cap (which is adjusted annually for inflation) are then considered ordinary income, provided the actual charges themselves are not in excess of the cap as well.

8. Indemnity pays a daily maximum benefit regardless of the actual charge incurred. Reimbursement covers the actual charges.

9. When the insured is actually receiving benefits from the policy.

10. The spousal premium waiver provides a premium waiver for both husband and wife when either one enters a claim situation that qualifies for the premium waiver.

NOTES

1 Nursing home data has it own table at http://www.hcfa.gov/stats/nhe-oact/tables/t7.htm, while home health care is found lumped in with "other" data at http://www.hcfa.gov/stats/nhe-oact/tables/t9.htm.

2 http://146.142.4.24/cgi-bin/dsrv?pc. Search on SIC number 8053 for nursing homes or SIC number 8082 for home health care.

How Long Are Benefits Paid?

» Overview

Long-term care insurance, like most other forms of insurance, stipulates a maximum amount of benefits payable over the life of the contract. This is called the **policy maximum**. For example, homeowners' coverage will pay for either the original cost or replacement cost of what was lost because of theft or fire. Auto insurance will pay as much as it costs to repair or replace the car. Even many forms of health insurance have a lifetime maximum—normally a seemingly high amount such as $1,000,000.

The NAIC Model Act includes a minimum benefit period in its definition of a long-term care insurance policy. It says long-term care insurance policies must have at least one year of benefits payable; specifically, it states that an LTCI policy must "...provide coverage for not less than twelve (12) consecutive months for each covered person..." However, there is no policy maximum in either the NAIC Model Act or Model Regulation. HIPAA is also silent on policy maximums.

» The Policy Maximum

Long-term care insurers offer a choice of policy maximums. This is done in recognition of the fact that people have different needs, preferences, and abilities to pay for insurance. There is no "one size fits all" when it comes to how much coverage someone obtains. The policy maximum (also called the **lifetime maximum**) is normally expressed in terms of a number of years or a total dollar amount or an approach that combines these two concepts. Choices in the lifetime policy maximum can range from as short as one year to seven or ten years or even unlimited coverage, which has no dollar or time limit. Most companies offer at least three choices for the lifetime maximum, and many offer many more choices. Most companies now offer an unlimited maximum that will pay benefits for as long as care is needed.

In the earliest policies, the lifetime maximum was defined strictly in terms of the years of benefits paid. If someone had a "four-year" policy, their coverage would end after they had received 1,460 days of benefit (four years X 365 days per year). Some policies had different lifetime maximums for facility care and for in-home care. For example, someone could buy a policy that provided four years of care in a nursing home and two years of care at home. Benefits could only be used in those exact combinations.

The original companies in the LTCI business resisted offering maximums longer than six years because of the challenges of accurately pricing policies with longer coverage durations. However, over time there was a better understanding of the long-term care risk, and companies began to offer 10- or 12-year maximums. These were similar to a $5,000,000 maximum on a medical insurance policy, in that few if any people would meet the maximum, but the risk to the insurer was limited. It was then recognized that the risk for these extended periods was not greatly different from the risk of having no maximum at all. Thus, the **unlimited maximum** was born. The term **lifetime policy** is sometimes used for policies with this feature because benefits continue for the life of the insured—there is no maximum number of days that benefits are payable. Benefits are paid as long as the insured continues to need care and receive covered services.

Both consumers and agents appreciated the fact that there was now an option that would continue payments as long as care was needed. People began to purchase much more of this option. Claim experience continued to show that a somewhat higher premium rate was adequate to support the unlimited maximum. Today, it is one of the more popular options with consumers.

» Counting Days

The original nursing home insurance policies handled policy maximums by counting the days on which benefits were payable. This worked fine when the policy paid an indemnity benefit whenever someone was in a nursing home. The full daily benefit amount was paid regardless of the cost of care, so counting the days that benefits were paid was equitable for both the claimant and the insurer. Also, this concept was easy for the agent to explain at the time of sale. A three-year policy maximum meant that the insured had access to 1,095 days of benefits.

When inflation protection was added to one of these policies, there was no impact on the maximum benefits payable within the policy. Because a day on which benefits were paid counted as one day against the policy maximum, the actual dollar amount paid on a daily basis was not an issue. Counting days was simple for everyone to understand.

The counting of days began to change when companies started offering coverage for providers other than nursing homes. The original comprehensive (nursing facility and home care) indemnity policies provided a daily benefit for home care equal to a percentage of the nursing home daily benefit. As an example, a policy would pay 50 percent of the nursing home benefit amount for home care and 75 percent for assisted living. If the nursing home daily benefit was $100, the home care benefit was $50 while the assisted living benefit was $75. Yet the insured did not receive any credit on the policy maximum when the daily benefit was reduced. A day on which benefits were received counted as a day against the policy maximum, even if the insured only received benefits of $50 on that day, compared to the $100 that would have been paid if they had received nursing home care on that day.

The insurer argument for this design was that the claimant was twice as likely to claim home care benefits as nursing home benefits—therefore the full day credit was equitable. Also, insurers were concerned that utilization rates would be higher than projected because home care is more desirable than nursing home care. They thought insureds might have an incentive to conserve using days of care at home if they knew that they would use up one day of their policy maximum for each day they received care at home.

Neither agents nor insureds bought this argument. Insureds and agents appreciated the simplicity of counting days, but they wanted the portion of unused daily benefit retained in the policy maximum. Insurers warned this would add to the cost of the policy, but people were willing to pay the proportional difference to ensure that they would receive their full maximum benefit amount.

In response to these concerns, some companies changed their way of counting so that someone who received care at home, paid at 50 percent of the daily benefit amount, would only use a half-day of the policy maximum. This got confusing when an assisted living benefit of 75 percent of the nursing home amount was added to the policy. Should the claim count half a day, three-quarters of a day, or a full day against the policy maximum? The simplicity of counting days for a policy maximum no longer existed. Things were getting complicated, and a new method was needed.

FOCUS QUESTION 1

Explain how counting days against the policy maximum changed from being a simple solution into an inadequate one.

_____

_____

_____

_____

_____

_____

_____

_____

_____

_____

» The Pool of Money Approach

The **pool of money** (or pool of funds) design provided the simplicity and fairness consumers and agents were seeking. In this approach, the policy maximum is an overall dollar amount. Benefits are paid until this total

TABLE 9.1

Policy Maximums Converted to a Pool of Money for
Common Options Using a Daily Benefit of $150

Years	Days	Pool of money
1	365	$54,750
2	730	$109,500
3	1,095	$164,250
4	1,460	$219,000
5	1,825	$273,750
6	2,190	$328,500

dollar maximum is reached. The policy maximum is still based on days, but in this design, the counting of days is just a way to establish the dollar maximum for the policy. Essentially, the lifetime maximum is calculated by multiplying the number of days (years) of coverage times the nursing home daily benefit amount. As an example, when the insured owns a three-year maximum at $150 per day, the new pool of money maximum is $164,250.

As benefits are paid, the pool of money is reduced by the actual dollar amount of the benefits paid. There is no longer a need to count days of care. Consumers and agents found this to be a fair and equitable approach.

Consider an example: An insured owns an LTCI policy that has a "three-year" lifetime maximum and uses the pool of money approach. The policy pays $150 per day for nursing home care and a home care daily benefit of 50 percent of the nursing home benefit, or $75. The insured has a pool of money of $164,250 available for paying claims. They receive home health care benefits of $75 per day for 15 days. The total amount of benefits they receive is $1,125, and this amount is credited against the policy maximum, not 15 days and not 15 times the nursing home daily benefit ($2,250).

Once reimbursement policies became more prevalent than indemnity policies, counting the number of days was no longer equitable for the claimant. The reimbursement design can pay for less than the full daily benefit on a regular basis since it pays actual costs of care, which can often be less than the daily benefit maximum. This leaves a difference between the amount reimbursed and the maximum daily benefit. The unused portion of the daily benefit remains available to the claimant in the pool of money design.

Also with the pool of money design, insureds can make their benefits last longer if they receive care at less than the full daily benefit amount, or if they don't receive care every day. Consider an insured with a lifetime maximum of $164,250. This is based on a "three-year" policy maximum, with a $150 per day nursing home benefit. If the insured is in a nursing home that costs $150 per day, their benefits would last exactly three years. But if they are in a nursing home that only costs only $100 per day, their benefits would last 164.5 days, or 4.5 years. If the insured receives all their care at home, costing $50 a day, their benefits would last nine years. And if they did not receive home care every day, which is common, their benefits would last even longer. Thus, the pool of money can enable insureds to make the most of their benefit dollars.

While the pool of money design has a slightly higher premium cost than a policy that counts days of care, it is much more appealing to consumers. Today this is the predominant approach to the policy maximum for a long-term care insurance policy.

FOCUS QUESTION 2

Explain the consumer appeal of the pool of money approach.

_____

_____

_____

_____

_____

_____

_____

Increasing the Pool of Money

Suppose a policy has a pool of money and also an inflation protection feature. The daily benefit amount will increase, so that if the pool of money amount stays the same, the amount of time benefits received will decrease.

As an example, a policy has a pool of money of $164,250, based on three years with a daily benefit of $150 per day. If the $164,250 maximum remains constant while the daily benefit increases by 5 percent for five years (to over $183 per day), the number of days the maximum benefit amount is payable would shrink from 1,095 to 868.

Essentially, under an inflation provision, the lifetime maximum for the policy must increase at the same rate as the daily benefits. That means that if daily benefits increase by 5 percent compounded annually, so must the lifetime maximum. While this concept is simple, the actual method for calculating the increased lifetime maximum is more complicated and will not be addressed here.

» Policy Limits for Specific Benefits

In addition to the overall lifetime maximum on all benefits, many policies also stipulate a limit on the dollar amount or length of time for which they will pay for specific types of services covered under the policy. Common examples are limits on the respite care benefit, bed reservation benefit, caregiver training benefit, and an equipment or home modification benefit.

Respite Care

Normally, an insured does not need to satisfy the elimination period of their policy in order to qualify for **respite care** benefits. However, to avoid having an insured continue claiming respite care benefits indefinitely, insurers limit the number of days this benefit is payable. There is a separate policy maximum for the respite care benefit that is expressed as a number of days or as a dollar limit. This is usually calculated on an annual basis — that is, it renews each claim year, policy year, or calendar year, depending on the company. The most typical respite care benefit provisions provide

14 to 21 days of respite care per calendar year. Some policies provide respite care up to a dollar limit based on the daily benefit amount (for example, $150 per day for nursing home care X 21 days per year = $3,150 of respite care expenses per year.)

Companies were originally fearful of abuse of the respite care benefit because it was not well understood. The original limits were for seven or 14 days—one or two weeks—a year. These fears were eased when claims actually began coming in and the claim representatives began to empathize with the situation of the claimants' caregivers. There was much more stress, strain, and exhaustion than fraud. These caregivers really need a break or at least some assistance. Based on this knowledge and experience, insurers have expanded the respite care benefit on average to 30 days— essentially one month a year.

Bed Reservation

The **bed reservation benefit (BRB)** was another area of learning for LTCI companies. Nursing homes that are at or near capacity are able to fill a vacancy as soon as one appears. Some facilities have waiting lists. Therefore, it is not unusual for a nursing home to charge a patient a fee to reserve their nursing home bed during a temporary absence such as a hospital stay.

Before the creation of the bed reservation benefit, when an LTCI claimant living in a nursing home needed treatment in the hospital because of a condition such as a stroke or heart attack, the facility would fill the temporarily empty bed. Then when the claimant was discharged from the hospital, there was difficulty in finding them a bed in the facility. The alternative was for the claimant to continue paying for the bed although it was not actually being used. Claimants' thought this was reasonable and paid for the room. Many insurers agreed that this was a justifiable financial loss in this situation and continued paying benefits.

The bed reservation benefit allowed for a formal agreement between the insurer and insured for the continued claim payment when a temporary hospital stay was required. To ensure that it was truly a temporary stay, a policy maximum for the bed reservation benefit was typically limited to seven days a year—one week. Again, the policy maximum for the bed reservation benefit was originally short because of the fear of fraud or abuse. The limit has since generally been lengthened to as much as three or four weeks a year, and some companies pay the benefit when the claimant leaves the facility for other reasons (such as visiting family at home), not just for hospitalization.

Caregiver Training

Many family caregivers need a little help learning the best methods to use in caring for their loved one. For example, they might need to learn how to safely move a disabled person from a bed to a chair, or how to handle delicate situations with a sufferer of Alzheimer's disease. LTCI companies recognized that it was less expensive to pay for some training for an informal caregiver than having the claimant go to a nursing facility.

The insurers that provide a **caregiver training benefit** typically limit the amount payable. This limit is a function of the daily maximum—a caregiver training benefit that pays expenses up to three or five times the nursing home daily benefit amount is typical. For example, if someone has a $150-per-day nursing home benefit, the policy might pay up to $450 or $750 for training an informal caregiver. This is normally a one-time policy maximum, unlike the respite care or bed reservation benefits, which generally renew annually.

Equipment or Home Modification

Some policies cover the costs of making minor home modifications (such as adding grab rails in the tub) or the cost of equipment (like an in-home electronic alert system or a wheelchair). Insurers find that the equipment cost or the cost of modifying the home is often less than the cost of receiving care in a nursing home. The **equipment or home modification benefit** is much like the caregiver training benefit. It is usually a function of the daily benefit and has a one-time policy maximum. For example, some policies pay expenses for equipment and home modification up to 30 times the nursing home daily benefit. For a $150/day policy, this would provide $4,500 for equipment and modification.

Providing these types of benefits was quite difficult with the policy maximum that counted days but much easier with the pool of money approach. A dollar-amount credit is made against the policy maximum for the actual amount paid each time the benefit is paid.

» Restoration of Benefits

Some companies offer a **restoration of benefits** feature, either as a standard policy provision or as a rider for an additional charge. This provision essentially "re-charges" or restores any of the policy maximum that has been used if an insured does not receive benefits for a specified amount of time.

Typically, the policy maximum is restored in full if the claimant recovers fully and no longer requires care for at least 180 days. Given the infrequency of this occurring, giving back the already used portion of the policy maximum is an inexpensive feature for the insurer. Another reason that this feature is unlikely to have much of an impact on the cost of coverage is that, since the likelihood of recovery is greatly diminished as the length of the disability increases, the amount of benefits used at the time the policy maximum is restored is generally very small.

However, companies were concerned that claimants would abuse this benefit. For example, an insured could use two-and-a-half years of their three-year maximum, then go off claim and have their children care for them for six months (thus satisfying the restoration of benefits requirement), and then go back on claim with a fully restored policy maximum. However, it was found that the risk of abuse was minimal, given the hardship that providing full-time care represented for family members and the high levels of stress involved in moving a loved one from a care facility back home, then returning them to the facility (or a different facility). Still, some companies address this risk by requiring that the insured fully recover (that is, no longer meet the definition of "chronically ill") and not require any long-term care (including family care) for 180 days in order for the benefits to be restored.

Unfortunately, a few agents misrepresent the restoration of benefit feature to consumers. They portray it as a way to obtain "lifetime" coverage while buying only a more limited plan (such as a policy with a three-year policy maximum). They claim that the insured can easily restore their lifetime maximum by not needing or receiving care for the specified time, but they neglect to explain that the likelihood of this happening is extremely small.

Because it is a benefit of minimal value and because there is the potential for agents to misrepresent or for consumers to misunderstand this benefit, fewer companies today offer a restoration of benefits feature. Some companies offer it as an option, with an additional premium.

FOCUS QUESTION 3

Describe the restoration of benefits feature and how it can be abused by consumers and by agents.

_____

_____

_____

_____

_____

_____

_____

_____

_____

» Summary

The policy maximum of LTCI policies has evolved, as long-term care insurance has become more consumer-friendly. The simple design of counting days of care served the long-term care insurance industry during its beginnings, until home care and the reimbursement model became more common. These innovations brought about the need for the pool of money approach.

The pool of money design has stood the test of time. It represents an equitable method of accounting for the benefits paid against the policy maximum.

On the other hand, when someone selects the unlimited policy maximum, the information in this chapter does not apply. Claimants can continue to receive benefits as long as they still qualify for benefits by exhibiting a chronic illness and receiving services.

Key Terms 🔑		
Bed reservation benefit (BRB)	Policy maximum
Caregiver training benefit	Pool of money
Equipment or home modification benefit	Respite care
	Restoration of benefits
Lifetime maximum	Unlimited maximum
Lifetime policy	

» Review Questions

1. Define "policy maximum."

2. What is the minimum length of time benefits can be paid by a long-term care insurance policy as mandated by the NAIC? What is the maximum?

3. What alternative method was devised when the "counting days" approach became inadequate?

4. What are some of the services or benefits that are commonly restricted to individual minimums in long-term care insurance policies?

5. What is the purpose of respite care?

6. Why has the bed reservation benefit expanded over the years from one week to as much as three or four weeks?

7. Why do insurers disburse funds to train informal caregivers?

8. What is an equipment or home modification benefit?

9. What changed in the insurance industry's methodology to enable insurers to offer the equipment or home modification benefit?

10. Given current trends, who is more likely to abuse the restoration of benefits feature—a consumer or an agent?

» Answers

1. The maximum amount of benefits payable to the insured over the life of the contract.

2. The minimum benefit is one year. The maximum is not defined; if they choose to, insurers can offer care as long as it's needed.

3. The pool of money approach.

4. The respite care benefit, bed reservation benefit, caregiver training benefit, and equipment or home modification benefit.

5. To allow informal caregivers to take a break.

6. Insurers, initially concerned about fraud and abuse, now see that this is not really a concern with regard to this benefit and look more favorably upon longer absences from the care facility.

7. It has been shown that providing informal caregivers with some basic training is more cost-effective than covering the expense incurred at a nursing home for the same kind of caregiving activity or function.

8. This benefit covers modifications to the insured's home and/or the purchase and installation of equipment. The resulting improvements assist the insured and reduce the need for more expensive nursing home care.

9. In calculating the policy maximum, the industry moved from counting days to the pool of money approach.

10. An unscrupulous agent.

10

Other Policy Provisions

» Overview

All standard forms of insurance are unilateral contracts. Consumers have a choice of accepting the contract as written or not. Consumers do not negotiate premiums and policy provisions. That negotiation occurs between the state insurance department and the insurance company. Companies are allowed to include clauses that are important to protect the risk they bear, while the states require inclusion of language consistent with consumer needs.

On the other hand, consumers have the ultimate decision-making capability when it comes to all forms of insurance. They are the ones who make the decision whether to purchase the coverage or not. They vote with their checkbook on whether they are willing to accept the terms and conditions set forth by the insurer.

In the insurers' search for a complete policy that meets state approval and protects the large number of people they have insured, additional contract language is required. These clauses do not fit neatly into any of the categories of the previous chapters, so they are covered here.

» Renewal Provisions

One such clause concerns the **renewability** of the insurance contract. The renewal provisions describe how insureds may keep their policies in force.

Conditionally Renewable

Given the extreme level of risk and uncertainty insurers faced with the original LTCI policies, they felt forced to enter the market with renewal language that protected themselves more than it protected the consumer. Therefore, the early policies were **conditionally renewable**. This is the type of renewal provision used by most automobile insurers—they can cancel a single individual's policy at any time for any reason, including excessive claim history. But with health insurance, insurers are not permitted to cancel a single individual's policy—cancellation must occur on a **class of insureds**.

A class of insureds is defined any way the insurer decides, but it cannot single out an individual insured. A class can include anyone who:

- is of a certain age (for example, over age 75),

- owns a certain policy form (such as a nursing-home-only policy),

- has the same coverage choices within the policy form (for example, a 20-day elimination period),

- resides in a particular state (such as all insureds in Iowa),

- has a specific policy issue date (for example, issued prior to 1996), or

- meets any other criteria the insurer deems appropriate given its experience.

FOCUS QUESTION 1

Give examples of groups of individuals who can be treated as a class of insureds by insurance companies.

_____

_____

_____

_____

_____

_____

Under the conditional renewal model, an insurer could not change the language of an insured's policy after the policy was issued, but it could terminate the policy. This approach afforded the insurer the protection it needed when entering a completely unknown line of business. However, there was little protection for the insured, only that the insurer needed to gain the approval of the insured to alter policy provisions. Essentially, the only assurance consumers had that the policy would remain in force was their trust in the company issuing the policy.

Although most of the early long-term care insurers started in the business with the conditionally renewable clause, there is no record of a company using the provision to cancel a group of policies. Before companies resorted to that extreme, they would either adjust premiums or transfer ownership of the block of business. There is a history of companies using these alternatives.

With the conditionally renewable clause, revising premiums was a viable option. Premiums are not guaranteed, so companies could raise or lower premiums depending on their claims experience. The premium adjustments were made on a class basis across insureds as defined by the insurer, using the same options listed above. There is a history of companies both raising and lowering premiums.

Given the limited peace of mind the conditionally renewable clause provided the insured, there was little acceptance of this type of contract on the part of consumers. They feared that someone could pay premiums for many years and then have the insurer cancel the policy just as they were approaching the need for long-term care services. If that happened, there would be no way for insureds to get their money back or receive any benefits. Regulators recognized this consumer concern. Finally, states began to pass regulations that prohibited conditionally renewable long-term care insurance. This trend was eventually reflected in the NAIC Model Regulation, which allows only the following forms of renewability— guaranteed renewable and noncancelable.

Guaranteed Renewable

Guaranteed renewable is the type of renewability most companies use. In this model, the company cannot cancel a policy for any reason other than nonpayment of premium. (The policy may also terminate when the insured has received the maximum allowable benefits under the policy, but this is not considered cancellation.) In other words, the insurer is guaranteeing to renew the policy every year as long as the premium is paid. In addition, the insurer cannot change any policy provision that raises rates or reduces benefits without the permission of the insured. This level of renewability is the minimum standard of the NAIC Model, HIPAA, and state regulations.

The guaranteed renewable provision does allow companies to adjust premiums in the future if this is warranted based on claims experience. Insurers feel strongly about maintaining this part of the renewability clause. This enables the insurer to share the risk regarding service utilization with the group of insureds.

The challenge in raising premiums on existing insureds is that insureds may find their new premium unacceptably high and let their policy lapse by not paying the new premium. A **rate spiral** can occur following a rate increase. As more healthy individuals leave the risk pool (the group of insureds), fewer people are paying premiums in proportion to the people making claims. This can cause the insurer to need another rate increase because premiums collected are insufficient to meet claims. This next rate increase causes more healthy people to leave the risk pool and an even greater shortage of premiums collected. As this pattern continues, premiums spiral upwards without an end in sight. This is a rare occurrence in the LTCI business, but regulators are concerned about the possibility of this happening, given the relative newness of the product, and they have taken steps to minimize it.

When there is a premium increase, many companies give insureds the right to receive decreased coverage for the same premium instead of paying an increased premium. This is an important feature that gives consumers another choice when rates increase, rather than simply having to pay more or drop their coverage altogether.

Noncancelable

A **noncancelable** policy offers the highest level of protection for the insured—neither the premium nor the contract can change. The insurer assumes all the risk that the assumptions used in projecting experience, including anticipated claim costs, will hold true. The policy is renewable every year at the same premium paid when the policy was originally issued, no matter what happens. The company does not have any way to obtain additional premiums from the insureds if its costs are higher than expected, nor can it cancel the policy except for nonpayment of premium or if insureds reach their maximum benefits allowed under the policy.

Years ago the term **level premiums** was used to describe the premium structure of guaranteed renewable LTCI policies. While the intent of this design was for premiums to remain the same, the insurer actually had a limited right to change them. Consumers who experienced a premium increase were confused, since they thought they had level premiums. The NAIC Model Regulation now has a requirement that many states have adopted regarding how premiums are described. A noncancelable policy is the only one that can use the term "level premiums." Language about the insurer's right to change premiums on a class basis is also required to help make consumers aware of this.

Consumers and regulators recognize that long-term care insurance has many unknowns that preclude the majority of insurers from providing noncancelable policies. For instance, there is limited history on utilization of services. One reason is that the service providers keep changing, and companies change their policies to accommodate these new providers. Also, there is limited data on an insured population—a group that is healthier than the general population. Finally, the motivation of the insured population is an unknown—are they more likely to access services because they have the additional funds to pay for care? Or are they less likely to utilize services because they have access to alternative, informal care support systems?

There are noncancelable policies for many forms of life insurance. The risk is better understood, and companies have extensive experience on which to base the pricing of these policies. In the past, many companies offered noncancelable disability income insurance. Unfortunately for them, the risks of this new model were unknown, and claim costs far exceeded expectations. Many of these companies sold their disability income business or stopped offering noncancelable policies.

Long-term care insurers are fully aware of this experience. There are a few companies experimenting with noncancelable long-term care insurance. But this is still the exception and not the rule. The unknowns listed above must become knowns, and the business must stabilize before this level of renewability is readily available on the market.

FOCUS QUESTION 2

Summarize the differences between noncancelable and guaranteed renewable policies.

_____

_____

_____

_____

_____

_____

_____

_____

» Limitations and Exclusions

The majority of the text of a long-term care insurance policy states what the insurance will cover. The limitations and exclusions describe what is not covered—they are what the insurer will not pay for.

Limitations and exclusions have been a concern since LTCI was first introduced. There have been some interesting experiments with exclusions over the years. At one time, some companies excluded mental impairments in such a way that excluded people with Alzheimer's disease—one of the primary reasons people need long-term care insurance. The differences between organic cognitive conditions like Alzheimer's disease (which is considered a legitimate long-term care need) and mental or nervous conditions like depression or schizophrenia (which are not long-term care issues) are now better understood.

The NAIC Model Regulation has a listing of permissible limitations and exclusions. In summary, these are:

- preexisting conditions;
- mental or nervous disorders of a non-organic nature (Alzheimer's disease must be covered);
- alcoholism and drug addiction;
- illness or treatment arising out of a war, armed forces service, participation in a crime, attempted suicide or self-inflicted injury, or non-fare-paying aviation;
- treatment when other payment methods are available or when there is normally no charge for the services;
- expenses for services payable under another insurance policy; and
- expenses reimbursable under Medicare.

Companies are not required to have all these exclusions in a policy. In fact, companies normally only include exclusions that they plan to use in their claim adjudication process. For instance, a company whose primary market is members of the military would not want to have the armed forces service exclusion.

The exclusions and limitations used by an insurer are considered "the fine print" of the insurance contract. Many years ago (before LTCI was even introduced), some companies would use much smaller fonts in their policies when describing what the company would not cover. Only at the time of claim did those who owned these policies realize what was not covered under the policy. Consumers and regulators did not appreciate this practice. Now regulations require companies to include the policy's limitations and exclusions in all marketing materials and disclosure forms such as the outline of coverage.

» Preexisting Conditions

Many consumers misunderstand the concept of **preexisting conditions**. The media have presented preexisting conditions as an evil, whereas they are simply a tool available to insurers to categorize their insureds and create like risk pools. The negative image may result from the use of the clause by some of the insurers who offered long-term care insurance when the product was in its infancy.

Post-Claim Underwriting and Regulation

A few of the LTCI pioneers regularly denied claims on the grounds that the insured had a condition when the policy was issued that would have precluded issuance of the policy had the insurer known about it at the time of application. Some of this was a result of the insurer not performing a complete review of the applicant's medical history at the time of application. This might have been because the insurer thought that the information was too difficult to obtain, or was too expensive to obtain on all applicants, or because the insurer unwisely trusted that the applicant had fully disclosed all health information on the application. These companies were able to issue policies within 72 hours of receipt of the application. When the insured filed a claim, the company would then seek all medical information in search of a condition that was present at the time of application that could be used to deny benefits. This practice—referred to as **post-claim underwriting**—is no longer an acceptable business practice in the long-term care insurance business.

The agents whose clients were subjected to this practice developed a poor reputation as a result of representing those companies. These agents told their clients that the insurance was in force, and the clients had peace of mind about their long-term care needs. But when they filed a claim, the frequent result was a denial of benefits or a rescission of the policy. Sometimes getting a refund of premium after the policy was rescinded would take months. As a result, agents stopped selling LTCI policies from companies that engaged in post-claim underwriting.

In addition, state regulators recognized the inappropriateness of this practice and worked to eliminate it. They started to scrutinize the applications companies used, in an effort to ensure that they were asking an adequate number of questions, including questions on prescription medications that were taken. Insurance departments began to require cautionary statements on the application and on the cover of the policy warning the applicant about the insurer's right to deny benefits or rescind a policy if there were incorrect or untrue answers on the application.

The NAIC Model Regulation includes a prohibition of post-claim underwriting. Companies are no longer able to use their own ignorance as a valid excuse to deny benefits when an insured files a claim after the insurer didn't ask for the medical information at the time of application. The NAIC Model implies that it is the insurer's responsibility to ask the applicant questions using the application. The purpose in asking is to obtain an adequate medical history to accurately assess the applicant's insurability based on the company's issuing guidelines.

For applicants over age 80, companies are required by the NAIC Model Regulation to go beyond the application to identify any preexisting conditions that are present at the time of application. The company must obtain a copy of a physical examination, an assessment of functional capacity, an attending physician's statement, or a copy of the applicant's medical records. Some states have lowered this age requirement.

The Model Regulation also addresses an applicant's use of prescription medications. A practice used by companies utilizing post-claim underwriting was not to investigate medications used by applicants or simply not ask about them. Regulations are now written to hold companies accountable for investigating why the applicant uses a medication listed on the application. If they fail to use this information when the application is submitted, the company cannot rescind the policy because of the condition for which a prescription is taken.

The applicant receives a copy of the application as it was submitted to the company. A copy is normally attached to the actual policy delivered to the insured. This policy will have cautionary language designed to focus the insured's attention on the application. If upon review of the application, the insured notices any omission or incorrect information, they are encouraged to contact the insurer for clarification. The insurer then makes a decision whether to further investigate the insured's medical history.

Rescission

An insurer has the right to contest a claim if it finds misstatements on the application during the first six months of coverage. The insurer's recourse includes **rescission** (annulment) of the policy or denial of the claim. Before taking such action, the company must prove the applicant misrepresented their medical history in such a way that was material to the issuance of the policy. For example, if someone did not disclose that they had a hip replacement just before applying for the policy, the company can cancel the coverage.

After the policy has been in force for at least six months but less than two years, the insurer must meet a higher standard of proof to contest a claim based on information found on the application. During this time, the company must prove not only that the condition left undisclosed on the application was material to the issuance of the policy, but that this condition is related to the reason the claim was filed. If the person in the example above with the undisclosed hip replacement filed a claim based not on the condition of their hip but rather on Alzheimer's disease, the company could not deny the claim or rescind the policy after it had been in force at least six months.

A third level of proof is required after the policy has been in force for two years. The company must now prove fraud—that is, that there was a deliberate intent to defraud the insurance company by misrepresenting the applicant's medical history in order to obtain insurance coverage. Fraudulent misstatements are difficult for the insurer to prove and can frequently involve legal interpretations of the medical records and the application by attorneys representing both sides of the issue. Continuing the example above with the person filing a claim based on Alzheimer's disease, the company would have to prove that this condition existed, the insured knew it existed at the time of application, and the insured had the specific intent of defrauding the insurer by applying for coverage.

FIGURE 10.1

The Different Levels of Proof Required to Rescind an LTCI Policy

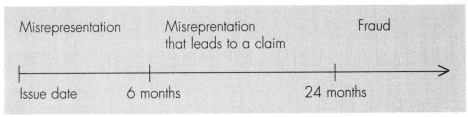

Explain how the burden of proof intensifies for rescission over the course of a long-term care insurance policy.

_____

_____

_____

_____

_____

_____

_____

_____

_____

All companies have similar rescission rights in their policies. When providing a replacement policy, companies are held accountable for the previous company's legal rights to use preexisting conditions or any other probationary periods. When a claim is submitted on the replacing policy, the new company must take into consideration the length of time the original policy was in force and the preexisting condition clauses contained in that policy. If six months have elapsed since issuance of the old policy, the new company must prove that the misrepresentation is related to the cause of the claim. After the old policy has been in force for two years, the new company must prove fraud in applying for the new policy.

Proving misrepresentation or fraud is difficult because of the variables involved in recording medical information during the application process. It is possible that the physician did not tell the applicant what was wrong, so the applicant could not provide the information. In some cases the applicant tells the agent taking the application about a condition or treatment, but the agent does not feel that the condition is significant enough to record it on the application. What must be proved to establish misrepresentation or fraud is that the applicant deliberately withheld their medical history from the company so that they would receive a policy from the company.

Some companies are more specific about how they treat an insured's preexisting conditions, and include a statement on the cover of the policy regarding preexisting conditions. The most common preexisting condition clause excludes benefits for six months after the policy is issued for any condition that existed six months prior to the issuance of the policy. As an example, when someone submits a claim three months after their policy is issued because of complications stemming from hip replacement surgery completed five months before the policy was issued, the claim is denied. Some preexisting condition exclusions will exclude benefits only for the first six months—that is, in the seventh month the insurer would begin to pay the claim. Other carriers take a more limited approach and deny any claim that begins within the first six months of coverage if it results from a preexisting condition.

Increasingly, many insurers are removing any preexisting condition exclusions and limitations from their policies, preferring instead to place an emphasis on clear and thorough underwriting at the time of application.

» The Right to Return

The early long-term care insurance policies were primitive by today's standards. There were many unknowns and ambiguities in the policy language. This was cause for concern by some new insureds. They wanted to scrutinize the policy before deciding whether to keep it or return it to the issuing company. They wanted a refund of all premiums paid if they decided to not keep the policy. Insurers wanted to limit the time for them to review the policy. An agreement was reached early on in the evolution of LTCI.

Long-term care insurance has an escape clause for the insured. This is referred to as the **right to return** or the **free look provision**. If a new insured has any doubt about whether their new coverage is right for them, they have the right to return the policy to the company within 30 days for a full refund.

The 30-day clock begins running when the policy is delivered to the insured. This is either when the agent physically delivers the policy or when the policy is mailed by the company to the insured. HIPAA has a limit on how long it can take to initiate delivery of a policy to the insured—this can be no longer than 30 days after the date of approval. This provision is designed to protect both the insurer and insured. The insured gets their policy in a timely manner, and the insurer knows in a timely manner whether the insured will actually keep the policy.

» Provisions Related to Lapse

The Premium Grace Period

Regulators and consumers expressed concern over a policy lapsing because of nonpayment of premium when the insured actually intended to keep the policy in force. This could occur when an insured maintained two residences and the premium notice was sent to the wrong residence or didn't get properly forwarded. Many insureds are retired, and some are blessed with travel opportunities—sometimes for extended periods of time. The premium notice might come while they are gone, and the policy would lapse before they returned home to make the premium payment. Sometimes a surviving spouse is not as proficient at paying bills as their recently deceased loved one, and the premium does not get paid on time. There are times when an automatic withdrawal from a checking account is returned to the insurer because there is not enough money in the account to pay the premium or the insured has changed accounts. Some people in the early stages of dementia are not timely in paying their bills and lose their long-term care insurance bills along with those for their telephone, natural gas, or electrical service. Or the insured might be in a care situation and unable to pay attention to the fact that the next premium payment has come due.

FOCUS QUESTION 4

Summarize possible reasons why the payment of insurance premiums may unintentionally be delayed.

_____

_____

_____

_____

_____

_____

_____

_____

_____

There are many other circumstances in which a policy unintentionally lapses because the premium is not paid on time. For this reason, all insurance policies have a **premium grace period**—a length of time after the premium due date during which the coverage remains in force although payment has not been received. The policy lapses—the insured no longer has access to the policy benefits—when the premium is not received by the end of the grace period. The grace period lasts at least 30 days.

After a policy lapses, a company's normal procedure is to reinstate the policy if the insured wants the policy back in force. The insured will pay past due premiums (from the premium due date to the date of reinstatement). They may need to reapply for the coverage, including going through new underwriting. But they will get a policy that bases premiums on the insured's original issue age and has satisfied some time toward the contestable periods.

Third-Party Notification of Lapse

In an attempt to avoid situations in which a policy lapses and must be reinstated, insurers and regulators developed the **third-party notification of lapse** provision. This requires insurers to send a notice to another individual designated by the insured before a policy lapses or terminates. The NAIC Model Regulation includes this provision.

When applying for insurance, the applicant can designate someone else to receive a duplicate lapse notice. It is recommended that this person be a trusted friend, family member, or advisor—a next-door neighbor or frequent social contact, a son or daughter, or an attorney or trust officer. Some consider designating their spouse as the person to receive the notice. This may be inappropriate when they live at the same address. The designated person's full name and address (home or business) must be given to the insurance company.

It should be kept in mind that the person receiving the lapse notice is not liable for the premium. The idea is to alert someone that the LTCI policy of someone they know will lapse soon if premiums are not paid. This person should (but is not required to) contact the insured to find out why the premium has not been paid.

When the applicant or insured decides not to designate someone else to receive the notification of lapse, they must waive their right to do so. This is normally done with a check box next to a statement explaining the right. After the policy is issued, the insurance company offers the insured an opportunity to change the designation no less frequently than every two years. Most companies allow an insured to make such designation at any time; it is just that they must be proactive about it at least every two years.

As explained above, a policy goes into a grace period the day after the premium due date if the insurer does not receive the premium. This grace period lasts for a minimum of 30 days. If no third party is designated to receive the lapse notice, the policy will lapse at the end of this grace period. However, the third-party notification of lapse can extend the normal grace period, because the policy cannot lapse until 30 days after the notice is sent to the third party.

However, this does not mean that a policy with a third-party notification of lapse must necessarily have a 60-day grace period. An insurer does not have to wait until the end of the initial 30-day grace period to send the notice to the third party. It can send the third-party notice as early as the premium due date. However, if it does so, it will have to send many more such notices, resulting both in higher costs and the "boy who cried wolf" syndrome. On the other hand, if the third-party notice is sent at the end of the initial 30-day grace period, the grace period is in effect doubled to 60 days, which an insurer may consider too long. Many companies compromise by sending the third party notification 15 days after the premium due date. This creates a 45-day grace period that is adequate for most people.

Lapse Due to Impairment

If an insured unintentionally lets their LTCI policy lapse because they suffer from a cognitive or physical impairment, it is not likely they will pass the underwriting standards required for reinstatement. Long-term care insurers have a special provision that allows some insureds to reinstate the policy without going through underwriting, if it is demonstrated that their unintentional lapse was due to a cognitive or functional loss.

When the insured is able to show that they suffered a cognitive impairment or loss of functional capacity during the policy's grace period, the insurer will reinstate the policy. The standards for impairment are the same as those for benefit eligibility. The insured has up to five months (insurers can extend this time period) after the end of the grace period (normally this equals six months from the premium due date) in order to make a request for reinstatement. Past due premiums are paid prior to the reinstatement or are deducted from the claim payment.

This clause is designed to protect those who missed a premium payment when they could have actually qualified for benefits. People in the early stages of dementia who begin to lose their proficiency in paying their bills on time are the most susceptible to this occurring. This problem is frequently identified when the person helping the insured file a claim is dumbfounded to learn benefits are denied because the policy has lapsed because of nonpayment of premium. Insurers and regulators recognized the appropriateness of reinstating policies in these situations and made it standard language of all LTCI policies. It is also part of the NAIC Model Regulation.

FOCUS QUESTION 5

Explain why it may make sense to reinstate a long-term care policy if the policy has lapsed because of nonpayment of premiums during a period in which the insured suffered a cognitive impairment or loss of functional capacity.

_____

_____

_____

_____

_____

_____

_____

» Nonforfeiture Benefit

A concern some people have when their policy lapses is that they "don't get anything back" after having paid premiums. They could pay premiums for many years, then get into financial difficulty and find their LTCI policy unaffordable. Or the insurer could raise premiums to an unaffordable level. Or the insured may just decide that they no longer want or need coverage for whatever reason. In any event, some insureds want some sort of financial compensation when they need or choose to let their policy lapse. A **nonforfeiture** value is created when the insured gets something back—these are values they do not give up, or "forfeit," when giving up their policy.

So that the premiums of an LTCI policy can remain the same as people age, insurers charge more than the actual risk would dictate in the early policy years. The insurer holds these "extra" premiums in reserves. The reserves build over time with both premium payments and investment returns. Although there are not reserves that are identified for a single policy, the insurer uses reserves to subsidize the premiums of individual policies in their later years. When a policy lapses, the reserves stay with the insurer and are used to keep other insureds' premiums level.

Some insureds felt they should have access to those reserves. With permanent life insurance, the premiums are level (using essentially the same concept of paying extra in the early years so that premiums are more affordable in the later years) and cash values are available upon lapse. These people wanted the same type of options available to them through their LTCI policy. However, to do so would increase premiums significantly.

HIPAA put a stop to any notion of cash values and certain other types of nonforfeiture values in a qualified long-term care insurance policy. Cash surrender values are specifically excluded from a qualified policy. The values generated in a qualified policy are not available for payment or assignment, or to be pledged as collateral for a loan. An insured cannot borrow from the values. Dividends are payable only to increase benefits available or decrease future premiums. Cash is payable only when the insured dies or surrenders the policy. Then the amount returned upon complete surrender cannot exceed the amount of premiums paid. Any refund received when the policy is surrendered is countable as taxable income to the extent the premiums paid were deductible. Thus, an alternative to life insurance-like cash value is required for a qualified policy.

Even discussing nonforfeiture values was new for an accident and health insurance policy. This type of policy had historically stayed away from having values available upon lapse. Because it costs extra to get something back from one's insurance, people have not looked for that type of benefit in their health insurance. In fact, most people have wanted the lowest premium possible for their accident and health insurance policies. But most accident and health insurance use attained age rather than issue age in determining the appropriate premium.

With encouragement from regulators and consumers in the early 1990s, a group of actuaries set out to design a nonforfeiture value that made the most sense for long-term care insurance.[1] The same options available in permanent life insurance were tested for application to LTCI. This group considered the following:

- cash surrender value,
- return of premium,
- reduced paid-up,
- extended term insurance,
- shortened benefit period,
- all of the above except return of premium in a combined rider, and
- a hybrid using cash surrender value to purchase a reduced paid-up.

The option that emerged as the most equitable was the **shortened benefit period**. Companies now make this available as an optional rider. This benefit is part of the NAIC Model Regulation and is a required option in most states.

The Shortened Benefit Period

In designing the shortened benefit period option for LTCI, one consideration insurers and regulators wrestled with was how many years premiums should be paid before benefits would be available under this rider. A short period would cause the price to go up, as many people would qualify for benefits. A long period would do the opposite—the price would be low because lapses tend to decrease the longer a policy is in force. Three years seemed adequate before any values were available.

The daily benefit amount payable under continued coverage was also a concern to regulators and insurers. It was determined that the daily benefit amount would be the amount that was payable when the policy lapsed, even if the policy had a form of inflation protection. The cost of the nonforfeiture rider would be too great if the daily benefits continued to escalate after lapse. Including an inflation purchase option in the lapsed policy made no sense because the insured had already made a decision that they did not want the policy or it was unaffordable when they stopped paying the premium.

Next, the length of the shortened benefit period was considered. Using a percentage of the policy maximum made some sense, but this was hard to calculate and then explain to an insured. Given consumers' expressed concern over getting something back for the premiums paid, it was determined that the total amount payable during a subsequent claim should equal the premiums paid. The length of time benefits were payable would equal the daily amount payable divided by the total premiums paid. These benefits were meaningless unless a minimum length of time was required. The NAIC Model Regulation defines this minimum as 30 days.

For example, an insured allows their policy to lapse after paying an annual premium of $1,000 for seven years. If the daily benefit at lapse was $125 per day, nonforfeiture benefit value is the greater of the following: the premiums paid to date ($7,000) or the daily benefit times 30 ($3,750). Therefore, in this example, the maximum benefit amount available to the insured after their policy lapses is $7,000, payable for expenses up to $125 per day.

Yet another consideration was how an insured would access benefits with the shortened benefit period. The consensus was that the benefit qualification criteria would remain the same and the elimination period would still need to be satisfied before the insurance company paid the claim. This design was the easiest to understand and would not add to the cost of the rider. People who had this rider would not lapse their policy to get more lenient qualification criteria, thus causing adverse selection at claim time. It was the most efficient way to administer the policy and was simple for regulators to enforce.

FOCUS QUESTION 6

Summarize the considerations involved in trying to determine the appropriate payment under the shortened benefit period.

_____

_____

_____

_____

_____

_____

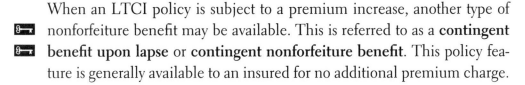

Contingent Nonforfeiture Benefit

When an LTCI policy is subject to a premium increase, another type of nonforfeiture benefit may be available. This is referred to as a **contingent benefit upon lapse** or **contingent nonforfeiture benefit**. This policy feature is generally available to an insured for no additional premium charge.

The contingency that causes the availability of this nonforfeiture benefit is a substantial rate increase. The amount of increase that comes under the definition of "substantial" varies by age and is defined in the NAIC Model Regulation. (See Table 2.1 on page 25.)

The contingent benefit upon lapse is available to insureds who do not have the shortened benefit period nonforfeiture option added to their policy. This makes sense because the people with this other option can elect to lapse their policy at any time to receive the shortened benefit period without premiums being due again.

An insurer must make the offer of the contingent nonforfeiture benefit whenever it raises rates by a percentage that exceeds those in Table 2.1. Companies need not include this language in their policies because of the complexity of the rider and the number of pages it would add to a policy, although some have chosen to do so. Rather, companies and most state insurance departments that have adopted this provision from the NAIC Model Regulation have agreed to administer policies issued after the inclusion of this regulation as if it were a part of the policy. If the insurer were to ever file for a rate increase or series of rate increases that triggered the definition of substantial, the state insurance department would then require them to make the contingent nonforfeiture benefit offer. Note that the contingent nonforfeiture benefit upon lapse was developed in the late 1990s and may not apply to older policies.

» Survivorship

A new optional policy provision has emerged that provides a benefit to a surviving spouse when their loved one's policy lapses because of death. Many companies refer to this as a **survivorship benefit** and offer it as an optional rider when both husband and wife own a policy.

The companies offering this option use a computer code to link the husband and wife's policies together or simply issue a single policy covering both people. When one spouse dies after paying premiums for a certain period of time, the spouse still living no longer has premiums due. Specifics on how this works vary from company to company.

One variable is how the company handles the nonpayment of premiums. If it simply waives the premiums of the surviving spouse's policy, it may be in violation of HIPAA, which considers this a benefit and requires that benefits be paid only to the chronically ill. A safer way to ensure that the policy remains tax-qualified is to consider the policy paid up and premiums no longer due. Both approaches accomplish the same thing, but technically they are different.

Another variable is the number of years the policy must be in force prior to death. Companies normally choose somewhere between five and 10 years. A consideration in counting these years is whether the lapsed policy was in premium-paying status the entire time. Excluding the time the waiver of premium was in effect is an alternative companies can choose. Another alternative is to consider only the length of time the surviving spouse's policy was in force. That is, rather than counting the number of years the deceased's policy had premium payments, a company can count the length of time the survivor's policy has been in force. This method does not penalize the widow or widower who lost their spouse soon after the policies were issued.

» Summary

The provisions discussed in this chapter are important features of a long-term care insurance policy. Furthermore, each provision has evolved since the beginnings of the LTCI business to provide a balance between the consumer's need for meaningful coverage and the insurer's ability to create a block of business that will endure for many years.

Consumers now have the assurance that a company will not cancel a long-term care insurance policy, and insurers maintain the ability to adjust premiums so they can continue offering this form of insurance. Consumers also have the assurance that if they answer the questions on the insurance application thoroughly and honestly, the insurer cannot contest their claim based on their prior health. And insureds can return their policy for a full refund of premium within 30 days of receiving the contract if they don't think it is right for them.

There are protections built into each policy to minimize the potential for lapse. If an insured allows a policy to lapse because of a chronic illness, the insured can reinstate it within a period of time without having to again qualify for the coverage based on the insurer's underwriting standards. If the policy lapses because the insured could not afford a significant increase in premiums, they will have some coverage without having to pay premiums again, through the contingent nonforfeiture benefit.

Key Terms 🔑

Class of insureds	Post-claim underwriting
Conditionally renewable	Preexisting condition
Contingent benefit upon lapse	Premium grace period
Contingent nonforfeiture benefit	Rate spiral
	Renewability
Free look provision	Rescission
Guaranteed renewable	Right to return
Level premiums	Shortened benefit period
Noncancelable	Survivorship benefit
Nonforfeiture	Third-party notification of lapse

» Review Questions

1. What early form of long-term care insurance offered the insurer a safe way out while leaving the consumer without protection?

2. Can an insurer cancel the health insurance coverage of a single individual today?

3. In terms of renewability, name the two kinds of policy that replaced conditionally renewable coverage. Which one is more common?

4. What is the name for the portion of the policy that sets forth what will not be covered?

5. What is the term used for the annulment of a policy?

6. What is the provision included in policies that ensures consumers will have adequate time to inspect their policy and return it within a specified period for a full refund if they're not satisfied? What is the length of the evaluation period?

7. What are the measures in place that are designed to prevent the lapse of a long-term care insurance policy because of nonpayment of premiums?

8. Name the benefit that came into play because insureds wanted to see some financial benefit if they allowed their LTCI policy to lapse after years of paying premiums.

9. What are the two kinds of nonforfeiture benefit that emerged?

10. Define "survivorship benefit."

» Answers

1. Conditionally renewable coverage.

2. Barring nonpayment of premium, no.

3. The two kinds are guaranteed renewable and noncancelable; the former is more common.

4. Limitations and exclusions.

5. Rescission.

6. This is called the right to return or the free look provision. The insured needs to evaluate and return the policy within 30 days to qualify for a full refund.

7. Insurers usually offer grace periods of a minimum of 30 days. During this time the policy stays in effect even if the premium remains unpaid. A designated third party may also be notified in the event of premium nonpayment so that necessary steps can be taken to remedy the situation.

8. The nonforfeiture benefit.

9. The shortened benefit period nonforfeiture option and the contingent nonforfeiture benefit.

10. This is a benefit paid by an insurer to a surviving spouse when that person's loved one's policy has lapsed because of death.

NOTE

1 Details are contained in the Final Report to the National Association of Insurance Commissioners' Long-Term Care Insurance Task Force from the National Association of Insurance Commissioners' Long-Term Care Insurance Nonforfeiture Benefits Ad Hoc Actuarial Group, June 2, 1992.

11

Calculating the Premium

» Overview

Premiums are calculated based on the age of the insured and the coverage choices made by the insured when they apply for the policy. The coverage choices that affect the premium cost, listed below, were discussed in detail in earlier chapters:

- what services and providers are covered,
- when benefits begin (the elimination period),
- how much is paid in benefits (the daily or monthly benefit amount and inflation protection),
- how long benefits are paid (the policy maximum), and
- any ancillary options.

This chapter explores how each of these coverage factors affects rates and premiums.

Actuaries have a different perspective from that of agents and consumers on the development of rates and premiums. They develop the formula that is used to create the rates that are then used to make the premium calculation. There are many factors that actuaries consider in developing rates. Rates are typically the unit cost for a given benefit, and the calculation of premiums consists of the application of those rates after factoring in the number of units selected and making other adjustments for optional benefits or features chosen. The units for long-term care insurance are the initial daily benefit amounts chosen. These are usually expressed in one-, five-, or ten-dollar increments. Companies file rates with state insurance departments. The rates are then used by an agent to determine the premium a consumer will pay for the coverage they select.

The rate formula developed by an insurer's actuarial department is based on many assumptions that the consumer and agent might never see. The actuary uses, at a minimum, assumptions about each of the following criteria in the development of the rates for each long-term care policy issued by the company:

- morbidity,
- mortality,
- field compensation schedules,
- amount put in reserves,
- interest rate earned on the reserves,
- persistency or lapse rate,
- home office expenses (see below),
- expected product mix,
- expected demographic mix of buyers,
- underwriting criteria used,
- claims philosophy,
- duration of claims, and
- other criteria.

FOCUS QUESTION 1

List five actuarial criteria used in rate determination.

_____

_____

_____

_____

_____

Home office expenses include:

- general overhead,
- underwriting,
- marketing,
- claims,
- billing and collection,
- system maintenance, and
- administration.

Some of these items are discussed in this chapter, mostly in a high-level overview when discussing the relationship among the choices the consumer makes. The technical aspects, the mathematical formula, and the specific impact of each criterion on the rate calculation formula are best left for an actuarial text.

» When Benefits Begin

When benefits begin is based on the specific services covered under the policy and the elimination period that is selected.

Covered Services

Generally, the more services covered under a policy, the more expensive the policy. A comprehensive policy generally covers both facility-based care and care at home. It is the most expensive type of policy because it covers and pays benefits for the entire continuum of long-term care services. A more limited type of policy would be one that covers only facility care or a home-care-only policy that doesn't provide any benefits for facility care. Depending on whether it is a nursing facility or home-care-only policy, a limited provider policy will either start or stop paying benefits when a claimant switches from a community-based provider to a facility-based one. This design limits the type of expenses for which the insurance company will have to pay benefits. There are some situations in which a more limited benefit policy could result in higher costs for the insurer. (For example, if someone only has nursing home coverage, they might be forced to receive care in that more costly care setting, even though their needs might be better met with care at home.) In general, however, limited benefit policies are less costly for the insurer because there will be situations in which the insured requires care but does not receive benefits because the service setting in which they are receiving care is not covered under their policy.

A continuing issue in the LTCI field is what to do with old nursing-home-only policies. These were generally purchased before assisted living communities became popular in the mid-1990s. Some consumers and regulators would like to see insurers add coverage for assisted living to these policies. Companies argue that this would have to be accompanied by an increase in the premium paid by the insured because of the expanded coverage. They claim that the frequency and duration of claims would likely increase beyond what was originally intended with these policies. (Furthermore, many of these policies are grandfathered under HIPAA and thus receive the same tax benefits as a qualified policy. If changes are made to these older policies, the insureds could lose the favorable tax status they now enjoy.)

There is some debate within the industry about whether expanding the service settings and provider types that are covered might not actually decrease claim costs because less costly care providers would be available to the insured. For example, if a policy covered both nursing home care and assisted living, the insured would likely prefer the less restrictive and less costly setting. Since many policies have a lifetime dollar limit, there is a built-in incentive for insureds to conserve their coverage and receive care in less costly settings or from lower-cost providers if those types of choices are included in their policy.

On the other side of the debate are those who argue that coverage is used to the maximum extent it is available, and that the more provider choices that are covered, the more opportunity there is to incur claim expenses. There is also some concern that provider charges might rise to reflect the availability of insurance benefits once a provider realizes that an individual was privately insured—a payment option that is typically more generous to providers than are other funding sources for long-term care.

The Elimination Period

Companies normally offer consumers a range of choices with respect to the elimination period. Choices may include some or all of the following: 0, 30, 45, 60, 90, 100, 180, or 365 days. Some companies also let the consumer choose the type of elimination period they prefer—one that counts days on which the insured receives a covered service, or one that counts days on which they are disabled, regardless of whether they received long-term care services on that day. This provides consumer choice, which in turn broadens the market for potential purchasers of the company's LTCI product.

A shorter elimination period means that the amount the insurer will pay for claims is higher, since the care costs for which the insured is responsible are limited to a smaller number of days. The likelihood of claims may also be increased with the shorter elimination period, since there is less out-of-pocket cost to the insured during the initial days of the claim, possibly making them more willing to receive paid care where they might otherwise have sought out informal or other care options. Also, since premiums are typically waived once an insured begins to receive covered benefits, a shorter elimination period increases premium costs simply because the premium waiver begins sooner than it would with a longer elimination period. This leads to fewer premium dollars collected and invested in reserves.

There are certain fixed expenses associated with any claim once it is submitted. Someone at the home office needs to manage the claim, a licensed health care practitioner must determine eligibility for benefits, and there are systems costs such as loading the claim in the system, generating letters, and even the first-class postage necessary for mailing these letters. Some of these expenses can be delayed with the longer elimination periods, and there is also the potential that they won't be needed if the insured recovers and no longer requires care prior to satisfying the elimination period. Typically, with a short elimination period, all the fixed costs are added as soon as the claim is filed, regardless of the claimant's life expectancy or the potential duration of the claim. Therefore, the load in the rates for administrative expenses is less with the longer elimination periods.

The utilization data considered when determining rates indicate that the longer someone needs care, the longer they will continue to need it. In other words, a claim is likely to last longer when someone has a 180-day elimination period than when they choose a 20-day period. This means that with a longer elimination period, the fixed costs for managing a claim can be spread across a longer claim.

With a federally tax-qualified policy, there must be an expectation that the claimant will have the impairment and the need for services for at least 90 days. This has had a positive effect on the rates charged for the shorter elimination periods because it is now understood that any claim is likely to entail more than just a quick recovery in a nursing home. For some of the very short stays, the cost of assessing the impairment, establishing the claim file, and maintaining records could actually exceed the dollar amount of the benefits paid. This short-term care is often more of an inconvenience for the insured than a financial drain on personal assets. Furthermore, the fact that Medicare is the primary payer for some of these short stays (under certain circumstances) and that the LTCI policy is the secondary payer takes away much of the inconvenience and consumer expense factors. Medicare coordination and the requirement that the insured won't qualify for benefits unless care needs are expected to exceed 90 days have slightly reduced the cost load companies need to impose on a shorter elimination period. This has provided some additional stability to the premiums for shorter elimination periods.

Some companies have found that working with the claimant early in the claim cycle allows them to reduce claim costs sufficiently to waive the need to satisfy the elimination period. The company may have a trained licensed health care practitioner conduct an assessment to certify that the claimant is chronically ill, develop the plan of care, and help implement the plan by actually scheduling formal and informal providers to deliver services. These people may also look for funding alternatives (such as Medicare) where the insured is eligible for them. The feeling is that this approach results both in better care for the claimant and lower actual charges and lower benefit payments. These savings can offset the savings the company would realize by having the claimant pay for care during the elimination period.

In the past, some companies had separate elimination periods for different benefits, such as one elimination period that had to be satisfied in order to access nursing home benefits and another to be met prior to receiving home care benefits. An insured could select a short elimination period for home care and a longer one for facility-based care. This would lower the rate for the facility side of the policy and provide the quick access to benefits on the home care side. The days on which a home care benefit was paid would sometimes also count against the facility elimination period. Companies found this concept difficult to explain and administer, and the perceived savings were never realized. A single elimination period for all providers is now the norm in the LTCI industry. This also complements the trend toward having a single pool of benefits for all types of covered services, rather than separate benefit amounts for different types of services.

These are some of the factors that are taken into account when an insurer's actuary determines rates associated with the various elimination periods available with a policy. Generally, because of these factors, the shorter elimination periods seem to have a disproportional load in the rate when compared to the longer elimination periods. This is not unlike other insurance (such as automobile insurance), where the lower deductible options are much more expensive than the higher deductibles.

» How Much Is Paid in Benefits

The amount of benefits paid at the time of claim obviously affects the amount of the premium. Two factors are taken into consideration when determining how much money is paid in benefits: the initial daily benefit amount chosen and the inflation protection method chosen, if any.

The Daily Benefit Amount

The daily benefit amount is the basis on which premium rates are typically calculated. Companies choose whether to base the benefit amount on units in one-, five-, or 10-dollar increments. This means they are willing to issue coverage in those sizes of units. One company might issue a policy with a daily benefit of $157 per day; another would want that rounded to either $155 or $160 per day; still another would want the rounding to occur at either $150 or $160 per day.

The premium is then calculated by multiplying the number of units times the rate per unit. This is where the concept of the difference between rates and premiums makes the most sense.

The premium is usually proportional to the number of units, unless the company adds in a policy fee or has a different rate structure (unit cost) for very small benefit amounts. As more units are chosen, the amount of money paid will increase, but the rates usually do not change based on the number of units chosen by the consumer. This is because the number of units chosen should not affect the underlying assumptions the actuary uses to determine rates.

FOCUS QUESTION 2

Explain how premiums and rates are treated differently in calculations.

_____

_____

_____

_____

The difference between a reimbursement plan and one that pays indemnity benefits affects rates. Normally a reimbursement plan will have a lower premium rate per unit because the actual daily benefit paid is not expected to equal the daily maximum on each claim that is filed. The difference between the daily maximum and the actual charges that are reimbursed (sometimes called **salvage**) saves the company some expense in the amount of claim that is paid. Even if the difference is small for each claimant and each monthly claim they submit, it can add up to a significant amount of money for a large block of business. Granted, this "extra money" could eventually get paid out, but this does not happen until the policy maximum is reached, which is usually years later. So the savings in the early periods can be invested as part of the reserves for a longer period.

In contrast, indemnity plans pay the full daily benefit regardless of actual charges—there are no benefit savings for the insurer. However, some of the administrative costs are less with an indemnity plan. The skill level of the person managing indemnity claims can be lower because they are not required to assess provider billing statements or understand Medicare's reimbursement requirements and amounts. They only need to know on how many days care was received and the daily amount that is payable.

A reimbursement plan that does not have inflation protection is not likely to produce significant savings from the difference between actual charges and the daily maximum. This is because the actual charges increase over time with inflation while the daily maximum stays the same, until actual charges are greater that the daily benefit. Thus, a reimbursement plan without inflation protection will eventually function like an indemnity plan, with the full daily maximum being paid each day on which benefits are payable. (Choosing a very large daily benefit will delay this effect.)

FOCUS QUESTION 3

Explain why the absence of inflation protection makes a reimbursement plan eventually function like an indemnity plan.

_____

_____

_____

_____

_____

_____

_____

_____

Inflation Protection

The method the insured selects to increase the daily benefit over time to keep pace with inflation has a dramatic impact on the rates used to calculate the premium. This is due not only to the different designs but also to the persistency assumption used in developing the rates.

Persistency refers to the percentage of insureds who continue in premium paying status. Policies that lapse because of unpaid premiums (voluntary lapses) and death (involuntary lapses) reduce a company's persistency. This is so important because when more people continue paying premiums, there are more people who have the potential for filing a claim. In other words, the risk pool is larger, and the likelihood of filing a claim increases as the people in that risk pool age.

Lapse rates refer to the portion of insureds who lapse each year. Normally companies experience higher lapse rates in the first policy year for a myriad of reasons. One of the most common is "buyer's remorse," where the insured decides for whatever reason that they really don't need or want the coverage that they just purchased. The **ultimate lapse rate** is the rate in which lapses occur on an annual basis over the long term of a block of business. Lapses are cumulative to a block of business—the number of lives that are insured decreases each year unless there are sales of the company's product that exceed lapses.

To understand the impact of lapse rates on a block of business, consider Table 11.1.

TABLE 11.1

The Impact of Lapse Rates

Ultimate lapse rate	Percentage who still own their coverage after 20 years	Percentage who still own their coverage after 30 years
2.5%	60%	47%
5%	36%	21%
8%	20%	8%
10%	13.5%	4%

What Table 11.1 says is that in 20 years, a company with an 8 percent ultimate lapse rate will have 20 percent of the original insureds still paying premiums, while a company with a 2.5 percent ultimate lapse rate will have three times that many—or 60 percent—still paying premiums. This gap grows wider every year the business stays on the books, as is evident in the last column of the table.

In general, the higher the lapse rates, the more favorably a set benefit can be priced. This is because when an insured lapses their coverage, they typically forfeit the premium dollars paid into the coverage up to that point. Those premium reserves are released and can be used to cover costs for other insureds who stay in the risk pool and do not lapse coverage. Generally, lapses in the later years of the policy have a more favorable impact on pricing than early-year lapses, when reserves are still small and start-up costs associated with making the sale might not be fully amortized.

The most common inflation design is described in the NAIC Model Regulation—all benefit amounts increase on a prefunded basis by 5 percent compounded annually for the life of the policy. An insurer's anticipated lapse rate has a significant impact on the rates for this coverage design. Companies that anticipate low lapse rates will generally offer this choice at a higher rate than companies that anticipate higher lapse rates. In other words, there is an inverse relationship between the rate charged and the anticipated level of lapses.

Consider that the amount paid at the time of claim is increasing automatically at 5 percent compounded annually. This causes the amount payable at claim time to double approximately every 15 years. A company will need to charge a hefty premium for this type of inflation option when three times as many people are still paying premiums after 20 years and each of those insureds' daily maximum is ever-increasing. Table 11.2 illustrates the amount payable in years 20 and 30, using the 5 percent compounded inflation option and assuming a three-year claim.

A design with simple inflation increases—where the annual increases are based on the original daily benefit—is less expensive than a design with compounding increases. This is because the daily benefit with simple

TABLE 11.2

Claim Amounts Payable Under a Policy with 5 Percent Compounded Inflation Protection

Year	Daily amount payable	Annual amount payable	Three-year claim at the maximum payable
1	$150	$54,750	$164,250
20	$382	$139,430	$418,290
30	$622	$227,030	$681,090

increases doubles only every 20 years, while compounding will double the benefit amounts approximately every 15 years. Table 11.3 illustrates the amount payable in years 20 and 30 using the 5 percent simple inflation option and the maximum payable for a three-year claim.

TABLE 11.3

Claim Amounts Payable Under a Policy with 5 Percent Simple Inflation Protection

Year	Daily amount payable	Annual amount payable	Three-year claim at the maximum payable
1	$150	$54,750	$164,250
20	$300	$109,500	$328,500
30	$375	$136,875	$410,625

Both examples shown in these tables illustrate the potential claim the insurer is liable for when inflation protection is included in a policy. Consider those amounts along with the percentage of insureds with a policy in force at the various lapse rates shown in Table 11.1. It is much less expensive to have 20 percent of original insureds with a potential claim of more than $400,000 than to have 60 percent of them with the same amount payable. The risk of not adequately funding for future claims is much higher for companies with low lapse rates than it is for those with high lapse rates unless the low rate of lapse was correctly anticipated and reflected in the policy's pricing. This is why lapse rates have such a strong impact on the prudent pricing of inflation protection with automatic increases.

The Future Purchase Option

Another form of inflation protection, the **future purchase option,** is the least expensive hedge against inflation in the initial policy years. Under the future purchase option, the insured generally has the right to buy additional coverage every two or three years without providing evidence of insurability. These offers to increase coverage typically continue until the insured has declined some specified number of previous offers or until the insured goes into claim. Premiums are lower at the outset because the individual does not pay for the inflation increases until the time they purchase those increases. Then they buy those increases at their current attained age. But over time, the total amount of premiums paid with the future purchase option approach will likely surpass the amount paid under the automatic options. This is because the insured pays the full rate for their current age each time they buy coverage, whereas the prefunded increases base their rate on the initial or original issue age. And age has a dramatic impact on the rate charged.

FOCUS QUESTION 4

List and briefly describe available methods of inflation protection in long-term care insurance policies.

_____

_____

_____

_____

_____

_____

_____

_____

There are many variables in future purchase options:

■ A future purchase option design that doesn't increase during a claim is less expensive than one that continues the increases during a claim.

- A future purchase option that ceases when the insured does not exercise the option is less expensive than one that continues the purchase options, regardless of whether the insured has exercised prior options or not.

- Some future purchase options are available for a number of years. In this case, the fewer the number, the less costly the option.

- Some future purchase options put a cap on the amount available for purchase—the lower the cap, the less expensive the option.

- A future purchase option with an indexed increase (such as the Consumer Price Index) is generally more expensive than one with a predetermined percentage increase.

- A future purchase option with a higher predetermined percentage increase is obviously more costly than one with a lower predetermined percentage.

- The frequency of the purchase option (such as every year versus every three years) will impact the premium rate—generally, the more choices made available, the higher the cost.

- Whether the insured must opt in (state that they want to exercise the option) or opt out (state that they don't want to exercise the option) also affects the rate charged. The "opt out" approach costs less, because there is less administrative work required; however, there can be added cost to the insurer when the insured doesn't realize that they have to specifically opt out to avoid paying an additional premium charge for the periodic coverage increase. The insurer may need to go back and make billing adjustments for insureds who did not intend to accept the increase offer but didn't realize that they had to opt out.

- A more expensive future purchase option design allows for the accumulation of each unexercised option. The problem with this design is that the likelihood of anti-selection—the insured waiting to exercise the option until they know they will soon file a claim—is much higher.

A reimbursement plan generally has a less expensive inflation option than an indemnity plan. This is because, with inflation protection, the gap between actual charges and the daily maximum payable continues over time, so that the insurer can continue to realize savings from salvage. This holds true unless the actual charges increase at a higher rate than the policy's inflation increase.

These technical product design choices are addressed during the product development stage by insurer personnel, rather than making all the alternatives available to an agent and consumer. The cost of administering all these variables would be excessive, and having them all available would only confuse those making the decision.

» How Long Benefits Are Paid

Policy Maximum

One of the most important considerations when comparing premiums for various policy choices is the selection of a **policy maximum**. The policy maximum refers to the maximum number of days benefits will be paid or the total dollar amount that will be paid in benefits over the lifetime of the person covered. Many policies today define the policy maximum (often referred to as the **lifetime maximum benefit**) as a dollar amount, rather than as limited specifically to a number of days or years. However, the maximum dollar pay-out is often derived by multiplying a time frame selected (such as five years) times the daily benefit amount the individual wishes to purchase.

Companies normally offer a choice of lifetime maximums, ranging from as little as one year's worth of coverage to an unlimited coverage option. Companies might offer three, four, or as many as seven options between these extremes. The minimum is 12 months, mandated by the NAIC definition of long-term care insurance; some states specify 24 or 36 months as the minimum amount of coverage that can be sold. Companies normally pick a number of years slightly higher than the allowed minimum— frequently that is three years. Some policies have no cap on the amount payable; this is referred to as an **unlimited lifetime maximum** or a **lifetime policy**. Under that option, benefits continue without a maximum as long as the person continues to meet the requirements for being in claim. Four, five, or six years is frequently the middle selection.

Although it is allowed, few companies offer a one-year policy maximum. While this length of time may be of benefit for some people, it is not likely to appeal to the majority of the market. Additionally, as mentioned above, since some states require at least a 24-month maximum benefit, many companies select that amount as their low option. Actuaries have found the difference in premium between three and four years of coverage to be most significant. But the difference in premiums between five and six years is less significant. As well, the difference between a six-year and 10-year maximum is significant, whereas the difference between a 10-year and unlimited maximum is less significant.

The same general principles that apply to short elimination periods also apply to short policy maximums—there is less time to spread the fixed costs of establishing a claim. Therefore, it appears as though there is a disproportionate load to the premium for the shorter policy maximums.

Continuance

When companies began to offer comprehensive policies that covered the entire continuum of care, rather than policies that covered only one level or type of care (such as facility care only), a problem arose. With the older policies, insurer personnel trying to predict insureds' use of covered services only had to worry about the claimants' potential time in a facility or the duration over which they might receive care at home. Now the people doing the pricing must think not only about the length of time someone might spend with one type of provider, but also about where they might go next and how much time they might spend and how much expense they might incur at the new level of care. The concept of how long a claim lasts and the levels of care to which it might correspond is called **continuance** or **channeling**.

Unfortunately, there is a lack of adequate information. Consider once again the care continuum. We have good information about each type of provider and service included in the continuum, the type of people it serves, and how long each type of care is used. But this is incomplete without knowledge of the interdependencies between providers and services. The available information about lifetime patterns of use and cost that take into account all the different types of providers and levels of care that an individual can move through is much more limited. Past research has focused separately on each type of provider in an effort to help them better provide care. Only recently has research looked globally at all the providers used as a person continues with their chronic illness.

» Nonforfeiture Benefits

The nonforfeiture benefit is another coverage choice to consider when calculating the premium. Unlike the previous choices discussed, the nonforfeiture benefit is an "either/or" proposition—either it is included in a policy or it is not. For individual long-term care policies that are federally tax-qualified, the purchaser must be offered the option of a nonforfeiture benefit, but they are not required to include it in their policy if they choose not to.

The nonforfeiture benefit adds to the premium cost because it means that the insurer will have to make a payment to the insured if they lapse their policy or die while it is in force. If there are no nonforfeiture benefits, the insurer will be able to keep the money it would have paid out and can use it to maintain policy reserves for the future claims of other insureds.

Nonforfeiture benefits do not increase home office expenses a great deal, but there are some increased costs. The insurer has to keep track of policies that have lapsed but that still have a shortened benefit period and process any claims. But this is not a significant contributor to the premium charged for this option.

The contingent nonforfeiture benefit is factored into the standard pricing because this is an automatic benefit made available to all consumers subjected to a rate increase beyond a certain percentage. It is not a choice given to consumers. Companies typically do not charge any additional premium to include this option in the coverage.

While inflation protection has an inverse relationship to lapses, the nonforfeiture benefit has a direct relationship—the more lapses a company is expecting, the more it anticipates paying out in nonforfeiture benefits. To take this one step further, the more paid out in nonforfeiture benefits, the less a company is able to keep in reserves for future claims. Although the benefit may seem insignificant, the policy reserves and the amount of money the insurer is able to invest are strongly affected when many policies include a nonforfeiture benefit.

FOCUS QUESTION 5

Outline how the nonforfeiture benefit affects insurers' premium calculations.

_____

_____

_____

_____

_____

_____

_____

_____

_____

» Age

Age at purchase has a significant impact on premium cost. Many of the other elements that influence the premium amount can be controlled to some degree by the insured—for example, they can lower premium costs by selecting a longer elimination period. But an individual cannot control age at purchase other than by buying today rather than waiting until they are older, when they will have to pay a higher premium cost for the same coverage.

The only exception to this rule is that some companies will allow an applicant to backdate their application to "save age" if they have recently had a birthday. Normally they will allow backdating up to six months. If, for example, someone's age change occurred four months ago, the issue date of the policy will simply reflect the date before the age change; however, the applicant also must pay premiums retroactive to the issue date. When the policy is issued, the application date does not change, but the policy will appear as though it was in force from the time of the backdated issue date.

Most companies use an applicant's actual age (that is, the number of years they had lived at their last birthday) for the purposes of determining the premium cost. This is simple for the applicant and agent to understand. Other companies use what is common in life insurance—the applicant's age at their nearest birthday, whether that birthday is the last or the next. Using this method, the applicant has an age change six months before and after their actual birthday.

Another option for companies is to have age bands. Rather than having rates for every age, they have rates for every few years. They can vary from two-year age bands to as much as they want. Five-year age bands are seen with some forms of health insurance. Some companies use age bands only with younger ages (commonly below age 40) because of the challenge of differentiating the risk between the various ages. Age banding means all applicants within a certain range of ages pay the same premium. An age change occurs only when the applicant crosses over into the next age band. Most long-term care insurance charges individual age premiums and does not use age bands except perhaps at the very youngest ages (that is, below age 40).

There is a direct relationship between age and LTCI premium rates—the older someone is at the time they buy coverage, the higher the rates. However, it is important to remember that premiums are designed to remain level based on the individual's age when they buy coverage; they would not be expected to pay a different premium rate each time they attain a new age, once they have purchased coverage.

FOCUS QUESTION 6

Outline ways insurers introduce flexibility into the consideration of an applicant's age when they prepare an LTCI policy.

_____

_____

When Should One Buy LTCI?

When is the best time of life to purchase long-term care insurance? There are different ways to approach this question. Some compare the total amount an insured would pay if they bought at different ages—say 50, 65, and 85. Assuming the same daily benefit, this calculation shows it being less expensive to purchase coverage at age 50. And the savings are even greater when (more realistically) inflation is taken into account and it is assumed that if a person waits until they are 65, they will have to buy twice the daily benefit they would have bought at 50.

Table 11.4 shows the calculation for one company's premiums when coverage is purchased at various ages. Except for the daily benefit, how the premiums were determined is unimportant for this exercise. The 5 percent compounded inflation option is assumed, and the initial purchase is considered at age 50. The daily benefit grows at 5 percent compounded, and age is included in the chart. Some rounding occurs.

TABLE 11.4

The Cost of Waiting to Buy

Age	Daily benefit	Initial premium	Total cost to age 85
50	$150	$3,360	$120,900
55	$192	$4,590	$142,400
60	$246	$6,620	$172,250
65	$314	$9,960	$209,200
70	$401	$17,790	$284,650

There is another consideration consumers should keep in mind—the longer one waits to buy, the greater the chances that one will be uninsurable and unable to purchase coverage. Therefore, it is generally in a person's best interest to purchase sooner rather than later.

» Putting It All Together

The premium of an LTCI policy is a function of these components:

- when the policy will start to pay benefits (which provider types and services are covered and the length and type of elimination period),

- how much the policy will pay in benefits each day (the daily benefit amount and the inflation provisions),

- how much the policy will pay in total benefits (the policy maximum), and

- any ancillary options (a nonforfeiture benefit or other policy rider).

The **premium rate** is based on all of these components except the daily benefit amount. The premium of a policy is calculated by multiplying the rate by the number of units of the daily benefit.

Table 11.5 shows a very crude method of calculating rates, using the choices discussed in this chapter, with two options for each choice. In this example, the rate at a certain age for a comprehensive plan (10) with a short elimination period (10), standard inflation protection (10), a long policy maximum (8), and a standard nonforfeiture benefit (3) adds up to $41 per unit of the daily benefit. One unit is $10, so a daily benefit of

TABLE 11.5

Choices and Rates

Choice	Option–Rate	Option–Rate
Covered services	Comprehensive–10	Limited–7
Elimination period	Short–10	Long–8
Inflation protection	Standard–10	Minimal–1
Policy maximum	Short–3	Long–8
Nonforfeiture benefit	Standard–3	Deluxe–5

$150 per day consists of 15 units. The premium for this policy is the rate (41) times the number of units (15) or $615 dollars per year.

This rough approach assumes that the different choices are independent of one another. This is only partially true—there are some interdependencies. For example, the inflation protection load for a long policy maximum is usually higher than for a short policy maximum. This is because the amount likely paid out is higher for both the inflation option and the long policy maximum. Another example is when purchase option increases to the daily benefit are allowed during a claim and the policy has a long policy maximum.

Some insurers have separate rate charts that are used for specific benefits chosen in combination with each other. Other companies simply apply rate factors to adjust for the cost of including certain riders or optional benefits. And some companies use both approaches, treating different benefit options with one approach or another. For example, nonforfeiture is usually a factor adjustment to rates (for example, 35 percent might be added to the cost of whatever policy is chosen), while if built-in automatic inflation protection is selected, the insurer would use the unit rates associated with that feature as it impacts the other plan choices. In both these examples, the combination is greater than the individual parts. For this reason, agents and state insurance departments look at the rates for a combination of choices (the covered services, elimination period, and policy maximum) and then the rates for each of the optional riders (inflation and nonforfeiture options) for each combined selection.

Today, most premium calculations are done by a computer program provided by the insurer to the agent. The rates for each option choice are loaded into the program. The agent and consumer make choices and input them into the program, and the program derives the premium. Some companies provide a worksheet and rate card that allow the consumer to calculate rates on their own to help them decide which combination of options they prefer.

» Summary

Calculating premium rates is a complicated mathematical process done at an insurance company's home office by actuaries. Many factors and assumptions unknown to the general public are taken into consideration in developing rates. No two unrelated companies will have exactly the same rates because of the breadth of the variables considered and because of differing company data sources and philosophies. Rates are developed for each consumer choice based on each product design. These rates are then filed with state insurance departments before insurers provide them to their agent distribution network.

The premium is a function of the rate (determined by the insurance company) for each choice at the consumer's age times the number of units (the daily benefit selected by the consumer).

Key Terms

Channeling	Persistency
Continuance	Policy maximum
Future purchase option	Premium rate
Lapse rate	Salvage
Lifetime maximum benefit	Ultimate lapse rate
Lifetime policy	Unlimited lifetime maximum

» Review Questions

1. Name the two factors or variables used to establish when benefits are scheduled to take effect.

2. Name the two factors that are considered when determining the benefit amount.

3. What is the difference between reimbursement and indemnity plans?

4. What do we mean by "salvage"?

5. Why is the administrative cost of managing an indemnity plan less than the corresponding cost of managing a reimbursement plan?

6. What is "persistency"?

7. Define "policy maximum."

8. Is the minimum length of a long-term care insurance policy's benefit maximum 12 months nationwide?

9. What are the most important reasons why one is better off by buying a long-term care insurance policy earlier rather than later?

10. Review the four components of an LTCI premium by listing them.

» Answers

1. The specific services to be covered under the policy and the elimination period that is selected.

2. The initial daily (or monthly) benefit amount chosen and the inflation protection method chosen (if any).

3. Reimbursement covers actual cost of care (with limitations and maximums as specified by the policy). Indemnity pays full benefits regardless of actual charges.

4. The difference between the policy's daily maximum benefit and the actual charges that are reimbursed.

5. The skill level of the person managing indemnity claims can be lower because they are not required to assess provider billing statements or understand Medicare's reimbursement requirements and amounts.

6. This term refers to the percentage of insureds who continue in premium-paying status.

7. The policy maximum is the maximum number of days benefits will be paid or the total dollar amount that will be paid in benefits over the lifetime of the policy.

8. No, some states specify 24 or 36 months as the minimum amount of coverage that can be sold.

9. The total cost of premiums paid to an advanced age is less when one purchases coverage at, for example, age 50 as opposed to age 70. Also, the longer one waits to buy, the greater the chances that one will be uninsurable and unable to purchase coverage.

10. The components are as follows: (a) *when* the policy will start to pay benefits (which provider types and services are covered and the length and type of elimination period), (b) *how much* the policy will pay in benefits *each day* (the daily benefit amount and the inflation provisions), (c) *how much* the policy will pay in *total* benefits (the policy maximum), and (d) any *additional options* (a nonforfeiture benefit or other policy rider).

12

Premium Adjustments

» Overview

Once the annual premium of an LTCI policy is calculated, adjustments are made for the frequency of premium payments and any discounts that may be offered by the company. This chapter describes these adjustments and also considers the impact that the current tax treatment might have on lowering the net premium cost for owners of qualified long-term care insurance contracts.

» Premium Frequency

Some people like to pay premiums with more frequent but lower payments. Rather than paying $1,200 per year, they'd rather pay $100 per month. However, insurers do not usually simply divide the annual payment by the number of months to determine the monthly payment. Generally, the more often premiums are paid, the more expensive the insurance is to the consumer. This is because of the additional costs to the insurance company—lost investment income, the increased cost of mailing premium notices, and the higher potential lapse risk associated with having to make more frequent payments.

Premium payments go to work as soon as the insurer receives them. The companies are able to use the premium payments by investing them. If there is a delay in receiving the payments—such as when payments are made monthly, quarterly, or semiannually—the company loses an opportunity to have the funds invested and earn a return.

The cost of sending a bill and collecting the payments through **direct billing** (mailing a premium notice to the insured) can add up quickly.

Although it is done with machines, sending a premium statement is not free to the insurer. There is the cost of the machine, programming the system, the paper and ink for the statement, the mailing, return envelopes, and the postage. Then there are the cost of opening the returned envelope, logging the premium payment, and depositing the check. These costs may seem low for one or two mailings, but they are significant when many thousands of premiums are considered. And the more frequently premium statements are sent, the greater these costs.

The most efficient method for premium payment for both an insurer and an insured is **electronic funds transfer (EFT)**. In this method, the insurer takes the necessary funds directly from the insured's savings or checking account. The direct expense to the insurer is very low once the electronic transfer is established, mostly because of the lack of human interaction in collecting the premium payment.

EFT has become the most common payment method used by insurers for monthly payments. In fact, many insurers no longer offer a monthly direct billing option. Those that still do normally charge a higher load for that option than for EFT. EFT can be used for less frequent payments (such as quarterly or semiannually), but this is not as common as monthly EFT because of the larger premium that is automatically drawn from the bank account. The potential for overdrawing the insured's account increases as the premium frequency decreases and the premium amount increases.

Insurance premiums are paid before the protection is provided. In other words, for a year's worth of protection, the premium is paid at the beginning of the year. Insurance is not like a retail purchase where payment for the good is made when it is received.

Insurers normally have **premium payment modes** that reflect consumer needs. These can include:

- monthly—12 times a year,
- quarterly—four times a year,
- semiannually—twice a year, or
- annually—once a year.

Some insurers allow for bimonthly payment (24 times a year) or biweekly payment (26 times a year). This is normally done only when payments are deducted from the insured's paycheck as part of employer-sponsored LTCI coverage.

Most insurers charge more for more frequent payment modes. This compensates the insurer for its lost investment income and the additional expense involved in collecting premiums more frequently. Some insurers, however, do not load for different payment modes and simply charge for monthly billing at one-twelfth of the annual premium. Some carriers set monthly premiums and derive other modal premiums based on a straight proportion, without a load for different modes.

FOCUS QUESTION 1

What are the two methods by which insurance companies can collect premiums?

_____

_____

_____

» Limited Pay

Some companies offer payment options in which premiums are paid for a limited period of time, rather than over the life of the policy or until premium waiver takes effect. Rather than paying premiums as long as the policy stays in force, payments are made for a predetermined number of years or up to a certain age. Common examples are:

- single pay—one premium payment,
- ten pay—paying premiums for 10 years,
- twenty pay—paying premiums for 20 years, and
- to age 65—making premium payments until the insured turns 65.

These **limited pay** options add to the premium amount, sometimes rather significantly, because premium payments stop while the policy remains in force. The company must collect enough in premiums in the early policy years so that sufficient reserves are established to cover the risk for the person's life expectancy. It is not unusual to load the rates for these limited pay options to protect against that risk.

The amount added will depend on the insurer's assumptions on issues such as persistency, investment return, and field compensation. In terms of persistency, these policies should have virtually no lapses except for death. People know what they're buying and understand they will overpay for the coverage in the early years in exchange for the peace of mind of having a policy that no longer has premiums due after a certain amount of time. As for investment, the companies are in essence investing the addition to the standard premium and then using the return on that investment to pay premiums after the insured goes beyond the limited pay period. This puts pressure on the company to at least meet its return expectations after premiums are due.

A limited pay design normally pays the agent less than the average commission rate for the first-year premium. But because the premium is higher, the agent will make about the same in the first year as with a standard premium. Some designs call for no renewal commissions, and certainly any applicable renewal commissions will cease after the limited pay period ends.

The limited pay design works independently of the premium frequency consideration. In fact, someone could pay for their limited pay policy using any of the previously mentioned modes. The limited pay premium is simply multiplied by the modal premium to establish the amount the insured will pay.

The biggest challenge an insurer faces with the limited pay design involves what happens after the premium payment period has ended and all premiums due have been paid. While premiums are still being paid on a policy, the insurer can make premium adjustments (on a class of insureds). But after all premiums have been collected, the policy is in effect noncancelable, in that the insurer has no way of increasing premiums when contractually no premiums are due. Thus, after the limited period has ended, the risk of estimating the correct rates rests solely on the insurer.

There is one company that offers a limited pay rider that does not eventually result in a noncancelable policy. The rider has a provision that allows the company to assess additional premium charges after the paid-up period if experience justifies it. Most insurers find that this approach runs counter to the objectives a buyer has when selecting a limited pay policy.

FOCUS QUESTION 2

Summarize the pros and cons of a limited pay arrangement for the consumer and the insurer.

_____

_____

_____

_____

_____

_____

_____

_____

_____

_____

_____

_____

» Policy Discounts

Most long-term care insurers offer discounts to their base premium for one or more reasons. There is the potential for significant savings if a company allows multiple discounts for different reasons and allows them to be applied simultaneously, wholly or in part.

The Spousal Discount

The most common discount is the **spousal discount**. Research suggests that the presence of a healthy spouse leads to a decreased utilization of long-term care services. In fact, fewer than 20 percent of nursing home users are married.[1] This is partly because the healthy spouse is often physically willing and able to care for the other.[2] This scenario leads to cost savings on claims for long-term care insurers, and this savings is passed on to insureds through a discount in the premium they pay.

The early spousal discounts were typically given when both husband and wife were issued LTCI policies from the same company. The discount was either on both policies or on the least expensive one. Discounts of 5 percent to 15 percent or more were typical.

As simple as this concept sounds, the actual implementation of a spousal discount is complicated for competitive and regulatory reasons. Some state insurance departments do not allow the rate charged for one person to be tied to the issuance of a policy on another person. In response, some companies ask that both spouses apply for the coverage but do not require that they both buy a policy. The application process enables the insurer to confirm that both spouses are healthy enough to provide informal support. Some companies have waived the need for a spouse to apply for or purchase coverage—they only require the presence of a spouse. Some states require this last approach; they argue that the research evidence supports the idea that lower claims costs are associated with the presence of a spouse, and therefore the discount should be based solely on whether there is a spouse, not on whether the spouse applies for or buys insurance.

Some companies have extended the concept of a spousal discount beyond married couples to include domestic partners or siblings. There may be requirements with respect to the documentation of the domestic partnership or the number of years that the partnership has been in effect. Typically, the discount for siblings or other family members other than a spouse requires that they live with the insured.

In another approach, some insurers offer an additional discount when three or more members of the same family purchase coverage. This discount is more a function of marketing efficiencies than an expected impact from informal supports.

Most companies maintain the spousal discount even if the couple divorces or one spouse dies. While the potential for claim savings from informal support is obviously lost when this happens, taking away a premium discount is distasteful to most insurers. Typically, the possibility of divorce and death is taken into account when the discount is initially priced. Some state regulations prevent the removal of a spousal discount in the event of the death of a spouse.

One drawback of the spousal discount relates to how an insurer establishes rates for single people. Before the introduction of the spousal discount, there was an assumption built into the development of rates that some insureds were married and others were single. Everyone paid the same rate regardless of marital, partner, or insurability status. In essence, the married people were subsidizing the rates of the single people. Now that the married insureds pay less for their coverage, the single people end up paying more. Some say that this is equitable because people are paying the applicable amount for the risk they bring to the insurer. However, there is much conflicting evidence on the actuarial validity of spousal discounts, especially for buyers at the youngest ages. Single people can have very resilient informal support networks, and married couples may not still be married at the time they require care, so the fact that they were married at the time of purchase may have no impact on future claim costs. Also, there is no requirement that spouses agree to provide informal care for each other in order to receive the spousal discount. The debate within the industry continues over whether a spousal discount is truly actuarially justified or simply a marketing incentive designed to obtain two sales with one visit.

The Preferred Health Discount

Another type of premium discount that is gaining in popularity is one for people that have a positive health history. This is called a **preferred health discount**. Companies are more likely now than 10 years ago to establish underwriting classes and to provide a discount for the more healthy insureds (and possibly charge a higher premium or require a reduction in coverage for less healthy insureds). The preferred health discount is defined differently by each company, but may include people who:

- do not smoke cigarettes,
- are physically and mentally active,
- have height and weight consistent with predetermined insurer guidelines,
- are taking only minimal medications, and
- have had no hospitalization or surgeries in the recent past.

These preferred rates for the healthiest applicants have helped to attract desirable consumers to companies offering them. An insurer might even offer two levels of preferred classes (preferred and super-preferred) to attract the "marathon runners" (or the healthiest of the healthy) to their company. This is a common consumer-driven practice with term life insurance that is now slowly emerging in long-term care insurance.

The drawback of offering a price break to preferred classes of insureds is that those insureds who do not qualify will pay more than when they were lumped in with the preferred risks. There is also very limited data to accurately identify the type of person who should receive the preferred health discount. There is much research on those needing long-term care services, but little on their health status six months or more before they needed care. Underwriters look at the potential causes of chronic illnesses (such as overweight and smoking) and then determine whether the applicant has any of them in their medical history. It is also difficult to determine the correct level of discount to give these people without making many (possibly unfounded) assumptions. Experience will reveal whether the companies offering these discounts based them on accurate projections.

FOCUS QUESTION 3

What are some of the drawbacks of offering a preferred health discount?

_____

_____

_____

_____

_____

_____

_____

_____

_____

Some insurers offer what are called **substandard rates** to applicants who do not meet regular underwriting standards. For example, if an applicant has a condition that the insurer feels is not totally uninsurable but poses a slightly elevated risk, the insurer may offer the insured coverage for a higher premium charge than someone else the same age would pay. Such applicants often agree to pay the higher rates because they may be considered uninsurable by companies that do not charge substandard rates.

Companies differ greatly in how they define a substandard risk and what they charge for that risk. One company might identify a condition as substandard, while another company would accept it as a standard risk. The additional premium cost for a substandard risk might be anywhere from 25 percent to 200 percent. Some companies that offer coverage to substandard risk individuals charge the same premium rate but offer only reduced coverage. For example, an insurer might offer nursing-home-only coverage for two years with a 90-day elimination period. In this way the company limits its risk by limiting the maximum coverage available to the insured. There are other innovative policy designs emerging to address the needs of substandard risk individuals.

An insurer may create several **underwriting classes**—such as super-preferred, preferred, standard, and substandard—in an effort to attract the greatest number of consumers possible. Having such classes enables the insurer to adjust premiums based on its experience within each class. These classes allow insurers to better analyze their experience and make better business decisions based on that experience rather than on general research data. This approach is fair for insureds, because they each pay premiums based on the level of risk they bring to the insurer. Classes are common in other types of insurance—for example, good drivers buy their automobile insurance from companies that have discounts for those without driving violations.

Group Discounts

LTCI companies interested in the business or employer market may have another type of discount—one for the employer group. An employer group is made up of at least three employees at a single business. Many companies allow spouses of employees to get the same discount, but these people do not count toward the three-employee minimum. Some insurers set a higher threshold on the number of employees that must be in a group before a discount can be provided.

A group discount may also be offered to **affinity groups**. These groups must consist of at least 10 people, and the group must have been formed for reasons other than to purchase insurance. Common examples of affinity groups are service clubs (such as Rotary or the Lions), college alumni associations, bank or credit union customers, or even investment clubs. Some insurers impose minimum requirements for group size or for enrollment in the long-term care program before a group discount is granted.

Each insurer has guidelines established to determine what constitutes a valid group and the level of discount available. Some companies even offer different underwriting protocols for the group depending on its size and the number (or percentage) of people who decide to purchase the insurance. The idea behind offering the employer and affinity group discounts is that healthy applicants who normally would not consider the coverage will purchase it because they get a discount not normally received.

The Multiple Policy Discount

A **multiple policy discount** is offered by a few insurers. It is modeled on the practice of property and casualty insurers that provide a discount when both automobile and homeowners' insurance is with the same company. A discount may be available for those who own life, disability income, or annuities with the same company from which they purchase their long-term care insurance. Having multiple policies makes the administration of each policy easier. As an example, the same medical records used to administer a disability income claim are used to administer an LTCI claim. The same claim representative might adjudicate both policies, thus saving a little more money for the insurer. These savings are passed on to the insured in the form of a discount to their long-term care policy.

Other Discount Considerations

These discounts can add up to significant savings for the insureds of companies that allow combining discounts. For instance, a healthy person (preferred rates) who is married (spousal discount) and owns life insurance from the same company (multiple policy) could receive three different discounts.

These discounts are part of a company's illustration system or rate card. The illustration system will ask the agent to identify which discounts the applicant qualifies for and then automatically takes into consideration the appropriate discounts as the premium is calculated. Using the rate card and a calculator to arrive at the premium will get the agent and applicant close to the correct premium. Because someone might qualify for multiple discounts that are subject to rounding using a calculator, the accuracy in hand calculating the premium is not as precise as using the company's illustration system.

» Tax Treatment of Premiums

Before HIPAA, lawyers, tax preparers, and individual taxpayers simply guessed at how the Internal Revenue Service would view long-term care insurance. Some decided to treat it like disability income insurance, while others treated it like health insurance. HIPAA, enacted in 1996, provided clarification.

As we have seen, HIPAA had an impact on LTCI product design by requiring that a policy have certain provisions in order to be federally tax-qualified. The purpose of owning a qualified policy is to obtain favorable tax treatment of both the premiums and benefits. (The tax treatment of a non-tax-qualified policy is still undefined by the IRS.) The taxation (or lack thereof) of the benefits for qualified policies was discussed in a previous chapter. This section looks at how someone can receive a discount on their taxes by owning a qualified contract, thus reducing the net cost of coverage.

The key sentence of HIPAA in this regard is as follows: "A qualified long-term care insurance contract shall be treated as an accident and health insurance contract." Accident and health insurance has received the most favorable tax treatment regarding both premiums and benefits. Premiums for an LTCI policy are treated by the IRS as accident and health insurance premiums as long as the policy is designed to meet the requirements for a qualified policy established by HIPAA. As a result, premiums for a qualified LTCI policy are in some cases deductible.

Individuals

To prevent insurers from creating a tax dodge for the wealthy, HIPAA placed limits on the amount of premiums an individual could deduct, based on their attained age in the tax year. These limits are found in Table 4.1 on page 90. When a couple files a joint return, each spouse can deduct premiums up to the limit. Thus, normally the limits for a married couple are double those for individuals.

LTCI premiums are included with an individual's or couple's unreimbursed medical expenses, which are deductible (for those who itemize deductions) provided they exceed 7.5 percent of adjusted gross income. Unreimbursed medical expenses are payments made for services or equipment for which insurance benefits are not available. Examples are eyeglasses, dentures, routine physical exams, experimental treatments or procedures, and for many people prescription medications. Medicare supplement insurance is counted as accident and health insurance and also included as an unreimbursed medical expense.

It should be noted that while some people's medical expenses are great enough for them to deduct their LTCI premiums, this is not the case for most people. Only a small minority of taxpayers are actually able to deduct these premiums.

Self-Employed Owners

Businesses are also able to deduct a portion of the premium for qualified LTCI policies. There are two classes of businesses in this respect: the **self-employed owner** and the employer. For these purposes, self-employed owners are those who are:

- partners or owners in a partnership, limited liability corporation (LLC), or limited liability partnership (LLP);

- S corporation shareholders who own more than 2 percent of the company's shares; or

- sole proprietors.

A self-employed owner must include their LTCI premium with their federal gross income. They can deduct as a business expense 70 percent of premiums (subject to the limits in Table 4.1) in 2002, and beginning in 2003 they will be able to deduct the full amount. The part of the premium (within the limits of Table 4.1) they cannot deduct as a business expense can be included as an unreimbursed medical expense on their personal income taxes, as described above for individuals.

FOCUS QUESTION 4

Name the three different kinds of self-employed owner.

_____

_____

_____

Employers and Employees

An employer that pays LTCI premiums on behalf of its employees may deduct the full amount as employee compensation. If a corporation pays the premiums only because the employee is also a shareholder, the IRS could decide that the premium was actually a dividend to the shareholder/employee.

Employees can exclude the premiums their employer pays on their behalf from their taxable income. When the employee pays all or part of the premium for employer-sponsored coverage, they may take the deductions off their personal income taxes as described above for individuals.

Other Tax Considerations

Many states have tax breaks for those who own long-term care insurance. States will offer either a tax credit or an income deduction. The credit goes against the amount of the resident's tax that is payable to the state. The tax credit is normally limited to a percentage of the premium, with a maximum credit of a few hundred dollars against the tax owed. The deduction will allow a reduction in the resident's taxable income before calculating the tax owed. The income deduction is normally allowed when the taxpayer does not qualify for the federal tax break.

The insurance industry continues to argue that when the government provides a tax benefit to purchase long-term care insurance, there is an offsetting saving to the state's Medicaid budget.[3] Many states have recognized this relationship and have embraced it with tax incentives.

» Summary

There are a variety of adjustments and discounts that help determine the premium of an LTCI policy. One common adjustment relates to the frequency and method of premium payment. Often insureds who make more frequent premium payments must pay more to compensate for the increased cost to the insurer. In some cases insureds who pay by means of electronic funds transfer receive a small discount, as this is less costly for the company.

There are also discounts based on preferred health and marital status, as well as discounts that apply when more than one person enrolls at a time (family and group discounts). Someone who is not a standard risk might pay an additional premium charge for their coverage.

The net cost of owning LTCI is reduced when the insured is able to deduct premiums from their income tax. However, this only occurs when the premium and unreimbursed medical expenses together exceed 7.5 percent of adjusted gross income.

Key Terms 🔑	Affinity group	Premium payment modes
	Direct billing	Self-employed owner
	Electronic funds transfer (EFT)	Spousal discount
	Limited pay	Substandard rate
	Multiple policy discount	Underwriting class
	Preferred health discount	

» Review Questions

1. Name the two methods commonly used to collect premium payments.

2. If an insured wanted to pay their premium annually, would the amount for a given year be due at the beginning or the end of that year?

3. What is the most common premium discount applied in long-term care insurance?

4. Why are insurers willing to offer a discount to individuals who are married?

5. What is the preferred health discount?

6. How can someone obtain long-term care insurance coverage if they do not meet regular underwriting standards?

7. What do we call the premium structure according to which an insurer pools risk by offering similar policies to people with similar risks?

8. What is the difference between an employer group discount and an affinity group discount?

9. Is a group discount the same as a multiple policy discount?

10. With what type of insurance did HIPAA group long-term care insurance?

» Answers

1. Direct billing and electronic funds transfer.

2. The beginning.

3. The spousal discount.

4. Research suggests that the presence of a healthy spouse leads to a decreased utilization of long-term care services. (However, actuarial support for this argument is not conclusive).

5. This is a discount for people who can show a positive health history.

6. Some insurers offer what are called substandard rates designed with this type of applicant in mind. Often the premium is increased or the benefit reduced.

7. Underwriting classes.

8. The former is designed for employees of a company (and their spouses); the latter is for members of groups or organizations (as long as they have not been formed for the specific reason of getting an insurance discount). The minimum number of people needed to qualify as a "group" is also different for the two categories.

9. No, the latter refers to multiple policies (such as medical expense and LTCI) purchased by the *same insured*.

10. Health and accident insurance.

Notes

1 http://www.milbank.org/0008stone/#whoneeds.

2 http://www.milbank.org/0008stone/#informal.

3 Cohen, Marc A., Kumar, Nada, and Wallack, Stanley S. 1994. "Long-Term Care Insurance and Medicaid." *Data Watch* (Fall) p.134.

 13

Group Long-Term Care Insurance

» Overview

In group insurance, coverage is provided to many people through some type of group vehicle like an employer or membership organization. This is an efficient method of distributing an insurance product, as an insurer can reach many consumers in a timely manner with minimal paperwork.

One of the purposes of group insurance is to ensure that people who might not purchase coverage on their own get the protection they need. Many people rely solely on their employer for their health, life, and disability insurance. Many employers make available these types of coverage to their employees under a group policy as part of the employee benefit package. Generally, everyone gets the same type of coverage, although everyone may not necessarily get the same level of coverage. (For example, all employees of a company may receive life insurance, but the death benefit may be twice earnings, so the coverage amount differs.) This approach provides efficiency of enrollment for both the sponsoring employer and the insurer.

Some people stay at an employer in part to maintain their group insurance because it provides such a good value and other employers may not offer such a comprehensive package of benefits. Therefore, group insurance can also benefit employers by helping them attract and retain employees.

A recent trend is offering flexibility in employee benefits. This is done in several ways:

- providing a pool of benefit dollars to each employee that they can use to pay for the benefit offerings they choose (the **cafeteria approach**);
- sponsoring **medical savings accounts**, the funds of which are available to pay insurance deductibles and coinsurance; and
- sponsoring **voluntary benefits**, whereby employees are able to purchase additional insurance products at their own expense but at discounted group rates and with the convenience of workplace enrollment and payroll deduction.

Popular voluntary benefits include dental insurance, supplemental life insurance, disability income insurance, and other coverages. A small but rapidly growing number of employers are offering group long-term care insurance on a voluntary basis to employees, their spouses, and their parents.

FOCUS QUESTION 1

Provide definitions for the following: the cafeteria approach, medical savings account, voluntary benefits.

_____

_____

_____

_____

_____

_____

_____

_____

» Defining Group Long-Term Care Insurance

The term "group" is used rather loosely in the LTCI field, but the NAIC Model Act provides a standard definition. According to the act, group long-term care insurance is an insurance policy issued to:

- employer(s) for past or present employees, or labor organization(s) for past or present members;

- current members and former members of any professional, trade, or occupational organization that was formed for purposes other than purchasing insurance;

- an association with a minimum of 100 persons that is formed for purposes other than purchasing insurance, has existed for at least one year, and has written bylaws; or

- another group in which the policy is issued in the best interests of the public, the policy offers an economic method of administering or acquiring the insurance, and the benefits and premiums have a reasonable relationship.

In a true group LTCI policy, a master policy is issued to the group sponsor (the employer or association) and certificates are issued to individual insureds. A group policy will gain regulatory approval in the sponsor's state of domicile even though insureds may live in multiple states. The individual certificates, which read much like individual LTCI policies, are issued in other states as long as statutes and regulations in those states are substantially similar to those that exist in the issuing state. The burden of proof for this extraterritorial jurisdiction is placed upon the state insurance regulators.

FOCUS QUESTION 2

Provide examples of groups that qualify for group long-term care insurance.

_____

_____

_____

_____

_____

_____

_____

_____

» Group Marketing of Individual Policies

Many insurers have recognized the market potential of employer groups and affinity organizations, yet they do not offer true group long-term care insurance. These insurers instead offer their individually issued LTCI policies with minor modifications on a group-marketed basis. Within the approved design of the individual policy, the insurer is permitted to alter benefits, lower rates under the franchise insurance law in states, or modify the level of underwriting required.

One advantage of using individual policies is the insurer's ability to bill the insured directly or to bill the plan sponsor, which in turn collects premiums from the insureds. Also, there is no concern about converting the policy when the insured's relationship with the sponsor as an employee or association member ends. The policy is portable because it is issued directly to the individual insured. The same portability is required of a group policy, where coverage must be continued on the same or a substantially similar basis even if the insured leaves the group. This is an important consumer protection feature that exists regardless of whether the policy is offered on a group or individual basis.

» Group Size

The size of the group often dictates the type of offering that is available. The larger groups usually have a true group plan, while the smaller ones are more likely to have specially designed individual policies. Some insurance companies, however, specialize in the smaller group market and have developed true group products for smaller employer groups.

The largest groups, those with more than 3,000 lives, will likely prefer a true group product. They will probably use a consultant to develop a **request for proposal (RFP)** from multiple insurers. This RFP might dictate how the product is designed and might specify policy procedures such as how insureds qualify for benefits along with other provisions in the contract. (The most extensive RFP was created by the Office of Personnel Management for the federal employees' long-term care insurance offering.) If a group is large enough, an insurer will develop a long-term care insurance policy for that specific group. After reviewing the RFPs, the consultant will select an insurer, or a consortium of insurers in the case of the federal government employees, to offer the long-term care insurance.

Medium-size groups are those with between 1,000 and 3,000 employees or members. This type of group is more likely to use an insurance broker to assist it in selecting the best product and insurer for its needs. Some groups may use an RFP in the selection process, but insurers are not likely to alter their standard group offerings for a group this size. Often, though, the standard group offering has enough flexibility to accommodate the requirements of the RFP. The competitiveness of the offerings for groups in this range comes from getting multiple insurers or multiple brokers involved in the process. These groups will receive a very competitive product the insurer offers to many different groups—one that they have on the shelf.

Small groups are those with fewer than 1,000 people eligible for the offering. These groups are more likely to have brokers working for them, searching for the type of plan with the right options for the group. Insurers are not likely to provide many concessions for these groups because the volume of potential participants is simply not large enough. However, some insurers specialize in the small employer market niche and can accommodate the desires of a small employer. Some of these groups will consider an individually issued policy for those who want to participate because of the ease in administering these types of policies.

Groups can be as small as three participants for employer-sponsored groups or 10 participants for affinity groups (although insurers can make their standard sizes higher than these minimums). A group this size will almost certainly use individual policies. There are many groups in this category, from small business owners to professional partnerships to investment clubs. In fact, there are many more of these smallest groups than there are larger groups, and on an aggregate basis there are more people in all these smaller groups than in the larger groups.[1]

Employers can "carve out" a small portion of a larger employee group for the purpose of offering long-term care insurance. (For example, they can offer LTCI only to management-level employees). The IRS has no discrimination rules as long as the **carve-out group** is based on objective criteria and it is fully insured. The sponsor can offer the coverage to all employees with a certain title (for example, the president and vice presidents), to specific classes of employees (all exempt, management personnel), to those with a specified number of years of service (those with more than 10 years), or to those with any other eligibility requirement that doesn't blatantly attempt to circumvent the law's intent. The best approach is to design the carve-out group so that it is broad enough not to subject the sponsor to challenges based on employment law. One example of a poor design is using owners of a corporation as the eligible group classification—the IRS could determine that the premiums paid by the employer were actually dividends from the company, are not deductible as a business expense, and are part of the owners' taxable income.

FOCUS QUESTION 3

What are some of the criteria used in defining carve-out groups?

_____

_____

_____

_____

_____

_____

_____

_____

» Securing a Group Sponsor

From the insurer's perspective, the first step in the group long-term care insurance process is securing a group sponsor. With large employer groups, this might mean gaining approval from the person in the human resources department who manages the employee benefits package. With smaller employer groups, this might mean meeting with the president, the board of directors, or the owner(s) to secure an approval to offer long-term care insurance. Affinity groups may require approval from the board of directors, benefit committee, or other decision-making entity within the group.

There are many reasons for employers to sponsor group long-term care insurance. This type of coverage rounds out a benefit package by filling in where other typical employee benefits have gaps. Health insurance pays for hospitalization, physician services, and medical treatment. Typically the only time health insurance pays for nursing home care or home care is when care is related to a short-term acute care episode. A group health insurance policy is not designed to provide protection for chronic conditions associated with the need for long-term care services. This leaves a gap in the employees' health coverage that threatens retirement savings and employee peace of mind.

Long-term care insurance can also pick up where a group long-term disability income policy leaves off. Frequently when someone is disabled, they have additional expenses for professional services needed to continue to live independently. These services might include assistance with taking a shower and getting dressed in the morning—in other words, they are the services typically covered by long-term care insurance. A disability income policy helps replace lost income because of a disability, but it does not pay for care expenses. An LTCI policy does. Having both types of insurance provides better protection against the potential financial loss of being disabled. Also, most disability policies end at age 65, yet the risk of needing long-term care is greatly increased at the older ages.

Offering a group LTCI policy may also help attract and retain employees. When unemployment is low and the worker has the upper hand in the employment market, employers can use their benefit package as a way of differentiating themselves from the competition. Long-term care insurance is relatively new to employee benefit offerings in that only a small percentage of employers provide it. When other employers are cutting back on their employee benefits, expanding one's own benefit package with group long-term care insurance can be a morale booster. This type of unique employee benefit may help sway someone's decision to join a different employer's workforce or stay with their current employer.

When long-term care insurance is offered to the members of employees' extended families, it can help minimize employee absenteeism caused by the responsibilities of caring for relatives. If an employee's family members do not have long-term care coverage, the employee may have to take time off work, arriving late or leaving early, to provide care. If employees' relatives have LTCI protection, they have the financial resources available to pay for professional services.

Employees who opt for LTCI protection will find premiums more affordable than if they wait to purchase coverage after retirement. This is because premiums are based on their age when they first enroll and are lower at the younger ages. Also, there is more disposable income available for long-term care insurance premiums while they're still working.

There is also a greater likelihood that the employee will qualify for coverage if they apply at a younger age. As employees get older, they become more susceptible to chronic conditions or other debilitating illnesses. This could make the purchase of long-term care insurance that requires underwriting more difficult to obtain—employees may become uninsurable.

Finally, with long-term care insurance, retirees will have a better retirement program and the peace of mind associated with having their retirement nest egg protected from the costs of long-term care services.

» The Sponsor's Responsibilities

An employer sponsoring long-term care insurance has certain responsibilities. It must select a carrier and provide input on the design of the specific plan offering. (Plan design is discussed in detail in the next chapter.) Once a plan is chosen, the employer must adapt its payroll deduction system to handle LTCI premiums, and it may approve the insurer's communication materials. Next, the employer supports the product rollout by making sure potential participants are made aware of the offering. This is often done through company-wide e-mail, posters, newsletters, payroll notices, and the like. After the rollout, the employer's ongoing responsibility consists of remitting premium payments and communicating the current list of eligible and covered employees to the insurer.

The sponsor's support of the plan is critical to its success. This support is most effective when the insurer is able to provide ample promotion and education that builds on the sponsor's communication and information program. The sponsor can use any combination of the following to create awareness of the new LTCI offering:

- internal newsletters,
- educational material mailed to the potential participants' homes,
- videotapes,
- posters,
- news stories,
- e-mail,
- websites,
- benefit fairs or seminars,
- payroll inserts, and
- departmental meetings.

It is essential that key human resource personnel be well trained in the LTCI plan so that they can answer potential participants' basic questions; more complex questions are referred to the insurer's group enrollment specialists or the agent representing the insurer.

Written material is the main communication vehicle. Whereas an individual sale includes a face-to-face meeting with an agent, a group long-term care insurance sale relies largely on the enrollment packet. This packet has to balance providing the details of the offering with simplifying it so that consumers can understand it. Without the sponsor's support, the potential participants will not open or read the enrollment packet. Many employers supplement the enrollment materials with worksite seminars and meetings to review and discuss the material.

The sponsor generally approves all written material before it is distributed to the potential participants. The material must balance the needs of all interested parties. The consumer has a need for easy-to-understand information. The insurer has a need to accurately disclose policy features and benefits. The sponsor has a need for information that will encourage enrollment. And state insurance departments require the insurer to file the material for approval (in states that require review of advertising materials). This requirement may result in different written material in different states for essentially the same product.

In the most successful programs, employers allow the insurer or the insurer's representative to make presentations during employees' regular work schedule (versus before work, during their lunch, or after work). It is best when all potential participants, including eligible family members, are welcome to attend. Even more successful are programs with mandatory attendance, although this is rare. The presentations begin with education on why long-term care insurance is important. This is followed by an explanation of the offering, including a walk-through of the enrollment packet, either at the same meeting or a subsequent meeting.

FOCUS QUESTION 4

Outline the responsibilities of group insurance sponsors.

_____

_____

_____

_____

_____

_____

_____

» Group Characteristics

Both the employer and the insurer want to see success in the rollout of a new employee benefit. Some insurers and sponsors measure success by the number of participants that opt for the coverage, while others judge in terms of the overall premium paid for the coverage. Insurers should look at the sponsor's demographics and stability before moving forward with group long-term care insurance.[2]

The age distribution of the employee group is critical. A healthy proportion of employees ages 40 to 60 is desirable. These are the people who are concerned with protecting their retirement nest egg and who are most likely to have had a personal long-term care experience. Younger employees generally have little interest in long-term care and see the potential need as too distant to worry about. They also are likely to have other, more immediate needs competing for their incomes (such as buying a home, paying for their children's education, and so on).

Since women are more likely to need long-term care and are also more likely to be caregivers, they often have a greater interest in LTCI. Therefore, a disproportionately male workforce may have lower participation results. Allowing spouses to participate in the offering will help with the success regardless of the gender percentages of the group.

Income levels also play a role in the success of a product offered to a group. Groups in which the average income is over $40,000 per year have better results. Sufficient discretionary income makes a big difference for the enrollment.

White-collar professions are more receptive to group LTCI than blue-collar trades. Employees accustomed to receiving their benefits from a union are not likely to participate in a program where they are required to pay the premium. Educational background will also play a role in the success—the more education a participant has, the more likely they are to enroll.

The length of tenure of employees is important. Sponsors that have long-term relationships with their employees generally are more successful with this product than those with high turnover. Employees who have been around a long time are more likely to look to the employer for benefits. Also, an employer with a good track record with other voluntary benefits is more likely to have success offering long-term care insurance.

Organizational stability is also important. Offering group LTCI when an employer is in financial difficulty, undergoing restructuring, or engaged in merger talks will result in few applications for the coverage. Employees are more interested in planning for the distant future when their immediate future is secure.

Employers with employees concentrated in one or a small number of localities are preferable. It is better to have 1,000 people in three locations than 1,500 people in 20 locations. A greater geographic concentration of employees allows for an easier rollout. Enrollment can gain momentum as those who have decided to purchase the coverage talk with other employees about the importance of the protection and the value of the offering.

Finally, much depends on the person in the company who will make the decisions about LTCI coverage. The decision-maker's personal experience with long-term care services and providers makes a difference in their commitment to the product and the subsequent success of the offering. If the president of the company (or another highly visible person) has had an experience with a spouse or parent needing long-term care services, the enthusiasm for the coverage can be felt throughout the organization.

FOCUS QUESTION 5

What are some of the considerations or factors that would influence one's decision to opt into group long-term care insurance?

_____

_____

_____

_____

_____

_____

_____

_____

_____

_____

_____

_____

» Summary

Group long-term care insurance has become a more popular offering with employers and affinity groups in the past few years. There are numerous reasons why LTCI is valued by both sponsors and group members.

A group LTCI offering is successful when there is a strong working relationship between the sponsor and the insurer. This partnership must maintain the focus on why the coverage is important for the potential participants and must provide the necessary support for the offering.

Key Terms

Cafeteria approach	Request for proposal (RFP)
Carve-out group	Voluntary benefits
Medical savings account	

» Review Questions

1. What are some of the differences between a group policy and a group-marketed individual policy?

2. Define a medium-size group for long-term care group insurance purposes.

3. What are minimum sizes for employer-sponsored and affinity groups?

4. Can insurers set their requirements higher than these minimums?

5. What are carve-out groups?

6. What is a group sponsor?

7. Name the types of insurance that group long-term care insurance can supplement.

8. Explain how group long-term care insurance offered by employers to employees and their families can reduce absenteeism.

9. Why might an enrollment packet differ from state to state even though the insurance offered is identical?

10. From the insurer's perspective, what age distribution is desirable in the employee group opting to buy long-term care insurance?

» Answers

1. LTCI policies that are individually issued contain minor modifications on a group-marketed basis; individuals who buy these policies are offered the modified terms owing to their membership in the group. Unlike a group policy, a group-marketed individual policy is portable without any conversion because it is issued directly to the individual insured.

2. Between 1,000 and 3,000 employees or members.

3. Three and 10, respectively.

4. Yes.

5. These are groups that employers can "carve out" of a larger employee group for the purpose of offering long-term care insurance. The group must be based on objective criteria and be fully insured.

6. The employer or affinity group to which the master policy is issued.

7. Health insurance (medical expense insurance) and disability income insurance.

8. If an employee's family members have long-term care coverage, the employee may not need to take time off work to provide care, as the family members have the financial resources available to pay for professional services.

9. Some state insurance departments require insurers to file their enrollment material for approval This requirement may result in different written material in different states for essentially the same product.

10. A large concentration of individuals of ages 40 to 60 is desirable.

NOTES

1 Lombardi, Lucian. 2001. "Marketing Group Insurance and Health Care Benefits, Trends and Insights, Phase Two." LIMRA International.

2 Much of this information is taken from "Who Buys Long-Term Care Insurance in the Workplace? A Study of Employer Long-Term Care Insurance Plans 2000-2001," for the Health Insurance Association of America by LifePlans, Inc., October 2001. The full report can be purchased from HIAA. The executive summary is available at http://membership.hiaa.org/pdfs/ExecutiveSummaryB-NBinWorkplace.pdf. Another excellent source available to LIMRA International members is "Characteristics of Group Long-Term Care Insurance Plans" by Patty Ash, found at http://www.limra.com/frames.asp?link=/abstracts/3578.asp.

14

Group LTCI Offerings

» Overview

Once a sponsor has committed to offering long-term care insurance, the plan design is developed. Larger sponsors usually use a consultant to develop a request for proposal (RFP), which includes a comprehensive list of all of the sponsor's considerations and preferences, including plan design. Sponsors not using the RFP process generally make all the same decisions, but they do so using less formal methods.

Determining the appropriate plan design choices to offer participants often involves negotiation among many parties—a benefits committee, the human resource department, senior management, and the insurance company. Similarly, in an affinity group, there might be a person or committee that has responsibility for managing the benefits and services that are offered to members. In smaller employers, the president, partners, or owners make these decisions.

» Designing the Offering

It is important to limit the plan options to a manageable number in order to simplify the decisions potential participants must make. This is particularly true in larger employer groups, where there may be little or no one-on-one communication about the coverage choices. Smaller organizations or small carve-out groups that plan to use individual policies are able to leave the insurer's full range of choices and options available to the potential participants, provided an agent or broker will be available to assist with the process of reviewing choices and selecting the appropriate coverage options.

The sponsoring entity essentially has to decide key aspects of the plan design that will best meet its members' needs. These aspects pertain to the following questions:

- When are benefits paid?
- How much is paid?
- How long are benefits paid?

Specifically, "when are benefits paid" refers to decisions about what services are covered and the nature and length of the elimination period. "How much is paid" refers to the daily maximum benefit or choice of benefit amounts and the type of inflation protection offered. "How long are benefits paid" refers to the policy's benefit maximum. Ancillary benefits, such as nonforfeiture options, are also considered.

The Options

Each option within each area is considered for a package to offer the potential participants. With respect to coverage type, most groups offer only comprehensive coverage, but sometimes a facility-care-only policy is appropriate as an option (for example, for retirees or those with more limited incomes.) Because of its limited appeal, insurers in the group LTCI marketplace simply do not offer home-care-only insurance.

The sponsor may select only one daily benefit amount or offer two or three choices. In part this depends on whether the potential participants live within one fairly homogeneous geographic area, or whether they live in different parts of the country with different long-term care costs. For a nationwide company, the daily benefit amounts might vary by geographic area.

The sponsor may want to offer only one elimination period to keep the choices simple, but sometimes a second choice might be offered. Similarly, most policies offer a choice of one or two policy maximums, as people have different preferences and abilities to afford coverage.

The insurer must offer a nonforfeiture benefit to the sponsor, but the sponsor can decline this offer, so that it is not available to participants. Similarly, the insurer must offer inflation protection to the sponsor, but the sponsor can decide not to pass that offer along to participants. A growing number of groups are offering 5 percent compounded inflation protection to each individual, given the importance of inflation protection. A purchase option inflation feature is sometimes available to participants, alone or in addition to the 5 percent compounded feature. (A few states require that these mandated offers of inflation protection and nonforfeiture be made directly to each individual, rather than only to the sponsor.)

Prepackaged Plans

The sponsor of a group plan may offer all of these choices to individual group members. Or it may group the choices into a series of **prepackaged plans**. The advantage of offering the choices "à la carte" is that someone might prefer a high daily benefit amount but a more limited policy maximum, or vice versa. When options are prepackaged, they may combine in ways that don't appeal to everyone. They may, for instance, combine all the "low" choices together and all the "high" choices together, but not allow individuals to "mix and match" if that is their preference. Both approaches can be effective — ultimately the choice depends on the demographics and preferences of the participating group.

The purpose of offering packages to potential participants is to simplify their choices, reduce confusion, and minimize the number of calculations required when making a purchasing decision. Table 14.1 shows three possible packages that offer gradually increasing (and more expensive) coverage.

TABLE 14.1

An Offering of Three Prepackaged Group LTCI Plans

	Plan 1	Plan 2	Plan 3
Covered providers	Comprehensive	Comprehensive	Comprehensive
Daily benefit amount	$100 per day	$150 per day	$200 per day
Elimination period	90 days	90 days	90 days
Policy maximum	3 years	5 years	Unlimited
Inflation protection	No	Yes	Yes
Nonforfeiture benefit	No	No	Yes
Premium	Low	Medium	High

What are the pros and cons of prepackaged group LTCI plans?

_____

_____

_____

_____

_____

_____

_____

_____

_____

Group and Individual Policies Compared

Table 14.2 shows how typical group coverage differs from the typical individual policy. The primary reason the average annual premium is

TABLE 14.2

Comparing LTCI Policy Design Characteristics in the Group and Individual Markets

Policy characteristics	Group market	Individual market
Covered providers	97% comprehensive	77% comprehensive
Elimination period	63 days average	65 days average
Daily benefit amount	$124/day average	$109/day average
Inflation protection	40% compounded, 0% simple, 48% purchase options	22% compounded, 17% simple, 2% purchase options
Policy maximum	6.3 years average	5.5 years average
Nonforfeiture	29%	Less than 1%
Annual premium	$722 average	$1,677 average

Source: "Who Buys Long-Term Care Insurance in the Workplace? A Study of Employer Long-Term Care Insurance Plans 2000-2001," prepared for the Health Insurance Association of America by LifePlans, Inc., October 2001.[1]

much lower in the group LTCI market is that the average age at issue is lower than in the individual market. For the data reported in the table, the average age in the employer group market is 50, and in the individual market it is 67. There are also often discounts associated with the economies of marketing insurance through a group sponsor.

» Renewability

All group long-term care insurance is guaranteed renewable. The insurer may adjust the premium for a class of insureds if actuarially justified, but it cannot cancel a policy. Only the sponsor can cancel a group LTCI policy, and some policies are written such that even the sponsor cannot cancel them, although the sponsor can stop offering the coverage to new insureds. And if a sponsor cancels a policy, insureds are allowed to continue their coverage on an individual policy basis, or to convert it to a group policy operated through a trust set up by the insurer for this purpose.

A sponsor may replace its group policy with coverage from a different insurer. The new insurer must offer coverage to all those who had coverage with the previous company. The new insurer cannot take into consideration any changes in an individual insured's health history, an individual's use of long-term care services, or their claim experience under the previous policy. The preexisting conditions that were covered under the old policy must be covered to the same extent by the new policy.

A participant or certificate-holder has the right to maintain the coverage in force if the sponsor elects to discontinue sponsoring the master policy for which that particular certificate was issued and does not replace the coverage with a similar policy within 31 days of terminating the previous coverage. The insurance company must make a substantially equivalent, individually issued policy available to the participants when a master policy is cancelled for any reason. This opportunity to convert policies is available at least six months prior to and one month after the cancellation of the group policy. The converted policy is offered without evidence of insurability, but a written application may be required. The premium for the converted, individually issued policy is based on the insured's age at the time of initial enrollment in the group policy. Some group policies are written such that the coverage simply continues as is, even if the sponsor elects to cancel or stop sponsoring the plan. In this approach, the only change the insured needs to make is to elect a method of paying premiums directly if they were previously being paid through the sponsoring group in some way (such as payroll deduction).

Group long-term care insurance also guarantees coverage that is fully portable. The insurer cannot terminate an individual's coverage because they no longer meet the eligibility requirements for the group insurance. This might occur when an employee leaves the company, divorces a spouse, or retires. If an employee divorces a spouse who was insured under the group policy, or if that employee dies, the spouse's coverage remains intact. Similarly, if an employee retires or quits, their coverage continues, although they may have to elect a method for paying premiums directly, rather than through the sponsoring group.

» Underwriting Options

The purpose of underwriting is to pool like risks. When like risks are pooled, each insured pays the premium appropriate for their risk. Consider, for example, automobile insurance and the way it is underwritten. Careful drivers who have not had an accident or traffic violation for a long time are able to get the best rates when they are pooled with other good drivers. The potential to improve rates occurs when a driver is over a certain age, is married, or has short commutes to work. Insurers have gained the experience necessary to recognize that these drivers have the fewest claims and present the lowest risk, so they get the best rates.

Insurance agents encourage drivers who qualify for this class of insured to take advantage of the low rates and any discounts available to them. Agents do not have good drivers purchase their automobile insurance from companies that specialize in 16-year-olds who drive sports cars. History tells the insurer that the 16-year-old is more likely than experienced drivers to have a claim soon after the policy is issued, so their rates are higher. The good driver knows that by buying from the high-risk insurer they would overpay for their insurance and subsidize the high-risk drivers.

The same concept holds true for all forms of insurance, including long-term care insurance. Insureds do not want to overpay for their insurance based on their risk class. Healthy people want rates appropriate to their health; people with chronic illnesses (the high-risk class for long-term care insurance) are grateful to find coverage anywhere. Ideally, each insured wants to purchase coverage for which they just barely qualified at a certain rate. This is because the least healthy person in a risk pool is subsidized by those with better health.

FOCUS QUESTION 2

Summarize the concept of underwriting—that is, pooling risk.

_____

_____

_____

_____

_____

_____

_____

_____

_____

_____

_____

Obtaining Underwriting Information

When pooling like risks by means of underwriting, the question of how much information is needed arises. Insurers must balance the cost of obtaining information against the benefit of having it. The best way to obtain information about someone's health history is to personally meet with the individual and with everyone who has ever provided health care for the individual—preferably all at the same time. Clearly, that level of detail comes with a huge price tag, so no company tries to obtain it.

All insurers require an individual seeking coverage to complete an application documenting what they know about their current health condition and health history. Some insurers continue their investigation into the applicant's risk profile by requesting medical records from all doctors seen in the recent past, by conducting a face-to-face assessment interview to evaluate the applicant's functional (physical) abilities, or by conducting an interview with the applicant over the telephone. Such an investigation gives insurers better data with which to identify and pool like risks.

This level of detail is typical in the individual market, but for several reasons underwriting is usually much more streamlined in the group market. First, the younger age of the population in the workplace and the mere fact that they are actively working is a good indication that they have at least a certain degree of health and functional and cognitive independence. Second, the detailed health history profiles typical in the individual market are usually not acceptable to the plan sponsor or the individuals considering insurance. The plan sponsor wants as many people as possible to receive coverage. If a group is large enough, insurers are able to use the experience of the group (rather than of individual members) to determine rates and premiums for that group. Insurers offer different levels of underwriting to employer or affinity groups to allow those groups the opportunity of using their experience as a single pool or joining with other groups in pooling their experience.

Insurers have several underwriting approaches to group policies. Sometimes a group sponsor can choose the approach it prefers, although there may be different premium charges or minimum participation requirements associated with different approaches. Sometimes the insurer sets conditions under which it will offer a sponsor each of these different underwriting approaches. Insurers also have rules about which types of applicants can be underwritten within each approach. Key elements of these approaches and these requirements are summarized below. The different underwriting levels are as follows: guaranteed issue, modified guaranteed issue, simplified or short-form underwriting, and full or long-form underwriting.

Guaranteed Issue

Typically, for large employers group health insurance comes with no restrictions—employees get coverage for themselves and their dependents regardless of anyone's current or past health conditions. Even people undergoing cancer treatments, those who have had surgery for degenerative heart conditions, or those who were born with birth defects are able to get the best major medical insurance available during open enrollment times. This epitomizes the concept of **guaranteed issue**.

With guaranteed issue long-term care insurance, the insurer anticipates a certain number of claims soon after a policy is issued. To some extent this is mitigated with LTCI because the guaranteed issue coverage is only available to employees who are currently actively at work, so the likelihood that they have physical or cognitive impairments is much smaller than the likelihood that they have a variety of health conditions (which might affect claims for medical insurance). Still, the insurer is likely to charge more to accept everyone into the group without any level of underwriting. In other words, the healthy participants will subsidize participants who are impaired enough to require benefits in the short term.

Guaranteed issue coverage is likely to be offered only when at least some of the following conditions are met:

- the employer group is relatively large;
- enrollment is limited to employees actively at work during a pre-set enrollment period (such as 30 or 60 days);
- a minimum number of employees agree to participate in the insurance;
- the employer is paying some or all of the premium cost;
- there are limits on the coverage (such as no lifetime benefits) that protect the insurer from adverse selection; and
- the carrier feels that the employer group does not present too great a risk because of the nature of the industry in which they are involved. (For example, the public sector is more handicapped accessible and usually has a higher proportion of currently disabled employees. Most insurers do not want to offer guaranteed issue coverage to this type of employer.)

Modified Guaranteed Issue

As an attractive alternative to guaranteed issue, many insurers offer a **modified guaranteed issue** option. This approach requires applicants to provide their health history but minimizes the detail. The insurer might only require that the person be actively at work and it may ask a handful of health questions that could automatically disqualify someone for the coverage.

How an insurer defines "actively at work" varies. It may require that a person be working full-time, that they work a certain number of hours per week, that they have missed only a certain number of days in the past year for medical reasons, and/or that they are not currently on claim with a disability income policy. An insurer may limit "actively at work" in terms of age—age 65 and younger is typical. Some insurers require an employee to have been hired at least 30 days before they are eligible to apply—this is meant to prevent someone from joining a company simply to get LTCI insurance.

The questions asked in modified guaranteed issue focus on the most common causes for a claim soon after policy issuance. A company may seek information for the past year, three years, five years, or ten years, or it may ask whether a condition ever existed. A different period may be used depending upon the condition. The most typical questions on a modified guaranteed issue application are the following:

- Do you currently require assistance of any kind with activities of daily living like bathing, dressing, toileting, eating, or taking medications?

- Are you currently receiving long-term care services, or have you received them within the past 12 months?

- Do you have any one of the following conditions: Parkinson's disease, Alzheimer's disease, a similar degenerative neurological condition, multiple sclerosis, metastatic cancer, multiple strokes?

This approach might also include questions on the following:

- heart problems,

- treatments for cancer,

- diagnosis of HIV or AIDS,

- dependency on insulin for diabetes,

- muscle problems associated with a degenerating nervous system,
- the presence of a cognitive impairment, and
- the use of assistance devices like a wheelchair or walker.

Because sponsors want the decision on whether coverage will be offered to an applicant to be made in a timely manner, additional medical information or functional assessments are not ordered or considered for active employees applying for coverage. Whether a certificate is issued to the person depends solely on the information provided on the modified guaranteed issue application. When someone is declined coverage, they might have the option of appeal by going through an additional level of underwriting.

Modified guaranteed issue is becoming more common than guaranteed issue, even for the larger companies. It may be preferred when the conditions for guaranteed issue described above are not met. Also, the insurer may offer a slightly reduced premium if the sponsor elects this approach over guaranteed issue coverage.

Simplified Underwriting

Simplified underwriting (or **short-form underwriting**) involves more questions than modified guaranteed issue but fewer questions than would be found on the typical application for individual coverage. The application used, sometimes referred to as a short-form application, asks about conditions that are automatically declined in addition to conditions that frequently lead to the need for long-term care services. A detailed listing of prescription medications is requested—this gives the insurer an indication of the conditions for which the applicant has received treatment from physicians.

An underwriter reviewing a short-form application might request additional health-related information or assessments. This can include a copy of the applicant's medical records, an attending physician statement, a face-to-face physical and cognitive assessment, or a personal history interview. All this is done to obtain more details on the applicant's health history and their ability to function independently without physical or cognitive limitations.

The use of more health-related information in simplified underwriting results in a greater ability to pool risks. It can also bring about greater stability of premiums, an advantage for insureds. Moreover, a slightly lower premium may be offered than if guaranteed issue or modified guaranteed issue is used. Or the insurer may be more comfortable including richer benefits like lifetime coverage. The disadvantage of this approach is the longer turnaround time from application to approval. The insurer and sponsor consider these trade-offs and select the approach that best meets their needs.

Full Underwriting

Full underwriting (also called **long-form underwriting**) involves the same level of inquiry used when issuing an individual LTCI policy. The application asks for an extensive medical history. The company's underwriting standards dictate the extent to which additional information is requested and reviewed. This approach takes the longest amount of time but does the best job of pooling like risks for stability of premiums. Generally, medical records from the applicant's physician are requested on all applicants over age 60 or 65. A telephone interview may be done for applications from those between the ages 65 and 74, and an in-person interview is typical for applicants aged 75 and older.

» Extending Coverage

Group medical, dental, vision, and life insurance are normally offered to employees and their dependents, including spouses and children. Because long-term care insurance is a multigenerational issue, many sponsors like to make the coverage available to family members other than just dependents. They include employees' parents, parents-in-law, grandparents, grandparents-in-law, and sometimes siblings or adult children.

Some sponsors extend group LTCI coverage to retirees. Frequently these individuals continue a relationship with their former employer through pensions, a 401(k) plan, or health insurance. Adding long-term care insurance simplifies the retiree's decision-making process in determining which company to buy their LTCI coverage from. Retirees' spouses are usually able to participate as well.

FOCUS QUESTION 3

What individuals other than current employees may be offered long-term care insurance under employer-sponsored group plans?

_____

_____

_____

_____

_____

_____

In almost all cases, relatives and retirees pay their own premium without any sponsor subsidy. Payment is normally done through either payroll or pension deduction (from the employee's paycheck or the retirement payment). Or the insurer can directly bill the participant or arrange to deduct the premium from their bank account.

Seldom is less than full underwriting offered to these potential participants. Unlike employees, nothing is known about their actively-at-work status or recent use of sick leave days. Insurers are reluctant to provide even simplified underwriting and will likely order medical records as part of the underwriting process. And sponsors are less concerned about the speed with which a policy is issued to a nontraditional participant or whether the individual is declined coverage. Retirees and parents of employees are usually subject to full underwriting. Spouses of active employees may receive full underwriting, or if they are under a certain age (such as 65), they may have to undergo only short-form underwriting.

These nontraditional participants, like other insureds, get discounted group rates, and they benefit from the fact that someone else did the due diligence in selecting a company from which to purchase their coverage. The advantage to the sponsor is that these additional participants help expand the pool of people insured under the program.

» Group Rates and Premiums

Rates for group long-term care insurance have the same relationship to coverage options as with individual policies. Rates are higher for greater daily benefits, shorter elimination periods, longer policy maximums, and for the addition of inflation protection and nonforfeiture. Premiums are calculated using the rate and the daily benefit maximum, just as with individual policies.

Employees may receive a full rate chart or only a summary premium schedule showing only the premium for each offering at various ages. This simplifies the decision-making process for the potential participant. The premiums shown in the offering are based on the premium payment frequency available to employees. An employer group using payroll deduction to pay the premium will have only one premium frequency available, while an affinity group where the members pay the premium directly to the insurer may offer a range of premium frequencies.

All forms of group insurance have **group rates** that are different from rates for individually issued policies. Normally, group rates are lower because of reduced administrative costs for billing and collection, underwriting, and policy issue. Also, group insurance commissions are smaller because a large portion of the agent's work is done with the initial sale to the sponsor. There may not be an agent role beyond that sale, or their role assisting individual applicants may be limited to a few group enrollment meetings, rather than extensive one-on-one contact. If the sponsor deals directly with the insurer, no agent compensation is payable. These reduced costs are passed on to the sponsor and participants in the form of lower rates.

There is a difference between group rates and **group discounts**. Group rates are the rates used to calculate the premium for those insureds that enroll in a group plan. Group discounts are used when individual policies are issued to members of a group. Here too the insurer can realize some administrative cost reductions, and these are passed on to the consumer in the form of a percentage discount off the standard individual rate. Discounts of 5 and 10 percent are common.

Since group long-term care insurance is guaranteed renewable, an insurer can adjust premiums as experience warrants, subject to the approval of state insurance departments. A premium increase resulting from an insured's decision to increase coverage is not considered a rate increase, as long as the rates for the base policy and each incremental increase in coverage remain the same. Many group contracts (as well as individual policies) allow insureds to apply to purchase additional coverage at attained age rates while the rates and premium for the previous coverage remains constant.

A sponsor can discontinue a master policy or replace it with another LTCI policy. If the sponsor cancels the master policy, the NAIC LTCI Model Regulation requires that each participant or certificate-holder be able to maintain their coverage in force by paying the premium for their policy. In these situations, the insurance company must continue to provide coverage to each certificate-holder as long as premiums are paid on time.

If a group is large enough, an insurer may offer it **experience rating**— that is, the persistency, participation, expense, and claims experience of the group is used to determine a rate for the group, and this rate is then used to calculate the premiums of group members. There are cases where several sponsors have joined together to form a consortium to buy group LTCI in order to have the necessary size to have their business experience-rated.

The NAIC Model Regulation has a special exemption from the rate increase disclosure requirements for group insurance. This exemption allows insurers to experience-rate some large groups without the additional burden of state insurance department oversight when a rate increase is filed. The insurer avoids the state insurance department's scrutiny of its business practices in pricing and paying claims, or in determining that a rate spiral exists. The sponsor must have at least 5,000 potential participants and 250 actual participants to qualify for this exemption.

Premium Payment

Most group long-term care insurance is paid for, either wholly or in part, by the individuals receiving the coverage. However, there are some employer sponsors who pay some or all of the premium on behalf of their employees. (Generally only employers pay any portion of participants' premiums. It is rare for affinity groups to pay a portion of the premium unless their dues are based in part on the cost of the insurance.)

When an employer pays the entire premium for a group LTCI plan, usually all eligible employees automatically have coverage. Because many people are getting the coverage, insurers provide the greatest level of flexibility on underwriting and other choices. A sponsor paying the entire premium normally does so only for employees. Ancillary participants, such as spouses or parents, must pay their own premium. Few sponsors pay the full premium for a very rich benefit plan.

A sponsor assuming a part of the premium cost can pay a percentage of the premium or a fixed amount toward the premium. Or it can pay the premium for a "base" or "core" level of benefits, with an option available to the participant to pay an additional premium for more coverage. This optional "buy up" is common with employers that recognize the importance of providing their employees with long-term care insurance but do not want to bear the entire cost of a rich benefit plan.

Plans in which the insureds pay the entire premium are the most common in group LTCI. These are referred to as **voluntary plans**. The majority of group sponsors are still reluctant to commit large resources to such a new insurance product without a better understanding of the value it brings to the participants. The best way to gauge this value is to have the participants pay the premium and then measure the level of participation. Some groups experience high levels of participation (20 percent or more), while others have such low participation that the group is cancelled.

Perhaps the most important reason most sponsors refuse to pay a portion of LTCI premiums is that medical insurance costs continue to increase at a greater rate than general inflation. This trend erodes employers' willingness to devote additional benefit dollars for long-term care insurance.

A sponsor can also carve out a class of employees to receive favorable premium treatment. It is possible to establish a premium payment class based on years of service, exempt or salaried workers, number of hours worked or volunteered, or age (defined within state and federal discrimination laws). This group should be broad enough so that the selection of group participants is not challenged based on employment law nor does the IRS challenge it based on ownership status. There are no tax-based nondiscriminatory requirements as long as everyone within the established group is treated equally and the plan is a fully insured accident and health insurance policy.

FOCUS QUESTION 4

What are some of the class definitions used by sponsors in establishing carve-out groups?

_____

_____

_____

_____

_____

_____

Premium Payment Options

The sponsor and the insurer work together to establish how the premium will be paid to the insurer. It is easiest for the insurer when the sponsor pays the full premium for the participants and remits that amount directly to the insurer. Of course, this is the most expensive approach for the sponsor.

Another method is for the sponsor to collect premium payments through payroll deductions and then remit those amounts to the insurer through list bill. This is a viable option when participants are paying at least a portion of the premium or the full premium. Establishing the conduit that allows the collection of premium and remittance to the insurer represents a cost to the sponsor, although most employers already have payroll deduction set up for other benefits, and it is simply a matter of adding long-term care to that structure.

The insurer and the sponsor work together to ensure that the proper premium for each participant is paid. Reconciling the premium payment with each participant's coverage is time-consuming when there are new participants, participants leave the group, or there are changes in participants' coverage choices.

It is easiest for the sponsor when participants pay the insurer directly. This is common with small groups or when the sponsor is not making any contribution to the premium. It is also seen with affinity groups and associations (since there is no payroll deduction). When insureds pay directly, the insurer administers each participant's group coverage much as it handles an individual policy.

Spouses of employees can either pay the insurer directly or have their premium deducted from their employed spouse's paycheck. Retirees can pay through pension deduction or be billed directly. Most insurers allow an employee to pay the premium for their parents, but they typically do so on a direct bill basis, which minimizes the variations in premium amounts in payroll deduction. Also, most employees could not support such a sizeable deduction from their paycheck, given that the premium for their parents is likely to be fairly significant because of their older age.

» Enrollment

Once the structure of the program is finalized, the sponsor and insurer determine the timing and methods by which participants will be able to apply for and obtain coverage. This is referred to as **enrollment**. There are three primary options for enrollment—paper, the telephone, or electronically.

In the past, all group insurance enrollments involved the submission of paper applications to the insurer or the sponsor. Using this option, employees can obtain applications from enrollment packets or in on-site meetings with insurer representatives or sponsor personnel. The paper application provides the most comprehensive documentation of a participant's choices and contains their signature attesting to their disclosure of health information. The printed enrollment package includes all the necessary disclosure forms and booklets. This is the most costly and most time-consuming method to use with large groups.

Many enrollments now make use of technology, either the telephone or electronic links. In telephone enrollment, the potential participant calls the insurer's toll-free number to enroll. They can either use a touch-tone telephone to respond to prompts, or customer service personnel can ask them questions and record the answers. Following prompts works best when the coverage choices are extremely limited and simple (as when employees choose among three prepackaged plans). When more complex options are available, the telephone prompting system becomes tedious, expensive, and error-prone.

Electronic enrollment uses computer screens to gather the necessary data from the potential participant. The information is sent to the sponsor or insurer using either Internet or Intranet links. Both methods follow up the submission of information with a written confirmation of the answers along with the required disclosure material. Either paper or electronic follow up is available, as the NAIC makes its long-term care insurance buyers guide available for electronic distribution and some insurers also have their specific disclosures available online.

The NAIC Model Regulation considers electronic enrollment methods valid applications, although the applicant cannot provide a signature. The insurer must first gain consent from the sponsor to use electronic means, and safeguards must be put in place to ensure the accuracy and confidentiality of the information gathered.

In most cases, there is a limited period during which employees can enroll. Some insurers do this to allocate their personnel to the various sponsors and to create a sense of urgency among potential participants. After the initial enrollment period, the sponsor can offer the coverage on an annual basis, during open enrollment of its medical insurance offerings, or every two to three years. Voluntary plan offerings that do not have underwriting concessions might have ongoing availability, although participation results are poorest with a continuously open enrollment. Even fully underwritten voluntary plan offerings can benefit from a defined and time-limited enrollment period. Another issue involves new employees—are they eligible immediately, or must they wait for the next enrollment period?

FOCUS QUESTION 5

Outline the pros and cons of the three enrollment methods.

_____

_____

_____

_____

_____

_____

_____

_____

» Summary

Group LTCI plans are in many ways similar to individually issued policies. They have the same benefit structure with a daily benefit, elimination period, policy maximum, and optional inflation protection and nonforfeiture benefits. But group coverage does offer some flexibility not found in the individual marketplace.

The level of underwriting can vary from group to group. It can range from the same level as individual policies to no underwriting. Rates and premiums can vary by the group rather than just the plan offering.

The biggest limitation of group long-term care insurance is that not everyone has access to a plan offering. Those who want the coverage must first have a relationship with a sponsoring organization.

Key Terms

Enrollment	Group discount
Experience rating	Group rate
Full underwriting	Guaranteed issue

Key Terms	Long-form underwriting	Short-form underwriting
	Modified guaranteed issue	Simplified underwriting
	Prepackaged plan	Voluntary plan

≫ Review Questions

1. What are some of the parties that may be involved in the negotiations over group long-term care insurance policies?

2. What are three key aspects of a group policy that need to be determined?

3. Is a nonforfeiture benefit universally available in group LTCI policies?

4. Explain the concept of guaranteed issue.

5. What are the levels of underwriting that fall between guaranteed issue (no-restrictions enrollment) and full underwriting (enrollment contingent on satisfying rigorous application criteria)?

6. What is the difference between group rates and group discounts?

7. What is experience rating?

8. Is the premium for group long-term care insurance paid by individuals or employers in most cases?

9. What is thought to be the most important reason why most sponsors refuse to pay a portion of LTCI premiums?

10. What are the three methods commonly used today to enroll participants in a group insurance program?

» Answers

1. These may include a benefits committee, the human resource department, senior management, and the insurance company.

2. How much will be paid in benefits, when, and for how long.

3. No. The insurer is obligated to offer a nonforfeiture benefit to the group sponsor, but the sponsor has the right to decline to pass this option along to group participants.

4. A guaranteed issue is when group health insurance comes with no restrictions—employees get coverage for themselves and their dependents regardless of anyone's current or past health conditions.

5. The two intermediate levels are modified guaranteed issue and simplified underwriting.

6. Group rates are the rates used to calculate the premium for those insureds that enroll in a group plan. Group discounts are used when individual policies are issued to members of a group.

7. Experience rating occurs when a group's persistency, participation, expense, and claims experience are used to determine a rate for the group, and this rate is then used to calculate the premiums of group members.

8. Individuals usually pay their own premium, though some companies may cover all or part of this expense as part of their benefit package.

9. Medical insurance costs continue to increase at a greater rate than general inflation.

10. Filling out a paper application, applying by phone, or applying electronically.

Note

1 The full report can be purchased from HIAA. The executive summary is available at http://membership.hiaa.org/pdfs/ExecutiveSummaryB-NBinWorkplace.pdf.

15

Long-Term Care Programs

» Overview

In the early years of long-term care insurance, many people were looking for creative ways of solving the problem of paying for nursing home care and home care. Most governmental bodies were unwilling to increase taxes enough to finance a new entitlement program for long-term care. The demographics showed that people were living longer and more people were coming into the age group that traditionally needs care. This situation would only get worse as the baby boomers entered retirement and old age.

» Public-Private Partnership Programs

The Robert Wood Johnson Foundation (RWJF) initiated an innovative demonstration project in 1988. The goal was to address a portion of the long-term care financing problem by creating an alliance between the public and private sectors to encourage more people to prepare themselves for the long-term care dilemma by purchasing private long-term care insurance. The program would include an educational campaign to help younger people recognize the importance of planning for the possibility of needing care and identifying insurance as an option that makes sense while the coverage is still affordable and they remain healthy enough to qualify for it.

RWJF's Partnership for Long-Term Care brought together state governments (the public sector) and insurance companies (the private sector). These two entities developed a set of standards that LTCI products should meet that went further with respect to consumer protection features than was typical of many policies at the time. The Partnership program concept stipulated that individuals who purchased these specially designed Partnership policies could qualify for Medicaid assistance if they needed long-term care and had used up their private coverage, without meeting the usual asset impoverishment rules of Medicaid. This combination provided those purchasing private insurance with a new way to avoid complete impoverishment if they should require care for an extended period of time beyond what their coverage provided. As a result of this arrangement, the public sector (Medicaid) benefits from more middle-income people choosing to purchase private protection instead of spending down to rely on Medicaid. And individuals benefit by having a "Medicaid back-stop" to their private coverage if they need care beyond what their policy provides, without having to meet the full asset impoverishment rules of Medicaid.

FOCUS QUESTION 1

Explain the benefits of the RWJF Partnership program for the public sector and individuals.

_____

_____

_____

_____

_____

_____

_____

_____

While enabling legislation has been enacted in several states, at present only four have fully implemented Partnership programs. These are California, Connecticut, New York, and Indiana. There are some differences in how these state programs operate but also many common elements. This chapter focuses on the basic principles and common elements of these programs.

Standards for Insurance Policies

When the Partnerships began, long-term care insurance was in its infancy. Finding a policy with meaningful home care benefits was difficult. True inflation protection was still emerging. Insureds often had to satisfy an elimination period more than once when they stopped using professional care covered under the policy. The Partnership policy was innovative in the way it addressed these issues and set new standards for LTCI policies that weren't yet in place for all policies.

Many of the LTCI policies sold during the late 1980s were nursing-home-only policies. The number of assisted living communities was growing, and home care was becoming the provider of choice for most people needing care. The designers of the Partnership program saw that the long-term care field was undergoing dramatic change and wanted to be sure that Partnership policies covered the full spectrum of emerging provider types. The original Partnership policies required that the insurer offer a comprehensive policy that covered care at home, in the community, and in a broader range of facilities. (It could offer a facility-care-only policy as well if it wished.)

The Partnership program also recognized the importance of inflation protection to the value of coverage and in minimizing insureds' out-of-pocket expenses. Therefore, Partnership policies are required to include automatic inflation protection that increases the daily maximum benefit at 5 percent compounded annually.

Partnership plans are also required to have an elimination period that is satisfied only once per lifetime, rather than requiring the insured to meet this requirement with each episode of care. The concern was that people with limited assets who needed care several times could, in some circumstances, spend down their retirement nest egg before qualifying for insurance benefits. A shorter elimination period would help the problem but could increase the insurance premium to the point that the policy would become unaffordable. The compromise settled on for the Partnership policies was to design the elimination period so that it would be met only once while the policy remained in force.

At the time the Partnership policies were developed, some companies only waived premiums when the insured was receiving care in a nursing home. If an insured was collecting benefits for home care or assisted living, they still had to pay premiums. There was the possibility that impaired insureds would forget to pay premiums and the policy would lapse. The potential for this unfortunate scenario was eliminated with two of the Partnership policy's requirements: First, the waiver of premium must be effective for care received in a nursing home or other type of residential care facility, and second, the insurer must obtain the name of a third party from the insured who could be contacted in case of nonpayment of premium, so that the policy wouldn't lapse because the insured forgot to pay premiums.

The early developers of long-term care insurance had always strived to avoid the managed care approach. LTCI insurers did not want to tell people where they had to receive their care and how much was reasonable to pay for services. But given the continuing evolution of providers and services, many claimants were not knowledgeable about the types of care that were available in their communities. Many ended up in nursing homes when that was not the best solution for them. The Partnership policies struck a compromise with the concept of care coordination. This would allow the insurer to use consultants to assist the claimant and their family in planning care and securing appropriate services. However, the insurance company did not require the insured to go to one provider or another, nor did it scrutinize the invoice when the cost seemed higher than expected. The insurer did not manage the cost of care but rather provided assistance to insureds to obtain the care best suited to their needs.

A fear of many potential buyers of long-term care insurance at the time was that their claim would be denied and they would have no appeal available to them. Although all LTCI policies have an appeal process, RWJF wanted to provide buyers of Partnership policies a higher level of comfort. RWJF mandated that the state office managing the Partnership would act as an intermediary to ensure that claim denials received careful scrutiny and that appropriate claims were paid in a timely fashion.

One goal of the Partnership program was to make private LTCI coverage more affordable to middle-income seniors. Certain features of the policies are designed to minimize cost. Partnership policies must offer short benefit durations, such as one or two years. (Policies with longer durations may also be offered but may not qualify for the same level of asset protection.) Certain minimum and maximum daily benefit amounts are mandated. And when they were initially introduced, it was common for Partnership policies to offer only the shorter policy maximums.

The Partnership also wanted to be sure that agents were properly trained and fully informed about this new program. Those who wanted to sell the Partnership policies were required to complete between six and eight hours of training on the program. This training was well received by agents, although it added to their already existing continuing education requirements.

FOCUS QUESTION 2

Summarize the problems identified and addressed by the Partnership program.

_____

_____

_____

_____

_____

_____

_____

_____

_____

_____

_____

_____

_____

_____

Changes in Medicaid Qualification

The four states that initiated RWJF's innovative program were California, Connecticut, Indiana, and New York. They received financial grants to make adjustments in their Medicaid qualification criteria to foster the growth of long-term care insurance in general and the Partnership policies in particular. To change their Medicaid qualification criteria, these states needed approval from the federal Department of Health and Human Services (HHS).

Medicaid qualification criteria vary from state to state, but in general a person is eligible for Medicaid only if their assets are below roughly $2,000 and their income is at or near the poverty level. In essence, one qualifies for Medicaid by being poor already or by "spending down" one's assets and income on care until one becomes poor. Minimizing the negative effects of this humbling asset liquidation process was one of the objectives of the Partnership.

These four states developed two different variations on Medicaid qualification criteria that received HHS approval. The **dollar-for-dollar model** was the original Partnership design and is still used in Connecticut and California's Partnership programs. In this approach, the Medicaid applicant can keep an amount of assets equal to the amount of benefits they received from their Partnership LTCI policy. This in essence increases the Medicaid-qualifying asset level to the amount of insurance benefits received plus $2,000 (the level for those without a Partnership policy). As an example, an applicant can qualify for Medicaid while keeping $102,000 if their Partnership policy exhausted its available benefits (policy maximum) after paying $100,000 in benefits. If the state has an income requirement in order to qualify for Medicaid, the applicant must still meet it.

The other model now used in New York and Indiana is the **total assets design**. This design allows someone who had a Partnership policy and exhausted that policy's benefits to retain all their assets and still qualify for Medicaid. The applicant must have received at least three years of nursing home benefits or six years of home care benefits or a comparable combination. Once the applicant's insurance benefits are exhausted, they are able to retain all of their assets regardless of the amount, and the asset transfer look-back rules do not apply.

These two models ease the qualification criteria for assets, but there is no change in Medicaid income criteria. That is, people owning Partnership policies can to some extent avoid liquidating their assets, but they still must spend almost all their income on care. Thus, the Partnership program does not make sense for those with significant pension or investment income.

Expanding the Partnership Plans

The funding from RWJF catapulted these four states into the limelight of the Medicaid and LTCI fields. Other states began to follow their lead. Then Congress included an amendment in the Omnibus Budget Reconciliation Act of 1993 (OBRA '93) that halted the expansion of Partnership plans. OBRA '93 stated that only plans approved by HHS prior to May 14, 1993 would receive grandfathered status and could continue as designed. Plans approved after that date must include provisions for recovering assets from the estate of Medicaid beneficiaries. The net effect is that for any new plans the asset protection provision of the Partnership plans is in place only while the insured is alive.

Some states have looked past OBRA '93 and tried to implement a Partnership-like plan. Washington and Illinois have programs in place, and in other states enabling legislation is regularly proposed. These plans do make it easier to qualify for Medicaid, but because of OBRA '93, there are no exemptions of assets from the estate recovery process (including the use of liens). These plans have not received much support from the insurance industry because of their administrative requirements and their limited market potential, given the need to recover assets from the insured's estate.

Limitations of the Partnership Plans

The Partnership plans are well designed and meet the needs of many residents in the states in which they're available. But they have a few drawbacks from a consumer's perspective.

One problem is that they are not completely portable. While the insured can receive care under their private Partnership policy in other states, they can only receive asset protection when applying for Medicaid in the state in which they purchased the policy. The one exception to this rule was created by recently passed legislation in Connecticut and Indiana, which allows for a reciprocal arrangement between those two states. But no other states allow for a break in their Medicaid qualification criteria if someone with an out-of-state Partnership plan applies for Medicaid. The insured is still able to collect benefits from the Partnership policy regardless of the state in which they receive care, but the Medicaid flexibility on spend-down rules are available only in the state where they bought the Partnership policy.

The other principal drawback of the Partnership programs is that, although insureds' assets are protected, once their insurance benefits are exhausted, they must apply for Medicaid and rely on Medicaid benefits to fund their long-term care. And although the Medicaid program does an excellent job in meeting the needs of many people, it has certain disadvantages compared to private long-term care insurance.

Not all long-term care services are covered by Medicaid, and not all providers accept Medicaid reimbursement. Some state Medicaid programs don't pay benefits for assisted living, and some pay for little if any care at home. The majority of nursing homes do accept Medicaid recipients, but many accept only a limited number, leading to waiting lists, and some do not accept Medicaid beneficiaries at all.

A Medicaid beneficiary must spend almost all their income to pay for their care. They can keep only a very small personal needs allowance ($30 to $50 per month depending on the state). The spouse of a Medicaid recipient still living at home is able to keep some income to live on, but only within certain limits.

Partnership Plans

The websites below provide information on Partnership plans in various states:

California   http://www.dhs.ca.gov/cpltc/

Connecticut   http://www.opm.state.ct.us/pdpd4/ltc/Insurer/insurer.htm

Indiana   http://www.state.in.us/fssa/iltcp/index.html

Iowa   http://www.legis.state.ia.us/Rules/2001/iac/191iac/19172/19172.pdf

Massachusetts http://www.state.ma.us/dma/masshealthinfo/over65/ltcins—IDX.htm

New York   http://www.nyspltc.org/

FOCUS QUESTION 3

Summarize the drawbacks of Partnership programs.

_____

_____

_____

_____

_____

_____

_____

_____

_____

» The CalPERS Program

The **California Public Employees Retirement System (CalPERS)** has launched a different kind of long-term care program. It is available to all California public employees, retirees, their spouses, parents, parents-in-law, and siblings.

The CalPERS Long-Term Care Program offers three plans—a comprehensive plan (covering facility and community-based care), a plan covering only nursing home care and assisted living, and a Partnership plan that meets the requirements of the California RWJF Partnership program. All three plans are federally tax-qualified and meet all the requirements of HIPAA. Coverage provisions and choices are similar to those of an employer-sponsored group LTCI plan. Because the program is not-for-profit and has no agent commissions, coverage is less costly than under private plans. The CalPERS plans are guaranteed renewable, which allows for future premium adjustments (just like the vast majority of private LTCI policies), but to date the program has actually expanded benefits without raising premiums.

The program is self-funded, meaning that CalPERS acts as the issuing entity and has established a separate trust fund for the program. As of April 2002, the program has over 158,000 enrollees, and in terms of premium dollars, it is currently the largest group long-term care program in the nation. (More information on the CalPERS program is available at: http://www.calpers.ca.gov/longtermcare/.)

» Summary

The RWJF demonstration project led to the creation of public-private partnership programs in a few states. These programs have helped meet the needs of the citizens of those states, and more broadly, they have helped raise awareness of the need for private long-term care insurance.

Although the self-funded CalPERS plan is currently unique, it has so far been successful, and people in the long-term care field are watching it closely. Public and public-private programs may eventually become more common as an alternative to using an insurance company's product to protect against the financial risk of paying for long-term care.

Key Terms 🔑

California Public Employees Retirement System (CalPERS)

Dollar-for-dollar model

Total assets design

» Review Questions

1. Give two reasons why it makes sense to purchase long-term care insurance early in one's life.

2. What was the role of the Robert Wood Johnson Foundation (RWJF) initiative in meeting long-term care needs?

3. Name the four states that have fully implemented Partnership programs.

4. What are the general criteria for Medicaid eligibility?

5. Name the two models of Medicaid eligibility modification adopted by states that implemented Partnership programs.

6. What was the impact of the Omnibus Budget Reconciliation Act of 1993 (OBRA '93)?

7. What is CalPERS, and who is eligible for it?

8. What are the three plans offered by CalPERS?

9. What enables CalPERS to keep costs down?

10. Give some reasons to watch CalPERS carefully as a potential model for success.

» Answers

1. At a young age LTCI coverage is still affordable, and the individual is healthy enough to qualify for it.

2. The initiative brought together state governments (the public sector) and insurance companies (the private sector) to encourage people to purchase long-term care insurance.

3. California, Connecticut, New York, and Indiana.

4. An individual is eligible for Medicaid if their assets are below roughly $2,000 and their income is at or near the poverty level. Exact criteria vary from state to state.

5. The dollar-for-dollar model and the total assets design.

6. It halted the expansion of Partnership plans. OBRA '93 stated that only plans approved by HHS prior to May 14, 1993 would receive

grandfathered status and could continue as designed. Since plans approved after that date must include provisions for recovering assets from the estate of Medicaid beneficiaries, the net effect is that for any new plans the asset protection provision of the Partnership plans is in place only while the insured is alive.

7. CalPERS stands for the California Public Employees Retirement System. Its LTCI program is available to all California public employees, retirees, their spouses, parents, parents-in-law, and siblings.

8. The plans are as follows: a comprehensive plan (covering facility and community-based care), a plan covering only nursing home care and assisted living, and a Partnership plan that meets the requirements of the California RWJF Partnership program.

9. It is not-for-profit and has no agent commissions, therefore coverage is less costly than under private plans.

10. It is a self-funded program that has managed to increase benefits while keeping premiums constant. And in terms of premium dollars, it is currently the largest group long-term care program in the nation.

16

Long-Term Care and Other Products

» Overview

This book has focused on traditional, stand-alone long-term care insurance policies. But there are also products that combine long-term care coverage with other types of insurance.

Life insurance and annuities have offered a type of long-term care coverage for many years. Insurers have combined LTCI with disability income insurance. Before Medicare supplement insurance became standardized in the early 1990s, some policies included expanded benefits for nursing home stays or home health care that would meet today's definition of long-term care insurance.

Under the NAIC definition, these products can be considered long-term care insurance if they provide at least one year of benefits in a setting other than a hospital, pay benefits when there is a loss of physical or cognitive abilities, or are marketed as long-term care insurance. When insurers file these products for approval, they will likely be subject to the state's LTCI regulations.

» Life Insurance with Accelerated Benefits

In the late 1980s and early 1990s, some insurers expanded their life insurance policies to include a payment of benefit for dread diseases and terminal illnesses. Many insurers still offer policies with this feature (known as **accelerated benefits** or **living benefits**) or make it an option for additional premium.

The idea behind this design was that someone with a serious illness is likely to have expenses not covered by their major medical insurance. Benefits paid by a life insurance policy can help offset some of those expenses and can actually help the insured keep their life insurance policy in force. Before there were accelerated benefits, insureds were sometimes forced to borrow heavily against their policy's cash value, cancel the policy to obtain the cash surrender value, or sell the policy in a viatical settlement. Accelerated benefits were a better alternative for all parties.

The dread disease and terminal illness rider on a life insurance policy allows for the payment of a portion of the death benefit in the event that the insured is diagnosed with one of a number of life-threatening illnesses. In other words, the payment of the death benefit is accelerated. The medical conditions identified in the rider require extraordinary medical intervention to sustain life, even if only for a short time. Some of these conditions result in the need for continuous artificial life support that can exhaust the benefits of a major medical insurance plan.

Benefit Eligibility

The NAIC Accelerated Benefit Model Regulation requires benefits to be paid under four conditions that dramatically limit a person's life span. These are:

- coronary artery disease resulting in an acute infarction or requiring surgery,
- permanent neurological deficit resulting from cerebral vascular accident,
- end-stage renal failure, and
- acquired immune deficiency syndrome (AIDS).

FOCUS QUESTION 1

Name the four life-threatening conditions specified by NAIC that qualify for accelerated benefits.

_____

_____

_____

_____

This list is designed as a floor rather than a ceiling. The NAIC Model Regulation emphasizes that a policy and a state's regulation should include but not be limited to these conditions. A state insurance department can mandate that additional conditions be covered, and an insurer's policy can include conditions not mandated if this is approved by the state insurance department.

Insurers can design a plan that pays accelerated benefits when someone is diagnosed with cancer, a heart attack, organ failure, a stroke, or other specific illness. But there is a problem with this approach—the severity of a single condition can vary greatly. There are forms of cancer that normally lead to death and others that are not life-threatening and do not require surgery or chemotherapy; some organ failures require a transplant, while others do not.

Some insurers require that any illness resulting in a limited life expectancy be certified by the physician as a terminal illness before the insurer will accelerate benefits on the life insurance policy. In these situations, the insurer doesn't pay benefits based on the cause but rather on the prognosis. An insurer may require a second opinion when receiving a prognosis that will trigger accelerated benefits.

Benefits

The amount of accelerated benefits is normally limited to a portion (frequently between one-quarter and one-half) of the face amount of the policy, with a dollar limit. The NAIC Model Regulation does not impose a maximum, allowing for insurer flexibility. Some policies that are available today pay the full death benefit for long-term care expenses and then pay an additional nominal amount at death. The dollar limit is normally a set amount, or the insurer will have a face amount limit that applies to the accelerated benefit rider.

Benefits are available as a lump sum (an option mandated by the NAIC regulation) or as monthly payments. Using an annuity contingent on the life of the insured is not allowed by the regulation. The benefits are usually paid on an indemnity basis, without scrutiny of receipts for medical treatment or other expenses.

HIPAA specifies that any life insurance accelerated benefits paid as a result of a terminal illness are considered a death benefit and not subject to income taxation. The NAIC Model requires that the first page of the policy and other related documents contain a disclosure of the tax consequences and recommend that the insured consult with a personal tax advisor.

Accelerated Benefits and Long-Term Care

A life insurance policy can have an accelerated benefit clause that looks much like a long-term care insurance policy. Many companies refer to this design as "living benefits," but the policy must contain the terminology "accelerated benefits." Benefits are payable when someone is chronically ill, and are either reimbursements for long-term care services or indemnity benefits. The services can include any and all that are included in a stand-alone LTCI policy—nursing home care, assisted living, home care, adult day services, respite care, etc. Another allowable design looks like the long-term care policies of the past, requiring a permanent confinement to a nursing home or a stay in excess of six months.

When long-term care accelerated benefits are distributed as monthly payments, the cash value and death benefit of the policy are reduced each month up to certain limits. For example, a policy may pay monthly benefits equal to 2 percent of the original death benefit until half of the death benefit is paid out (in effect making the policy's accelerated benefits payable for 25 months). The cash values decrease by a similar amount either as a loan or a lien against the death benefit payment. According to HIPAA, any life insurance accelerated benefit paid to an insured who meets the definition of a chronically ill individual (that is, they suffer from a cognitive or ADL impairment expected to last 90 days or longer) is considered a death benefit and not subject to income taxation.

A difficult situation arises when a policy is owned or assigned to someone other than the insured, or when the beneficiary designation is irrevocable. One such situation could occur when a life insurance policy is purchased and then assigned to an irrevocable trust for estate tax reasons. The face amount is already "spent," so any reduction in death benefit will cause the life insurance policy's primary purpose to become secondary. The

NAIC Accelerated Benefit Model Regulation does allow for the addition of accelerated benefits as long as the insurer obtains a signed acknowledgment of concurrence for pay-out from the owner, assignee, or beneficiary. Insurers have the right to forbid the addition of an accelerated benefit rider to such life insurance policies.

FOCUS QUESTION 2

Explain the complication involved with accelerated benefits when a life insurance policy is owned or assigned to someone other than the insured, or when the beneficiary designation cannot be changed.

_____

_____

_____

_____

_____

_____

Waiver of premium for accelerated benefits is an option the insurer will normally offer. This is either part of the life insurance waiver benefit or built into the accelerated benefits rider. When accelerated benefits are claimed, the insurer must disclose any premium-paying requirements to ensure that the policy does not lapse.

Additional Regulation of Accelerated Benefits

In addition to the NAIC Accelerated Benefit Model Regulation, the NAIC Long-Term Care Insurance Model Act includes provisions governing combination life insurance and long-term care insurance policies. This encompasses all life insurance riders that are marketed as long-term care insurance. There is a life insurance policy illustration or a policy summary that is given to the insured at the time of policy delivery that must include the following:

- an explanation of how the long-term care benefits interact with other components of the policy, including deductions from death benefits;

- an illustration of the amount of benefits, the length of benefit, and the guaranteed lifetime benefits (if any) of each covered person;
- all long-term care exclusions, reductions, and limitations;
- a statement that the inflation protection option is not available;
- a disclosure of the effects of exercising other rights under the policy;
- a disclosure of any guarantees regarding the cost of insurance charges for long-term care; and
- the current and projected maximum lifetime benefits.

Once the insured is receiving benefits, the insurer must provide a monthly report outlining the benefit payment status. This includes all long-term care benefits paid during the month, the total benefit amount remaining under the policy, and an explanation of all policy charges related to the payment of long-term care benefits. These charges are normally a reduction in death benefits or cash values.

The NAIC Long-Term Care Insurance Model Regulation addresses replacement when a life insurance policy is involved. The insurer must follow the long-term care insurance replacement guidelines when a life insurance policy with long-term care benefits replaces a long-term care insurance policy. The insurer must follow both the life insurance and long-term care insurance replacement guidelines when a life insurance policy with long-term care benefits replaces a like policy.

Given that the concept of loss ratio is normally related to health insurance, the combination life insurance and long-term care insurance policy receives different loss ratio treatment in the Long-Term Care Model Regulation. Life insurance policies that include long-term care insurance benefits funded by a reduction of the death benefit need not meet the loss ratio requirements if the following criteria are met:

- The cash value accumulations including long-term care have a guaranteed interest rate that is at least equal to the accumulations without a long-term care benefit.
- The life insurance nonforfeiture benefits meet the state's minimum life insurance nonforfeiture requirements.

■ The required policy illustration or a policy summary is provided at the time of purchase and a monthly policy summary is provided while in claim status.

■ The life insurance illustration complies with the state's life insurance illustration requirements.

■ A detailed actuarial memorandum is filed with the state's insurance department.

When the life insurance policy meets these criteria, it is considered to provide reasonable benefits in relation to premiums paid. The policy is not subject to the same loss ratio requirements as a stand-alone long-term care insurance policy.

The insurer's policy is not subject to the same rate increase disclosure and pricing requirements as a stand-alone LTCI policy when the long-term care benefits are incidental to the policy and other basic requirements are met. Long-term care insurance benefits are incidental to the overall value of a policy when the long-term care benefits provide less than 10 percent of the insurance policy's total value according to the NAIC Long-Term Care Insurance Model Regulation. The values measured begin on the date of issue and continue for the life of the policy. Measurement of the value of the benefits can include assessment of the separate base and long-term care premiums, the annual cost of insurance charges, or an analysis of the present value of benefits. The other requirements include those listed above for the loss ratio exclusion and integrate annuity nonforfeiture and disclosure laws.

There is also a special exemption for combination life insurance policies regarding the delivery of a shopper's guide. Agents selling these policies are not required to deliver the guide as long as the policy illustration provided to the applicant meets the disclosure requirements of the Long-Term Care Model Act listed above.

» Annuities

Insurers offering annuities have long recognized the importance of providing financial protection for their annuitants in the event that they need long-term care services.

There are three designs that waive annuity surrender charges: the nursing home waiver, the terminal illness waiver, and the disability waiver. In addition, recently an underwritten annuity has emerged as a means of paying for long-term care services.

- The easiest design for insurers and annuitant to understand is the **nursing home waiver**. Surrender charges are waived when the annuitant enters a state-licensed nursing home. The waiver is normally effective after 90 or 180 days of confinement in the facility. (This eliminates many of the short stays related to rehabilitation from surgery or other acute conditions.) This design normally doesn't apply to other long-term care services such as assisted living or home care.

- The **terminal illness waiver** is triggered much like life insurance accelerated benefits for a terminal illness—it applies when a physician certifies that the annuitant has a limited life expectancy. The length of time required varies according to the insurer and is stated in either months (normally six) or years (one or two). Upon submission of adequate proof that a terminal illness exists, the insurer will eliminate the surrender charges on the annuity.

- The **disability waiver** is based either on the annuitant's inability to work or their functional impairment. When someone is unable to earn a living because of a sickness or injury, some insurers will waive the annuity surrender charges. Inability to work is defined as in disability income insurance policies, with variances related to total and partial disability. A disability waiver for functional impairment is based on ADLs and cognitive impairments much like a long-term care insurance policy. The disability waiver is the least common of the three surrender charge waivers.

- The **underwritten annuity** works much differently than the surrender charges waiver designs. When someone applies for the annuity, the insurer collects medical information to underwrite the case. But rather than rejecting the unhealthy applicants, the insurer will actually pay a higher monthly income amount to those with a shorter life expectancy. These annuities are also referred to as **impaired-risk annuities** and are really designed for individuals in a financial crisis seeking to obtain income from assets.

FOCUS QUESTION 3

Describe the three surrender charge waiver designs.

_____

_____

_____

_____

_____

_____

_____

_____

A few insurers offer unique options to annuities that address long-term care needs. In one, the annuity has two accounts. One account pays a regular interest rate, and the proceeds can be withdrawn for any purpose; the other pays a significantly higher rate, but the proceeds are only available when the annuity owner demonstrates a functional impairment—such as the eligibility criteria for long-term care insurance benefits. Another unique annuity product pays a higher monthly benefit after the annuitant demonstrates a loss of functional independence. More innovative designs will emerge as the importance of this type of option for paying for long-term care services gains stronger consumer recognition.

» Medicare Supplement Insurance

Medicare supplement insurance (also called **Medigap insurance**) is designed to fill the gaps in Medicare's benefit package. Before the passage of the Omnibus Budget Reconciliation Act of 1990 (OBRA '90), insurers were free to offer any benefits they chose in their Medicare supplement insurance. Some policies paid benefits for such things as skilled nursing facility care for a year or home health care for an extended period of time. However, as a result of OBRA '90, the NAIC developed standardized Medigap plans. With exceptions in a few states, all policies must now conform to one of these plans, and they are much more restrictive in terms of what benefits can be provided.

Some plans provide benefits related to long-term care, but none really meet long-term care needs in any meaningful way. For example, Plans C through J cover the copayment for days 20 to 100 in a skilled nursing home. However, this benefit is of course only available to those who qualify for Medicare's nursing home benefits—that is, those recovering from an acute condition.

» Continuing Care Retirement Communities (CCRCs)

Continuing care retirement communities (CCRCs), called **life care communities** in some parts of the country, do not fall under the classic definition of long-term care insurance. Nonetheless, they are worthy of a discussion in this book, as they are a form of risk sharing, just like long-term care insurance, and they are an alternative in long-term care planning. State insurance departments frequently regulate CCRCs, although they are subject to different regulations than LTCI.

CCRCs offer the entire continuum of living and care arrangements in one community. This includes independent living, home care, assisted living, and nursing home care. CCRCs may offer housekeeping services, transportation, meals, wellness services, and personal assistance. The best facilities address the physical, mental, social, spiritual, and intellectual needs of the residents in order to promote their independence and dignity. The advantage to the resident of living in a CCRC is that no matter what services they need, they can find them in the community.

The physical layout of CCRCs varies dramatically. Some have a campus-like setting with many acres of independent ranch-style homes and separate buildings for assisted living and nursing home care. At the other end of the spectrum, there are high-rise buildings with apartments for independent living on some floors and assisted living and nursing home care on others.

Financial Arrangements

There are three basic financial arrangements utilized by CCRCs. The **extensive agreement (Type A)**, sometimes referred to as a **life care agreement**, is the one that most closely resembles insurance. The resident pays an initial lump sum or entry fee when they move in, and thereafter a monthly fee of a predetermined amount. This monthly fee generally pays for the resident's care, no matter what services or level of care they need (although there can be exceptions, such as home care service received in independent living).

The **modified agreement (Type B)** also has an entry fee and monthly fees. However, these payments cover only limited long-term care services, such as a specified number of days of care each year. Once the resident's care exceeds the limits, they must pay an additional charge for services received. This charge is likely less than what someone from outside the facility would pay and may possibly be paid by a third party. This design is similar to an inverted elimination period — the initial services are covered while the extended care is not.

The **fee-for-service agreement (Type C)** is the furthest from the concept of insurance. There are an entry fee and monthly payments, but the amount of the monthly payments varies according to the services received. The owners of these facilities might encourage the residents to finance their care through an LTCI policy.

When someone applies to live in a CCRC, they undergo a form of underwriting. The community may have income standards to ensure that residents are able to fulfill the financial arrangement they enter into. A potential resident's insurance coverage, including long-term care insurance, is also considered. A person's independence or health status may be reviewed to ensure that they are capable of living on their own.

Like insurers, CCRCs must build reserves for unexpected or deferred expenses in order to ensure long-term financial stability. The amount of reserves varies by facility and the assumptions used in the pricing model. Bankruptcy was a problem with a few CCRCs before the risk was fully understood, so state regulation may require semiannual or triannual appraisals or financial statements.

FOCUS QUESTION 4

Outline the parallels between CCRCs and insurance.

_____

_____

_____

_____

_____

_____

_____

_____

There is a body within the CCRC industry with requirements that go beyond the regulatory environment. The Continuing Care Accreditation Commission (CCAC) has established stringent standards that a facility must demonstrate it meets to earn and retain accreditation. The goal of this program is to ensure that the facility strives for excellence, has sound financial management, and encourages residents to remain independent.

» Summary

The opportunities for combining long-term care benefits with other insurance products are endless. This chapter identified the most common combination products. The challenge facing insurers with these products is designing them to provide meaningful benefits, gaining state insurance department approval, motivating and training agents to offer them, and having consumers embrace them with a purchase decision.

CCRCs offer access to quality long-term care services with interesting funding alternatives. Long-term care insurance can play a positive role in the financial planning of those residing in CCRCs.

Over time, insurers and providers of long-term care services will find additional innovative means of paying for the care that a large number of people will ultimately need. Knowledge of these alternatives will help everyone involved with long-term care insurance provide much-needed advice to the buying public.

Key Terms	
Accelerated benefits	Living benefits
Continuing care retirement community (CCRC)	Medicare supplement insurance
Disability waiver	Medigap insurance
Extensive agreement (Type A)	Modified agreement (Type B)
Fee-for-service agreement (Type C)	Nursing home waiver
	Terminal illness waiver
Impaired-risk annuity	Underwritten annuity
Life care agreement	
Life care community	

» Review Questions

1. What are accelerated benefit riders on life insurance policies?

2. How can accelerated benefits help the insured keep their life insurance policy in force?

3. Are accelerated life insurance benefits taxable?

4. When are long-term care insurance benefits deemed incidental to the overall value of a life insurance policy?

5. Name the three designs that waive annuity surrender charges. Which one is the least common?

6. What is the alternative that has emerged alongside the established annuity surrender charge waiver designs?

7. What coverage fills the gaps of Medicare benefits?

8. In a word, how would you describe the scope of continuing care retirement communities (CCRCs) or life care communities?

9. Name the three basic financial arrangements found in CCRCs.

10. Why does state regulation require semiannual or triannual appraisals or financial statements from CCRCs?

» Answers

1. These riders allow for the payment of a portion of the policy's death benefit while the insured is still alive, provided certain conditions are met.

2. Before there were accelerated benefits, insureds with serious illnesses were sometimes forced to borrow heavily against their policy's cash value, cancel the policy to obtain the cash surrender value, or sell the policy in a viatical settlement. With accelerated benefits, such actions are often not necessary.

3. No, these are normally treated just like death benefits and are therefore not taxable.

4. When the long-term care benefits provide less than 10 percent of the insurance policy's total value.

5. The nursing home waiver, the terminal illness waiver, and the disability waiver—the last being the least common.

6. The underwritten annuity, also known as the impaired-risk annuity.

7. Medicare supplement insurance—often called Medigap insurance.

8. Comprehensive—CCRCs offer the entire continuum of living and care arrangements in one community.

9. Extensive, modified, and fee-for-service.

10. In the early days, bankruptcy was a problem with some CCRCs because the risks associated with this type of enterprise were not fully understood.

›› Key Terms

Key terms are indicated in the text by boldface and this symbol ▣— in the margin. Key terms are introduced, defined, and explained on the page or pages listed below.

Index

Frequently Asked Questions About the HIAA Examination

What material does the examination for the HIAA course The Long-Term Care Insurance Product cover?

The 16 chapters of the textbook *The Long-Term Care Insurance Product: Policy Design, Pricing, and Regulation.*

How many questions are on the exam, and how much time do I have?

There are 75 questions. You have two hours. (Some test formats have fewer questions. Inquire with the person who will be conducting your exam.)

What is the format of the questions of the exam?

All questions are multiple choice.

EXAMPLE ▶ *In a tax-qualified LTCI policy, the definition of "substantial assistance"*

a. *must be based on hands-on assistance.*
b. *must be based on stand-by assistance.*
c. *may be based on hands-on assistance, stand-by assistance, or another standard.*
d. *may be based on either hands-on or stand-by assistance but not on another standard.*

(The correct answer is d.)

Some questions are multiple-option multiple choice.

EXAMPLE ▶ *Which of these LTCI policy models pay a set daily benefit amount regardless of the actual cost of services received by the insured?*

I. *Disability*
II. *Indemnity*
III. *Reimbursement*

a. I and II only
b. I and III only
c. II and III only
d. I, II, and III

(The correct answer is a.)

A few questions are application questions. These require you to determine which of the facts given in the question are relevant and then apply your knowledge to reach a conclusion.

EXAMPLE ▶ *Carl has an LTCI policy with a 60-day elimination period. The policy is tax-qualified, so it also has a 90-day certification requirement. Carl's physician certifies that he has a physical impairment that will last more than 90 days. When will Carl be eligible for benefits?*

a. *He is eligible immediately.*
b. *He will be eligible after 60 days.*
c. *He will be eligible after 90 days.*
d. *He is not eligible for benefits.*

(The correct answer is b.)

You should be able to answer the question by applying your knowledge of elimination periods and the 90-day certification requirement.

Are there questions on the statistics and numbers in the textbook?

Yes, but not very many. For a few simple and important numbers, the exact figure must be known.

EXAMPLE ▶ *Under the NAIC definition of long-term care insurance, the minimum period that coverage can be offered is 12 months. The student would be expected to know this number.*

For statistics and other more complicated numbers, however, an approximate idea of the number is sufficient.

EXAMPLE ▶ *The text reports that the annual cost of nursing home care has gone up from about $18,000 in 1980 to over $50,000 currently. The student should know that costs have risen dramatically but would not be asked for specific figures.*

Is information from the figures and tables of the textbook covered in the exam?

Yes, the figures and tables found in the 16 chapters are covered, but exam questions focus on the main points, not details.

EXAMPLE ▶ *Table 11.4, "The Cost of Waiting to Buy," looks at premiums and the total cost of coverage to age 85 of someone who buys at age 50 compared to someone who buys when they are older. The student would not be asked the exact figures, but rather would be expected to understand that the older the age at purchase, the higher the premiums and the total cost.*

If I can answer all the focus questions and review questions, will I be able to pass the exam?

Not necessarily. The focus questions, review questions, and key terms are intended to direct the student to the most important information and ideas, but they do not cover everything that might be asked on the exam.

I have a lot of experience in insurance. Can I pass the exam without reading the textbook or studying?

Possibly, but you should be aware that the examination is based on the most common practices in the insurance industry. What your company does may differ. The safest approach is to read the textbook and see if you know the material. This will go very quickly if you already have a lot of knowledge.

HIAA's Courses and Professional Designations

For more than 40 years, the Health Insurance Association of America's Insurance Education Program has offered current, comprehensive, and economically priced courses for professionals seeking to advance their understanding of the health insurance industry. Since 1958, more than 500,000 people have enrolled in these courses. Many enrollees are employees of health insurance companies or managed care organizations, but consultants, third-party administrators, agents, brokers, and other health insurance professionals also study with us. In addition, an increasing number of noninsurance professionals, including health care providers, economists, consumer advocates, and government officials, are taking HIAA courses to gain a better understanding of the operations of our industry and to advance their careers in their own fields.

Courses include:

- The Fundamentals of Health Insurance (Parts A and B)
- Managed Care (Parts A, B, and C)
- Medical Expense Insurance
- Supplemental Health Insurance
- Disability Income Insurance
- Long-Term Care Insurance
- Financing Long-Term Care
- The Long-Term Care Insurance Product
- Long-Term Care Insurance Claims
- Health Insurance Fraud
- Customer Service for the Health Care Environment
- HIPAA for the Home Care Provider

- HIPAA for the Physician's Office
- HIPAA for Insurers
- HIPAA Privacy Regulations

The completion of HIAA courses leads to four widely respected professional designations: **Health Insurance Associate (HIA), Managed Healthcare Professional (MHP), Long-Term Care Professional (LTCP),** and **Health Care Anti-Fraud Associate (HCAFA).** The HIA designation has been in existence since 1990 and is currently held by more than 16,500 professionals. The MHP, offered for the first time in 1996, is held by more than 4,000 designees. The LTCP and HCAFA designations are currently being introduced.

And coming soon. . .additional courses and new designations in disability income and medical management.

For more information, visit our website (www.hiaa.org) or call 800-509-4422.

Other Books from HIAA

» Long-Term Care: Understanding Needs and Options

This book provides an introduction to the field of long-term care and long-term care insurance. It begins with an explanation of what long-term care is, who needs it, and how and where it is provided. It then looks at various ways of paying for long-term care and the limitations of each. It examines long-term care insurance, describing how it works and why it is often the best solution to the problem. Finally, it discusses the ways salespeople and insurance company personnel can bring this solution to the people who need it.

» Financing Long-Term Care Needs: Exploring Options and Reaching Solutions

The second book in HIAA's long-term care series explores in greater detail the various methods of funding long-term care, helping the reader understand the advantages and disadvantages of each and the role that each can play in a person's long-term care plan. Methods covered are personal savings and assets, family assistance, Medicare and Medicaid, reverse mortgages, annuities, life insurance, and long-term care insurance (both individual policies and employer-sponsored coverage).

» The Health Insurance Primer: An Introduction to How Health Insurance Works

This book, together with *Health Insurance Nuts and Bolts*, serves as a complete introduction to the health insurance field. The authors assume no prior knowledge and begin by explaining basic concepts and terminology, but they progress to an in-depth examination of such topics as the various kinds of health insurance, health insurance contracts, underwriting, and sales and marketing. *The Health Insurance Primer* is an excellent choice for beginners in health insurance.

» Health Insurance Nuts and Bolts: An Introduction to Health Insurance Operations

The introduction to the basic facts and concepts of group and individual health insurance begun in *The Health Insurance Primer* continues in *Health Insurance Nuts and Bolts*. Topics include managing the cost of health care; policy issue, renewal, and service; claim administration; pricing health insurance products; government regulation; and fraud and abuse.

» Medical Expense Insurance

For those who have a basic understanding of the concepts and functioning of health insurance, this book provides more specific information on medical expense insurance, the most common kind of health insurance in America. The text begins by describing the two coverages that provide health insurance to most Americans: group major medical insurance and individual hospital-surgical insurance. Subsequent chapters discuss the following topics: marketing and sales, pricing, contract provisions, underwriting, policy administration, claim administration, and industry issues.

» Managed Care: Integrating the Delivery and Financing of Health Care, Part A

An introduction to the field of managed health care, this book explains what managed care is, introduces the concepts on which it is based, and describes how it works in the real world. The book presupposes no prior knowledge of either managed care or insurance. Topics include the development of managed care, cost control techniques, measuring and improving quality, types of managed care organizations, and the involvement of government in managed care.

» Managed Care: Integrating the Delivery and Financing of Health Care, Part B

Part B of HIAA's managed care series covers operational issues and problems. Topics include the governance and management structure of managed care organizations; selective medical provider contracting; network administration and provider relations; marketing and member services; claims administration; financing, budgeting, and rating; legal issues; accreditation; and regulation.

» Managed Care: Integrating the Delivery and Financing of Health Care, Part C

Part C of this series examines current issues in managed care, operations and problems in specialized areas of managed care, and the role of managed care in government health benefit programs. Topics include public and private purchasing groups; consumers and physicians; managed care for pharmacy, dental, behavioral health, and vision benefits; and managed care for federal employees and military personnel, in the Medicare program, and in state government programs.

» Supplemental Health Insurance

This book is intended to provide those who have a basic knowledge of health insurance and supplemental health insurance with more specific information on the major supplemental products in the marketplace. In addition, the gaps in health coverage that led to the need for additional insurance are discussed for each product. Topics include Medicare supplements, hospital indemnity coverage, specified disease insurance, accident coverage, dental plans, specialty plans, and the supplemental insurance market.

» Health Care Fraud: An Introduction to Detection, Investigation, and Prevention

This book provides an orientation in how health care fraud is perpetrated and what is being done to combat it. It looks at how some of the most common fraudulent schemes operate, how these schemes are detected and investigated, and the laws that can be brought to bear against them. Fraud perpetrated by health care providers, consumers, and others is included, and fraud involving not just medical expense insurance but also managed care and disability income insurance is covered.

» Customer Service Strategies for the Health Care Environment

In an easy-reading style, this text focuses on practical ways to create a customer-driven organization. It also covers accreditation issues. Readers learn how accreditation surveyors identify and review customer service initiatives, review assessment guidelines, and find solutions to common customer service problems. The book features many valuable resources that can be used for self-study or for training staff and developing quality customer service programs.

» HIPAA Action Items for Home Care Providers

HIPAA regulations are here to stay, and home care providers must comply with the new rules. This practical guide cuts through information overload and gives readers a jump-start on compliance efforts. Clearly written and easy to follow, the book was designed specifically for home care organizations and providers. It is the first in a series of innovative HIPAA texts and courses that help those in the health care field organize compliance efforts and explain HIPAA to staff, patients, and business associates. Other titles include *The HIPAA Privacy Primer, HIPAA Action Items for the Physician's Office, and HIPAA Action Items for Insurers.*

**These books may be ordered
by calling 800-828-0111**

The HIAA Insurance Education Program

Gregory F. Dean, JD, CLU, ChFC
Executive Director

Deirdre A. McKenna, JD
Executive Director of Business Programs

Joyce Meals
Assistant Director

Leanne Dorado
Manager of Education Operations

Kevin Gorham
Fiscal Manager

La'Creshea Makonnen
CE Credit Manager

Yolaunda Janrhett
Registration Coordinator

Matthew Grant
Internet Coordinator